Books by Leon Stover

Anthropology and History

The Cultural Ecology of Chinese Civilization
China: An Anthropological Perspective (with Takeko K. Stover)
Imperial China and the State Cult of Confucius (McFarland, 2005)
Stonehenge and the Origins of Western Culture
Stonehenge City (McFarland, 2003)

Fiction

Stonehenge (with Harry Harrison)
Stonehenge: Where Atlantis Died (the above revised and expanded)
The Shaving of Karl Marx

Criticism

La Science Fiction Américaine
Robert A. Heinlein
Harry Harrison
The Prophetic Soul: A Reading of H.G. Wells's "Things to Come" (McFarland, 1987)

The Annotated H.G. Wells (McFarland)

Volume 1. *The Time Machine* (1996)
Volume 2. *The Island of Doctor Moreau* (1996)
Volume 3. *The Invisible Man* (1998)
Volume 4. *The War of the Worlds* (2001)
Volume 5. *When the Sleeper Wakes* (2000)
Volume 6. *The First Men in the Moon* (1998)
Volume 7. *The Sea Lady* (2001)
Volume 8. *Man Who Could Work Miracles* (2002)
Volume 9. *Things to Come* (2007)

Anthologies

Apeman, Spaceman (with Harry Harrison)
Above the Human Landscape (with Willis McNelly)

Science Fiction *from* Wells *to* Heinlein

Science Fiction *from* Wells *to* Heinlein

Leon Stover

McFarland & Company, Inc., Publishers
Jefferson, North Carolina, and London

Facing the title page: illustration for "To Follow Knowledge" by Frank Belknap Long in *Astounding Science Fiction*, December 1942.

Fig. 80 is reproduced with the kind permission of Advent Publishers, Inc. Fig. 121 is with kind permission of Harry Harrison. I am grateful to Henry Holt and Company for plate XVI. Fig. 107 is reproduced from a 1968 cartoon in the Chicago *Tribune*. Ten items of interior art and five magazine covers are from seven different Hugo Gernsback periodicals under the Ziff-Davis imprint. Eighteen items of interior art and 16 magazine covers are from *Astounding Science Fiction* and from its earlier and later incarnations, *Astounding Stories* and *Analog Science Fiction/Science Fact*.

The present work is a reprint of the illustrated casebound edition of Science Fiction from Wells to Heinlein, *first published in 2002 by McFarland.*

LIBRARY OF CONGRESS CATALOGUING-IN-PUBLICATION DATA

Stover, Leon E.
Science fiction from Wells to Heinlein / Leon Stover.
p. cm.
Includes bibliographical references and index.

ISBN 978-0-7864-3892-1
softcover : 50# alkaline paper ♾

1. Science fiction, English—History and criticism.
2. Science fiction, American—History and criticism. I. Title.
PR830.S35S86 2008 823.0876209—dc21 2001044931

British Library cataloguing data are available

Manufactured in the United States of America

McFarland & Company, Inc., Publishers
Box 611, Jefferson, North Carolina 28640
www.mcfarlandpub.com

To the memory of
Dr. Walter J. Wild
(1954–1999),
astrophysicist, friend, former student

[Science fiction] is designed to reach those qualities of mind which are aroused only by things vast, things cataclysmic, and things unfathomably strange.

—G. Peyton Wertenbaker,
letter to the editor of *Amazing Stories* (July 1926)

Table of Contents

Preface

Those unread in the history of science fiction are likely to think of hideous visitors from outer space, and for good reason. Invading aliens go back to *The War of the Worlds* (1898) by H.G. Wells, a venerable SF theme exploited by Orson Welles for his 1938 Halloween radio broadcast that incited a still-remembered national panic. Indeed, my departmental chairman once reported to the dean that my work dealt with H.G. Welles: a conflation of names often seen. Some literary snobs still think the scientific romances of H.G. Wells are nothing more than empty fantasies, not real literature.

Wells's aliens are invading Martians, octopoidal monsters (fig. 1 on page 2) that actually save mankind from itself; his nineteenth-century novel has unsuspected philosophical deeps written with artistic care. Much derivative SF is epigonal; more often than not aliens have been pictured as hellbent on killing all earthmen and raping their women. See fig. 2 on page 2 for a perfect illustration of this perverse exobiology.

In today's reported landings of UFOs, the aliens among us descend from the same source. They are invariably described as having a lightbulb-shaped head, vestigial nose, and slit for a mouth.

This image traces to the visiting alien of a 1934 American novel who critiques human folly. See fig. 3 on page 2. His large brain resembles the cerebral dome of Wells's octopus-like invaders (actually food sacs in the sea-dwelling model).

Science fiction is usually justified on the ground that it anticipates new science. Never; science always is ahead of fiction. (The nature of nature is not as you like it in stories of super-science.) *Applied* science is a different matter. With the advent of R & D (scientific Research and engineering Development), SF could imagine new technology that often got developed. Indeed, magazine SF began at the very moment the R & D industry emerged. At that time the genre dished out mainly gadget stories.

Fig. 1. *H.G. Wells's octopoidal Martian, from the serialized version of* The War of the Worlds.

Fig. 2. *Octopoidal rapist, from the French science fiction comic book,* Metal Hurland, *1960s.*

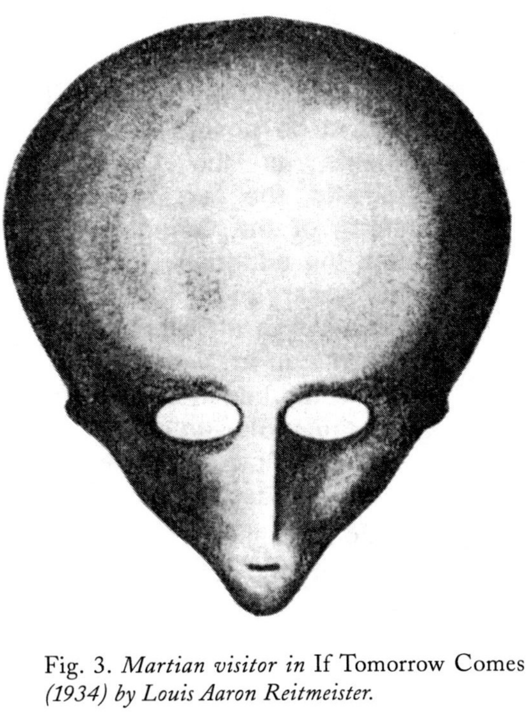

Fig. 3. *Martian visitor in* If Tomorrow Comes *(1934) by Louis Aaron Reitmeister.*

Today R & D is the world's biggest business, while SF as a paraliterature has all but vanished: assimilated into other genres (like high-tech spy thrillers) and reduced to nothing but special effects in movies and television. Ironically, television is the one mass-produced gadget that SF detailed from the start.

This book tracks the literary trajectory of SF from the scientific romances of H.G. Wells to Robert Heinlein, his principal heir in the pulp magazine era. Heinlein's early stories belong now in the canon of American letters. He did more than write informed engineering fiction: He used it to authenticate his reflective culture criticism and thoughtful view of history to come.

For that reason I have chosen him as the terminal point of this requiem for the genre, based on thirty years of teaching it, over sixty years of reading it, and experience writing and editing it.

By chance, I was the first to bring SF into the academy, followed by many others. Now that the genre is dead, it is memorialized in Ph.D. programs.

At best, it delivered a certain intellectual grittiness and grandiose cosmic vision. By the time Robert Heinlein came along, the magazine of his choice had achieved a distinction for good writing and sophisticated thinking unbested in any other.

Given the posthumous descent of the genre into the barbarism of today's popular culture, I look back on those more innocent magazine days with fond memories.

Leon Stover, Ph.D., Litt.D.

Part I
Science Fiction

1

American Dominance

The naming "science fiction" is an American act, after a British precedent. Every writer in the business bows to H.G. Wells, with a nod to his French rival Jules Verne.

In 1962, SF authors—not all of them dominant Americans—formed a professional guild, Science Fiction Writers of America (SFWA). At that time, SF ranked third in sales after mystery and romance. No longer. The SFWA is a sepulchral monument to a dead but not yet buried genre. It survives, half alive, on the margins of a print culture itself half killed by aggressive television.

Go into any large chain-linked book store and gaze at the classified paperback section with its tagged genres: western, mystery, romance, and spy thrillers. Under science fiction are paperback originals done by SFWA members, books the stores return by unopened boxfuls, unless on the invoice the manager notices a salesworthy name. Meanwhile, hardcover books that used to be classed as SF are filed under General Fiction, done by non–SFWA bestselling authors like Michael "Jurassic Park" Crichton.

Look closer at the paperback section. You will find about five feet of shelving given to spin-offs from the long-running *Star Trek* television series: novelizations of episodes, plus quantities of trivia about every detail of their production. Other books on that shelf provide blueprints of the Starship *Enterprise*, the pseudoscience of its warp drive, and encyclopedic coverage of the galactic cultures it visits.

These books are farmed out by a huge franchise to SFWA members without benefit of royalties. They are reduced to that: crumbs from the table. The scriptwriters and producers themselves, however, are not SFWA members. Familiar with all the SF clichés, they tap a mass audience unversed in the old magazine literature. *Star Trek* may be a passing fad, but it is not the passing out of sight of genre SF.

Another sign of the times is the advent of big-budget SF films that do not advertise as such. Derived from cheaper movies that did, the expensive special effects lavished on today's productions are the center of attention.

A good example is *The Postman* (Warner Brothers 1997). A further diversion from content is the starring role of Kevin Costner, a big box-office draw. Who would guess that *The Postman* goes over one more time a favorite SF theme? Based on a 1985 novel by David Brin, one of those few successful SFWA authors whose paperbacks are not returned from an overload market, it is a post-holocaust story set in near-future America. However, things turn out for the best in a benevolent catastrophe (see Chapter 8).

The most persevering SF writer in the terminal post–Heinlein era is Harry Harrison. Coming up under the same great editor who cultivated Heinlein and other notables (Chapter 4), he survives a shrinking market by promoting his work as anything *but* SF. A recent Harrison opus, a trilogy titled *Stars and Stripes Forever* (1998), is promoted as an "epic of alternate history"—another of SF's hallowed traditions that now goes unacknowledged. At first glance it looks to be yet another routine alternative South-Wins-the-Civil-War, as done in Ward Moore's SF classic, *Bring the Jubilee* (1953), but it soon departs. Choosing his counter-factual with exquisite care, Harrison posits a premature death for Prince Albert, leaving Queen Victoria without his restraining advice on her wish to side with the Confederates. The result of her meddling is a second American Revolution as generals Grant and Lee combine forces to fight the same old common enemy. The consequences are so plausible that we learn much about real contingencies in history. In this age of carnality, it is remarkable how exciting he can make a work of intellectual substance. He reflects credit on the asexual pulps out of which he emerged.

One who earlier decided to escape identification with SF is Kurt Vonnegut, who thus gained respectful reviews, greater sales, and bestsellerdom. A true lover of the genre, he contrived to write SF while marketing it as another species.

The alternate history theme first gained respect with Robert Harris's *Fatherland* (1992) in the Hitler-Wins-World-War-II sweepstakes, earning the author a big-budget movie contract. Len "spy thriller" Deighton did almost as well with *SS-GB* (1978). But when Philip K. Dick in *The Man in the High Castle* (1962) played that number thirty years before Harris, it impacted only SF fans. A businessman-writer like Harrison is not content with fandom's acclaim; he goes after bigger game and is destined to become a major *American* author disconnected from his generic past, as had Heinlein before him.

Other literary lights of bestseller fame who have smuggled SF into their work for an unsuspecting public are Michael Crichton, who does it all the time, and crime writer P.D. James who did it once in *The Children of Men* (1993). She is here heavily indebted to Brian Aldiss for his *Greybeard* (1964) on the same theme (a sterile future with no more children). Likewise did Crichton for *The Andromeda Strain* (1969) mine Harrison's *Plague from Space* (1965). These examples are enough to show how much the genre is blurred by SF writers seeking mainstream acceptance, even as mainstream writers wish to capture the SF ambiance. The end result is the genre's demise.

How the genre got started in the American pulp magazine industry is for the dying brood of loyal fans the high point of Western culture; nothing if not fanatical are they. Their icon is Hugo Gernsback, a Belgian electrical engineer who removed from Luxembourg to New York in 1904. There he founded a publishing empire embracing every aspect of new technology, starting with radio (see Epilogue).

In April 1926 he launched *Amazing Stories*, the first of the SF pulps, given to "amazing inventions of the future." In it he advanced the term "scientifiction," later refined in the June 1929 issue of *Wonder Stories* as "science fiction." *Wonder Stories* was one of seven SF magazines he initiated before they were imitated by other pulps.

From the turn of the century there had been much interest in the new consumer products of programmed innovation flowing out of the R & D industry. The first American corporation to attach a research laboratory to its production facilities was General Electric in 1900. News of what scientific research and engineering development had wrought at G.E. and other corporations were regularly reported by *McClure's*, the nation's premier general magazine. But when Ida Tarbell began her famous muckraking series on the Sinclair Oil Trust, it turned to investigative journalism as a specialty.

The slack was taken up by Hugo Gernsback with *Modern Electrics* (from 1908), all about radio, which became *Electric Experimenter* (from 1914), and finally the more broadly envisioned *Science and Invention* (from 1920). Its August 1923 issue, the special "scientifiction" issue (see plate III), was such a hit that Gernsback then conceived *Amazing Stories* to do more of same. Heinlein told me this is where he discovered science fiction while a junior in high school.

Amazing had come rather late to the market for specialty magazines. The first of these were the so-called dime novels, from the 1840s, and which established the categories of fiction now tagged crime, western, romance, etc. The dime novel entered a boom period in the 1870s, whose main publishers were Beadle & Adams and Frank Tousey. Number 451 of Tousey's Wide Awake Library, for example, is *The True Life of Billy the Kid* (1881), which I know to be altogether fiction from my long-ago service as vice curator of the Lincoln County Historical Museum in New Mexico (known locally as the Billy the Kid Museum). See fig. 4. It is a booklet of 16 pages, eight by 12 inches, and set in very small type. The cover is printed with a crude steel-plate engraving. Price: five cents (some other dime novels cost up to 25 cents). The inside cover lists hundreds of titles classified as pirate stories, sea stories, city stories (high life and low life), and stories of exploration, adventure, and romance.

The other dime novel series, Beadle's Popular Library, advertised wild West, border, mining, ranching, Secret Service, detective, robber, city, and sea life. Dime novels sold in the millions, and the industry hired hundreds of hack writers who specialized in one category or another.

The dime novel died out by the turn of the century, replaced by the pulp magazine. Its standard format was 120 untrimmed pages of unfinished woodpulp paper, seven by ten inches, with enameled color cover and interior illustrations. The price ranged from 10 to 25 cents. At its height during the 1920s and 1930s, the pulp industry produced a

Fig. 4. *Example of the western genre in Tousey's dime novel series.*

plethora of titles at the rate of about 20 million copies a month. The use of woodpulp, uncleansed of the sulphuric acid applied in its chemical processing and unmixed with linen content, was peculiar to legislation of the day. Sponsored by the pulp industry itself, the ruling allowed its products to be shipped at lower freight rates than other printed material: this is a time when periodicals were sold much less by subscription than by direct sale at newsstands, railway stations and in drugstores, then a major outlet. Consequently, every pulp-magazine collection is today dissolving into brownish tatters and acidic decay.

Science fiction art, in particular, was often so richly done by exceptional talents that it is impossible to dissociate the genre from them. Indeed, Brian Aldiss has dedicated a whole book to the subject, *Science Fiction Art* (1975). Another is *One Hundred Years of Science Fiction Illustration: 1840–1940* by Anthony Freeman (1974), who gets a century's worth out of it by tracing some anticipatory images back to Isidore Grandville and Albert Robida. Robida's futuristic frolics as in *Le Vingtième Siècle* (1882), *La Vie électrique* (1883), and *La Guerre au vingtième siècle* (1887), were especially well known to the magazine artists. Sometimes a cover done for a rejected story, minus title, would be used anyhow. Science fiction art thus had a momentum of its own, apart from the captioned interior line drawings which perforce must bear on story content; whereas the cover paintings often have no such bearing—the science fictional ambiance is all. Those done by Hubert Rogers for what became the premier magazine, *Astounding Science Fiction* (*ASF*)—John Campbell's editorial baby—are by far the most elegant. See plate IV for a striking example. In this painting, Rogers dramatizes the transcendental moral greatness of physical greatness—those giant rocketships in their gigantic cradles dwarfing human figures, who are but selfless agents devoted to the religion of technology and progress. Incidentally, cradled rocketships preceded the later and more familiar tail-finned types standing upright for vertical takeoff and landing. How these others landed is not explained.

The first of the pulps was *Argosy* (plate II:1), given to adventure stories, from 1896. Street & Smith Publications, a rival of Tousey's in the dime novel trade, eventually absorbed the latter and, seeing the shape of things to come in *Argosy*, originated the next three pulps: *Detective Story* (1915), *Western Story* (1919), and *Love Story* (1921). See plates II:2, 3, 4. Only after the "story" locution in these pioneering titles did there emerge an explicit *Adventure Story* magazine (fig. 5). Thereafter, specialized versions like *Jungle Stories* proliferated. Fig. 6 shows its ripoff of the Tarzan saga by Edgar Rice Burroughs, begun in 1914 in *All-Story* (= all adventure).

Another example of the specialized adventure magazine is *Sea Stories* (fig. 7), of which *Pirate Stories* (fig. 8) is a subspecies. New categories were generated by conflating existing ones: Detective + Love = *Spicy Detective* (fig. 9). Western + Love = *Range Romances* (fig. 10). Titles like *Spicy Detective* remained in its pulpish underground before surfacing in the enormously popular Mike Hammer series of paperback originals by Mickey Spillane (Frank Morrison), which emphasizes sex and sadism more than mystery. *Range Romances* was tame compared to the likes of *Spicy Western*. Its more lascivious content surfaced in movie westerns in 1945 with *Duel in the Sun*, nicknamed "Lust in the Dust."

Moreover, each and every sport (boxing, baseball, football, others) had numerous titles given to them, even cross-country racing (fig. 11). I shall not further illustrate the endless topicality of puerile pap, which did not fail to include all branches of the armed

Fig. 5. *The premiere pulp genre, adventure, gets its name in this magazine title.*

Fig. 6. *Adventure localized to a jungle setting.*

Fig. 7, left. *Adventure on the high seas.* Fig. 8, right. *High seas adventure limited to piracy.*

services (navy, army, air corps, marines) as narrowed subdivisions of the more general *War Stories*. Cosmopolites had their regular fare in *New York Stories* and *Parisian Stories*, not to mention any other specialty. The point here is to see SF as a late-coming part of *The Pulp Jungle*, title of the 1967 autobiography by Frank Gruber, who worked every genre in the list. Not so the SF writers loyal to their own small niche. But they almost alone prevailed when the pulps died.

Yet some notable mainstream authors got their start in that pulp jungle. Ring Lardner wrote for *Baseball Stories*, Upton Sinclair for *West Point Stories*, Theodore Dreiser for *Ghost Stories* even as he served as a Street & Smith editor, on whose company time he created his epic *Sister Carrie*; Tennessee Williams for *Weird Tales*, a subspecies of the supernatural genre along with *Horror Stories* in which tradition Stephen King has made such a remarkable career, going so far as to script and act in movies based on his own prolific output (notably *The Shining* of 1980 directed by Stanley "*2001*" Kubrick). Ray Bradbury, very much the darling of highbrow critics, likewise began in *Weird Tales*: epigonal Edgar Allan Poe grotesquery. How telling it is that he appeared only once in *ASF*. Its editor John Campbell deemed him lacking the right stuff, which is never the literary right stuff for belletristic critics.

I remember as a boy reading *Railroad Stories*, debating with a schoolmate the virtue

Fig. 9, left. *Sex and crime combined.* Fig. 10, right. *Cowboy romance, sex and western combined.*

of trains over airplanes defended by him and appearing in one of the aviation magazines (whose cover art reproduced the latest craft in exquisite detail): a partisan battle that led to fistfights. That tells how much the pulps incited juveniles to partisanship for one or another title. (How stupid of you not to like what *I* like!) I also recall other schoolmates disputing over their favorite characters in the hero pulps, *Operator 5*, *The Shadow*, *Doc Savage*. It was not until another pal put me onto *Astounding Science Fiction* that I switched loyalties, strengthened by parental disapproval. When my father (head of the Pennsylvania State Department of Education) returned home the day of this exciting discovery, he caught me, caution abandoned, openly reading it outside the privacy of my room; whereupon he pulled me by the ear and directed that I deposit the offending rag into the trash can. Middle class parents of the time believed pulp magazines a Bad Influence on youth, and even forbid their children to visit the Rexall Pharmacy unattended, where rack after rack of the mind-rotting stuff was on tempting display. It was warred upon by teachers, clergy, and parents alike, just as the same coalition today rallies against harmful television programs. Or rather, the campaign (orchestrated in my home state by said Education Department) was more like the War on Drugs: zero tolerance. There was no V-chip for the pulps, to select good from bad. This classed excellent *ASF* with the spicy titles and their *Playboy*-like covers, the *real* object of concern—not to mention

Fig. 11. *The ultimate in pulp topicality, cross-country racing in a special issue of* Sport Story.

the cheap science-fiction that also featured sexy babes (always in the tentacled grip of some rapist monster). But *ASF*, under John Campbell, was perhaps the most literate magazine of *any* sort; and its covers, often featuring astronomical art, were never vulgar. With its compound sentences, large vocabulary, and complex ideas, it ranged beyond anything brought into decent homes by subscription, *Good Housekeeping* being the preeminent organ of bourgeois respectability. That night after the ear-pulling incident I sneaked outside the house and from the trash barrel recovered the forbidden fruit, the start of a secret collection with me still. Yesterday's garbage is now a treasure, as university libraries pay dearly for such relics of popular culture in all fields, lately the subject of awakened academic interest.

Always it was the four main categories—adventure, detective, western, and romance—that dominated the pulps until they in turn yielded to paperbacks during the 1940s, which carried forward the same categories. Their final lodgment is in television programming. Significantly, when SF came on the scene in 1926, it modeled after the adventure story format, whatever else it purported to be as a fictionalized extension of Hugo Gernsback's *Science and Invention*, itself not hesitating to go beyond reporting on actual developments to extrapolating. Look at fig. 12, a typical cover for Gernsback's *Electrical Experimenter*, which projects a means of "suspended gravitation" by some imagined electromagnetic field. This develops into a handheld controlling device in the non–story related cover art for the August 1928 issue of *Amazing Stories* (fig. 13). No, the flying man is not Buck Rogers of the comic strips with his anti-grav backpack, although the same issue includes a story by Philip Francis Nowlan, "Armageddon 2419 AD," which inspired the later newspaper cartoons.

In this particular and others, *Amazing* owes to the so-called juvenile heroes like Frank Reade, a sort of young Tom Edison combined with wild West adventures. See fig. 14. Only later did SF adopt a more sophisticated stance, modeled after the British tradition of the scientific romance exemplified by H.G. Wells (Chapter 2). But it took quite a while before Wells the Father was recognized for what he really had to offer.

On the masthead of *Amazing Stories*, Gernsback proclaimed "Extravagant Fiction Today—Cold Fact Tomorrow." Amazing inventions of the future were the subject.

Fig. 12, left. *"Suspended gravitation" as a speculation in Hugo Gernsback's* Electrical Experimenter. Fig. 13, right. *Personal anti-gravity realized in* Amazing Stories, *extending the possibility in fig. 12.*

Scientifiction oldtimers joke that they could not sell to *Amazing* unless they came up with at least three patentable ideas per story. This worship of technological progress had to reduce to wonders no less marvelous than those in medieval miracle stories. By the 1950s there were more than 90 magazines in the field. (If that seems a lot, one should not forget that other genres were much more numerous.) Exhausting every synomym in *Roget's Thesaurus*, typical examples are (in alphabetical not chronological order):

Air Wonder Stories
Amazing Stories
Astonishing Stories
Astounding Science Fiction
Astounding Stories
Fantastic Adventures
Fantastic Stories
Marvel Science Stories
Marvel Tales
Miracle Science and Fantasy Stories
Science Wonder Stories
Startling Stories
Stirring Science Stories
Super-Science Stories
Tales of Wonder
Thrilling Wonder Stories
Unknown Worlds
Wonder Stories

When synonyms for "amazing" ran out, other titles evoking wonder were minted—*Cosmic Stories*, *Planet Stories*, and *Space Stories*; *Nebula*, *Universe*, *Infinity*, *Beyond Infinity*,

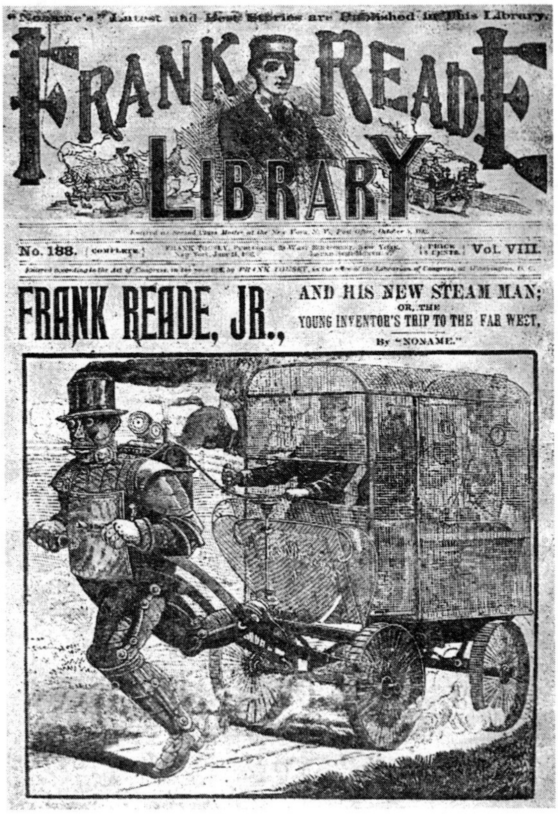

Fig. 14. *Frank Reade, boy inventor, with his Steam Man pulling the family buggy through Indian territory.*

and much else of other-worldly cast. Action takes place in the future, itself often the explicit subject, as in *Vision of Tomorrow* and *Worlds of Tomorrow*: a wonderful future made perfect by a masterful technology, giving rise to a saving tektopia of a new and improved material culture. This was in fact thematic at the New York World's Fair of 1939, billed as "The World of Tomorrow." But it would be a mistake to assume that science fiction, as it matured, invariably defined itself as futurist, even though an early band of fans aspiring to writerhood called themselves "The Futurians" and were led by the young Frederik Pohl, who came to exemplary maturity in later years. He recalls those boyish days in his memoirs, *The Way the Future Was* (1978).

When Gernsback introduced *Amazing Stories* as a new category into the pulp jungle, he had no stable of writers to fill the monthly issues to come. Instead he started off with some serialized reprints of Jules Verne and H.G. Wells novels (with short stories of the latter complete in one issue). He advised his readers: Go thou and do likewise. They did. One of them, the fannish letter writer in the magazine's first year, G. Peyton Wertenbaker, cited in my epigraph, did indeed go on to become one of its writers. Like the others, however, he had not the faintest glimmer of what Verne and Wells intended (see Chapter 3), and neither did Hugo Gernsback, who put them forth as models. For him engineering fiction, gadgetry, and innovative products were the essence. Whereas the other pulps could be written by any assortment of polyvalent hacks, Gernsback called for specialists true to his own vision, even if he had to cultivate them himself—which he did by forming the Science Fiction League. He got this going by publishing a letters column (thereafter a feature of all SF magazines but untypical of the pulps), giving names and addresses so the fans could write to each other and league together in local clubs. These by 1953 unified in World Science Fiction Conventions that give the Hugo Award.

Gernsback set the pace with a serialized novel in 1911–1912 runs of his *Modern Electrics* (fig. 15), 12 installments in all. Its title is of unparalleled crassitude, the writing the worst ever to blind the eyes of Western man. Yet it was the magic formula that set magazine SF in motion, reprinted in *Amazing* just to make sure the message got drilled in. This is the notorious *Ralph 124C41+: A Romance of the Year 2260*. Ralph's number is an idiotic rebus of prophetic significance: one to foresee for one. The plus sign indicates that he is one of the planet's ten geniuses, whose inventions show the way to a tektopian future.

Ralph, in consultation with various industrial enterprises around the world, develops better things for better living. Among his products are florescent lights, automatic packaging, plastics, jukeboxes, liquid fertilizer, tape recorders, stainless steel, loudspeakers, microfilm, vending machines that dispense hot and cold foods and liquids, solar power units, spun glass, a synthetic fiber like nylon for wearing apparel, new medical technology, and spaceships. All of these things that Ralph did were made possible by real-life industrial research: the very enterprise Gernsback regularly reported on in *Science and Invention*.

Fig. 15. *The April 1911 issue of* Modern Electrics, *with the first installment of the Ralph saga running into January 1912.*

Figures 16–21 offer a gallery of illustrations by the house artist Frank Paul that accompanied the *Amazing* reprint of the novel. The spaceship is the element providing adventure, as Ralph goes in pursuit of the story's two villains—a human and a Martian out to steal Ralph's girl. Benevolent Ralph and the villains prefigure the tension between technophilic and technophobic SF that soon developed. The diagram (fig. 22) showing how a radar-like device (in the novel, it is termed an actinoscope) works was a device much imitated by the earliest fans turned writers in the crude Gernsback image.

Kurt Vonnegut is one of those sophisticates who, while denying himself the science fiction label, yet expresses heartfelt affection for the old vulgarity in *God Bless You, Mr. Rosewater* (1965). The title figure is a fan of Kilgore Trout (Theodore Sturgeon, the eminent *ASF* writer, himself technophobic).

> Trout's favorite formula was to describe a perfectly hideous society, not unlike his own, and then, toward the end, to suggest ways in which it could be improved. In 2BR02B he hypothecated an America in which almost all of the work was done by machines, and only people who could get work had three or more Ph.D's.

This is exactly the scenario in Vonnegut's *Player Piano* (1952). The 2BR02B rebus for "to be or not (nought) to be" plays on Ralph's name. Trout, however, sees nothing

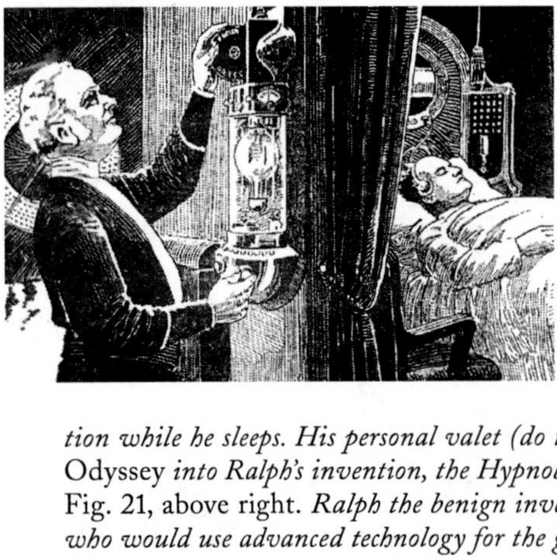

Fig. 16, top left. *Television as Ralph's world-linking invention. Illustration for reprint of the story in* Amazing Stories, *as are figures 17–20.* Fig. 17, top right. *Ralph provides solar power for Paris, a pollution-free source of energy for a sanitary utopia.* Fig. 18, above left. *Clean city of the future, with flying arches and aircraft overhead, as Ralph and his research partner roam it on motorized roller skates; wires dangling from their metal helmets indicate instant radio communication with a global village. Cell phones, however, got there centuries earlier.* Fig. 19, above center. *Ralph's contribution to medical technology, which makes the crudities of surgical invasion obsolete.* Fig. 20, left. *Although devoted to science and technology, Ralph does not neglect his cultural education while he sleeps. His personal valet (do they still exist in the 27th century?) inserts an audio tape of Homer's* Odyssey *into Ralph's invention, the Hypnobioscope, which transmits information to the brain while one is asleep.* Fig. 21, above right. *Ralph the benign inventor serving humanity fights with a spaceship against his evil rival, who would use advanced technology for the gain of personal power.*

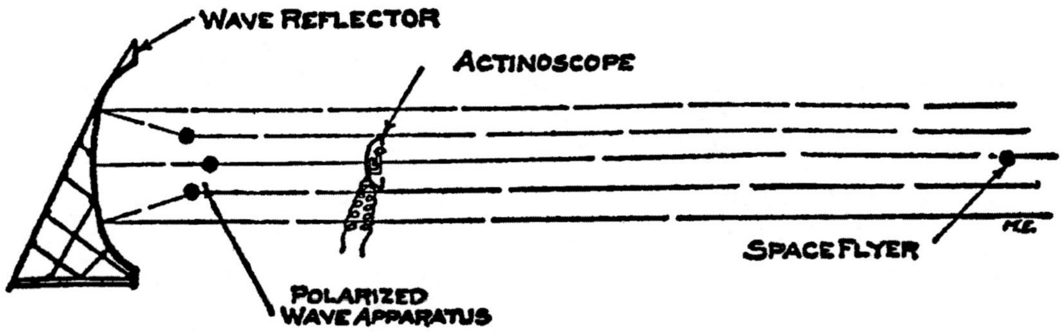

Fig. 22. *Ralph's device for detecting space flyers, here diagrammed by Gernsback in the* Modern Electrics *serial.*

humane in the growth of labor saving technology. It created "a serious overpopulation problem, too," for which he has his own ironic solution.

> All serious diseases had been conquered. So death was voluntary, and the government, to encourage volunteers for death, set up a purple-roofed Ethical Suicide Parlor at every major intersection, right next door to an orange-roofed Howard Johnson's. There were pretty hostesses in the parlor, and Barca-loungers, and Muzak, and a choice of fourteen painless ways to die. The suicide parlors were busy places, because so many people felt silly and pointless, and because it was supposed to be an unselfish, patriotic thing to do, to die. The suicides also got free last meals next door.
>
> And so on. Trout had a wonderful imagination.
>
> One of the characters asked a death stewardess if he would go to Heaven, and she told him that of course he would. He asked if he would see God, and she said, "Certainly, honey."
>
> And he said, "I sure hope so. I want to ask Him something I never was able to find out down here."
>
> "What's that?" she said, strapping him in.
>
> "What in hell are people *for*?"

Vonnegut's first novel, *The Sirens of Titan*, was a paperback original but fannish readers were not amused by his black humor. When he tapped the general market for it, with more expensive hardcover books, he hit gold. A change of readership made the difference, not his writing.

The title sirens are beautiful Tralfamadorian women stranded on Titan who somehow beckon one Malachi Constant from Earth to fly an untested spaceship there and bring a vital message. The message is encoded in all human DNA, planted there ages ago by the Tralfamadorians, aliens exactly like us except wiser and happier. Unlike humans with their fixed view of time, the Tralfamadorians' vision is extratemporal—past and present seen entire. The message? All it said was how, on the needed occasion, to replce a broken part in the spaceship stranded on Titan. They figure again in *Slaughterhouse-Five* (1969), whose narrator is gifted with an extratemporal viewpoint and in the end is transported to Tralfamadoria, a utopian planet of sensual delights. The Lotus Land that the hero of Homer's *Odyssey* spurns is here the answer to modern ills.

Strange to say, Hugo Gernsback was not as crass as he may seem. In the second year of *Amazing*, June 1927, he ran a very un–Ralphlike story heretofore unnoticed. The story is "Solander's Radio Tomb" by Ellis Parker Butler, the American humorist not otherwise known for SF. But he captured a definite moment in the history of radio that rings perfectly true.

The father of radio, Lee de Forest (inventor of the audion tube that made it possible), grew distressed that his baby had become a vehicle for jazz music and commercial ads—he had dreamed of quality broadcasts, classical music and poetry, as reported by Tom Lewis in *Empire of the Air: The Men Who Made Radio* (1991). Solander's tomb is a radio tomb because within its monument is installed a receiver and giant loudspeaker, one of those new technologies invented by Ralph (early radio had to be listened to with earphones).

Outraged citizens were removing their dead.

Fig. 23. *Illustration in the June 1927 issue of* Amazing Stories *for "Solander's Radio Tomb," with original caption.*

The station to which the tomb was attuned broadcast only solemn organ music for the benefit of the whole cemetery. Then the station changed to jazz. Fig. 23 (with original caption) illustrates the dead being removed by their horrified families.

The perfect example of the genre come to sociological maturity, barely 14 years after it began as engineering fiction, is "The Roads Must Roll!" by Robert Heinlein. Appearing as a cover story in the June 1940 issue of *Astounding* (see fig. 24), it rated seventh place in the SWFA anthology, according to votes cast by member writers for the top stories in the history of magazine science fiction.

The "Roads" are mechanical roads basic to the continental economy of a North Amer-

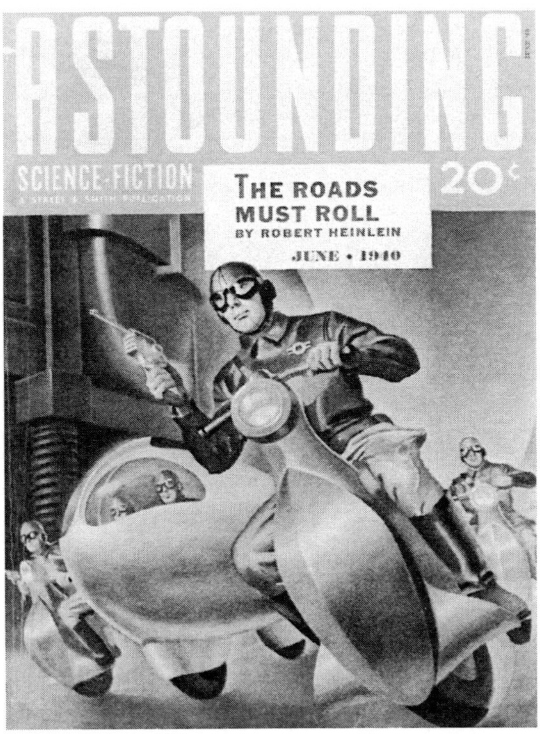

Fig. 24. *Heinlein's labor police, trained by the U.S. Academy of Transport, crack down on unenlightened transport workers still given to striking against the public interest.*

ican Federation in the then-future of 1970. On the premise that transport is civilization, the roads "Must Roll" at all costs, else their commercial lifeblood stops its circulation. The story is pertinent as ever in light of the air controllers' strike of 1981, which almost brought to a halt a national economy heavily dependent on air transport. The controllers calculated they were the key link in the chain of economic interdependency, with the power to disrupt everything if their unionized-labor demands were not met. Such a vital public service could not be allowed to hold the nation hostage and so President Ronald Reagan fired them and brought in a new generation of controllers.

In "The Roads Must Roll!" it is the system's maintenance engineers—the "rotor men"—who go on strike. The tension is between this older generation of unionists and a new one trained as paramilitary cadets in the United States Academy of Transport. The public spirited Transport Cadets, in this time of transition, just barely gain the edge and the crisis is averted.

Had Heinlein written this story in the Gernsbackian manner, the rolling roads would have been treated to a loving explanation of the system's wonders in every technical detail, complete with diagrams like Hugo's in fig. 22. A technophobic version, on the other hand, would feature noise pollution or some other undesirable side effect. But Heinlein's way was rather to write about a labor problem and the question of public duty regarding key technicians. The mechanical roads are displayed neither as glorified artifacts of progress nor as demonstrations of the converse—they are merely assumed as furniture of the future for a sociological discussion. "No, it's not the machines, it's the men."

The story has yet a larger context of world historical significance. It is but one episode in a centuries-long series of evolving events in the so-called Future History stories, collected in *The Past through Tomorrow* (1967). The mechanical roads are a solution to the problem caused by automobiles.

> The automobile made possible huge cities, then choked these same cities to death with their numbers. In 1900 Herbert George Wells [actually in 1901, in his *Anticipations*] pointed out that the saturation point in the size of a city might be mathematically predicted in terms of its transportational facilities. From a standpoint of speed alone the automobile made possible cities two hundred miles in diameter, but traffic congestion ... cancelled out the possibility.

Wells had the same solution, moving ways, for the gigantic urbanism of A.D. 2100 in *When the Sleeper Wakes* (1899). This is the very feature Gernsback chose to illustrate with technophilic glee when he serialized it in *Amazing* (see fig. 25). Indeed, gigantic urbanism was itself a tektopian dream for him (see fig. 26, as related to fig. 18).

Heinlein so much admired the novel that, when he got his copy autographed by the author in 1935 (during an American lecture tour), he preserved it as his "most treasured possession." That was four years before his first story, "Life-Line," in the August 1939 issue of John Campbell's *Astounding*, which brought him instant fame in that magazine and kept him there as its top author. Until the onset of World War II, he wrote about 30 percent of its copy under one name or another. The Heinlein name was for the Future History stories, "Anson MacDonald" for those outside them (see fig. 27), and yet

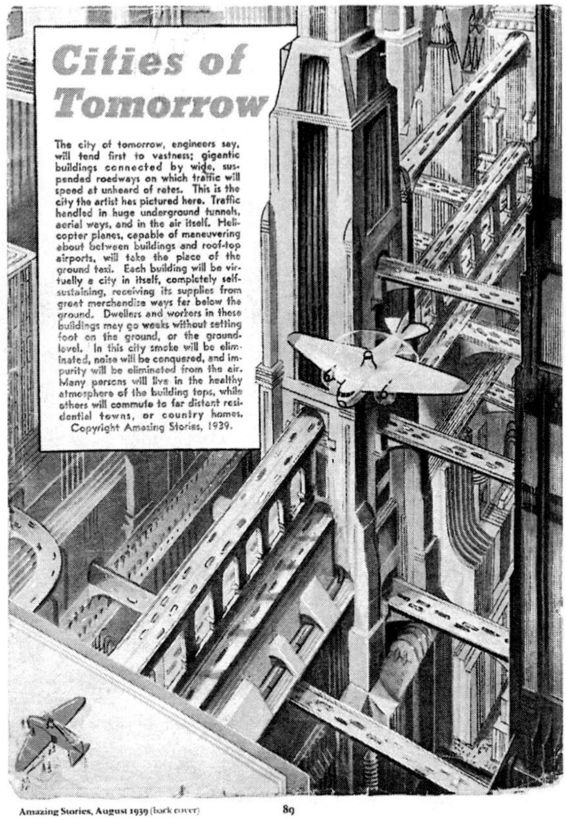

Fig. 25, left. *The moving ways of* When the Sleeper Wakes *by H.G. Wells as featured in the serialized* Amazing Stories *reprint.* Fig. 26, right. *"Cities of Tomorrow," illustrated editorial by Hugo Gernsback on the back cover of* Amazing Stories, *August 1939. What is hideous for Fritz Lang in his 1926 film classic,* Metropolis, *is here a utopian glory.*

other names for quite different stories. The pulp tradition had it that certain authors of whatever byline were associated with particular lines of story telling. Besides, it would not look good if one dominant writer hogged the show; it would look like the editor's stable of reliable authors was small. Who then can blame Campbell for promoting Heinlein under various avatars when he got what he wanted in a new and literate SF? For him the discovery of Heinlein, and the high standard he set, was the making of *ASF* (the revered initials for *Astounding Science Fiction*) as by far the best magazine in its field.

At Heinlein's death, he willed me his autographed copy of *When the Sleeper Wakes.* Now it is *my* most treasured possession. But however indebted the son to the Father, Heinlein is the most distinguished of the offspring. He remains the genre's last testament, even as he enters the canon of American letters.

American dominance began with the circulation of *Astounding Science Fiction* all over the world, a good model. Foreign SF writers never went through a Gernsbackian phase, nor ever descended into the worst depths of the American pulp industry. They bypassed all that and started afresh in book publication. It was SF and only SF, however, that had this impact, not other categories of pulp fiction. Thus when SF emerged as a worldwide movement (what else to call it?), it was American influence that propelled it.

British authors naturally were the first to respond, given the transatlantic language community. They often wrote for *ASF* and American readers more often than not were unaware of their national identity. The most popular of these, for his acerbic wit, was Eric Frank Russell.

Brian Aldiss later won international fame as one of the great modern masters of the genre. A voracious reader in his youth, when he worked for an Oxford bookseller and devoured the stock, he of course knew the British tradition (Chapter 2). But it was *ASF* that got him writing.

Fig. 27. *The Anson MacDonald byline used by Heinlein in "Waldo,"* Astounding Science Fiction, *August 1942. The technical term for the kind of device here illustrated is now "servomechanism," but when engineers at the atomic bomb factory in Los Alamos actually devised such for the handling of radioactive material they called them "waldos," a word still to be found in many dictionaries. This at a time when Campbell's* ASF, *often written by scientists and engineers, was read for new ideas by members of the R & D community (see Chapter 4).*

How he learned about it is an interesting story he told me. He says that American ships used to arrive with tons of unsold pulp magazines used as ballast. Magazine dealers would sort through this mass and pick out some of them for resale at marked down prices. Brian Aldiss found his first copy of *ASF* in one of these shops and then resolved to write such stuff himself.

In Japan, another country now highly receptive to SF, it was not *ASF* that got things going out but *The Magazine of Fantasy and Science Fiction*. A late entry in the pulp market, it began publication in 1949 with a higher grade of paper and with highbrow expectations that prevailed after most other SF magazines died out. A Tokyo publisher, Hayakawa-shobo, brought out a translated edition and later admitted Japanese stories into it.

The firm specialized in SF books, mainly translations of American authors but with a growing number of Japanese works. The company's president, whom I met in 1963, was (and is) a science fiction fan, favoring especially the works of Robert Heinlein, story collections and novels. He threw a big dinner party for Heinlein in 1985 on the occasion of the translated edition of *Job*, which included a learned essay by an eminent scholar on the novel's philosophical complexity.

Science fiction in Japan has had widespread support. While a visiting professor at Tokyo University, from 1963 to 1965, I attended meetings of the country's foremost SF club, which published its own fanzine, more elegant than anything seen in America. All my graduate students were intensely interested in American SF writers. They persuaded me to give extra sessions on the subject, which decided me to begin teaching SF when I got back to the States.

After 1950, American science fiction movies had no rivals. Before World War II, Germany held the lead with two notable Fritz Lang silent productions, *Metropolis* (1926) and *Die Frau im Mond* (1928). The former still is held by some to be superior to anything Hollywood ever produced. This is Euro-centric snobbery.

At the end of Chapter 3, I discuss Jules Verne and H.G. Wells on film. Verne does badly by Hollywood, but Wells fares better, especially in the productions of George Pal who specialized in science fiction movies. They may not be true to Wells but they *are* leading productions for their slickness.

The same may be said of the following films. They are not always good SF from the literary point of view, but always they set the international standard for professional quality.

Destination Moon (Eagle-Lion 1950), produced by George Pal; screenplay by Robert Heinlein, adapted from his own novelette in *Short Story Magazine* (September 1950): The film is cited for "advocating and promoting the exploration of space" in NASA's posthumous award to Heinlein of its Distinguished Public Service Medal (see Chapter 6). Story and film appear the same year because Heinlein went to Hollywood with contacts and proposal already prepared in advance; the magazine story is just for the record. He also secured for himself a position as technical advisor.

Private enterprise, seeing the future of world-unifying commerce in space travel, builds a rocketship that lands four scientist-astronauts on the moon 19 years before the Apollo 11 landing, a government project. The ship takes off and lands on tail fins, typical of SF magazine art.

The trip is realistic in every detail possible to special effects. When the astronauts land they wear realistic space suits, with proper constant-volume joints and goldfish-bowl helmets. The lunar mountains off in the distance and skyscape are murals done by Chesley Bonestell, already established for his astronomical paintings on the covers of *Astounding Science Fiction* (and the artist who painted the work chosen for the lower half of the cover to the present book). He would go on to do more spectacular work for George Pal in his other science fiction movies to follow.

The Thing from Another World (RKO 1951), produced and directed by Howard Hawks in black and white; based on the story "Who Goes There?" by John W. Campbell, writing as Don A. Stuart (*ASF*, August 1938): Science fiction fans, myself included, flocked to the premiere on 2 May 1951 at the Criterion Theater in New York City. The great John Campbell was coming to the screen, not as the now famous editor but as the legendary Don A. Stuart, author of a decisive body of work that changed the direction of SF, leading it at its best to philosophical sophistication.

We expected to see that exhibited in the film. Nothing of it survived. How disappointed we were may be reckoned by consulting the original story (see Chapter 4). It celebrates the triumph of reason as a group of research scientists based in Antarctica cope with a presence embodied in one of them. It began to make itself known after they recover an alien craft buried in the ice for millions of years. Given the scientific ethos they live by, all understand that problem-solving is a collective effort, and has been throughout the history of science. None are separate from that tradition.

The film opens with a few promising scenes. An army unit stationed in Antarctica comes across a tail fin projecting from the ice. The military already is a bad association for Hollywood, deepened by the research scientist attached to the unit. He is the typical mad scientist, out for his own vainglory in allowing "the thing" to flourish just so he can study it as the first to know the secrets of a hostile alien. A metal detector reveals the shape of the craft under the ice, as the men in a striking image spread out and stand in a circle. A flying saucer. The unit excavates it and finds a frozen body in it. Thawed out, the huge body comes to life and starts a rampage of destruction, unstopped by lopping off its arms with axes. The scientist concludes that the alien is a monstrous vegetable that regenerates its limbs.

Once again tampering with the unknown is the perennial theme, going back to Mary Shelley's *Frankenstein*, with ungodly results. The film goes against everything Campbell stood for in defending the scientific enterprise. Man's best hope is learning to know the unknown, probing the nature of nature. What makes the movie version notable is that it is a Howard Hawks production. The film critics loved it as one more outstanding example of his perfection of film noir. That is not good enough for SF critics.

The Day the Earth Stood Still (20th Century–Fox 1951), produced by Julian Blaustein in black and white; based on the story "Farewell to the Master" by Harry Bates (*ASF*, October 1940): The 1950s were rich in science fiction movies, good and bad; this one surely is the best of the decade, perhaps the best of any decade before science fiction no longer was advertised as such in Hollywood's promotional material. (This paralleled the decline of SF in print. The genre, however, had not exhausted itself; it continued under other names or as a nonspecific aspect of general entertainment.)

The film opens with a flying saucer landing on the White House lawn, a topical play on the mystery of the first UFO sightings in 1950. It sits there passively as crowds, army troops and television camera crews gather. Elmer Davis and H.V. Kaltenborn, well-known radio newscasters in the 1940s, report to the world; Drew Pearson, in his trademark fedora, appears before a camera in his own television studio.

Finally a ramp breaks out of the gleaming white hull, which later proves impossible to penetrate with diamond drills or acetylene torches, and reveals not a sign of where the door had opened. Down the ramp walks a man (no weird-looking alien) dressed in some shiny tight-fitting black fabric, and wearing a close-fitting helmet of lighter color that shows only a narrow gauzy band at the eyes.

The unearthly man, Klaatu, is played by the dignified Michael Rennie. He is one of the two stars who give the film its memorable class. The other is Patricia Neal who plays Helen Benson, a home owner in Washington, D.C.'s, residential Georgetown district. Klaatu, later driven into hiding, finds refuge after seeing a room-for-rent sign in the front window of Helen's house. He gives his name as a Major Carpenter, and gets along easily with the two-member family, Mrs. Benson and her young son, Bobby Benson (Billy Gray), Helen being recently widowed by the Korean War, which explains her need to rent out a room. Klaatu is sympathetic, with a real liking for the American people, despite what happened the moment he stepped off his ship.

Coming down the ramp, he is followed by a mighty robot, Gort, made of seamless white metal that yet flexes with his movements. Klaatu extends his hand with a strange object and a soldier instantly shoots him down. Gort's visor lowers and sends out a disintegrator ray that destroys all weapons arrayed against him: handheld rifles, artillery, tanks. None of the men are harmed. The strange object in Klaatu's hand was a gift for the President of the United States, with which he could have viewed Klaatu's home planet. He is its ambassador.

Only wounded, he is carried off to Walter Reed Military Hospital and put under tight security. He says he has travelled 250 million miles of space, which implies Mars: not very plausible. The doctor determine that Klaatu's body is physiologically like ours, right down to breathing air at our atmospheric pressure. Astronomers already knew that Mars had carbon dioxide at low pressure for atmosphere. But Mars long was the socialist planet in SF, pointing the way to Earth's future.

Klaatu escapes in the civilian clothing left in his room and ends up in Mrs. Benson's home. Meanwhile Gort stands guard by the ship, so motionless and passive that army engineers were able to encase him in a solid block of clear Lucite. The area is cordoned off with barbed wire and patrolled, with a battery of bright lights trained on Gort at night.

Bobby takes the likable Mr. Carpenter, new to D.C., to an amusement park and buys ice cream cones for both. Carpenter says he has no money to repay him, so gives him two diamonds in exchange. The boy is nonplussed and receptive to Carpenter's homily on capitalist greed and the warring of sovereign nation-states. Next they visit Arlington National Cemetery, where the alien comments on the wastefulness of war: unpatriotic words if spoken by a U.S. national at the time.

Bobby's mother, returning from work, is worried to find the boy gone, Mr. Carpenter as well. She searches Carpenter's room and uncovers a small packet of other diamonds. Now she is really worried, and goes out looking for the two. Just then they return and the boy gives an excited account of meeting with Professor Barnhardt. Mrs. Benson is impressed, although she does not yet know the story behind it.

After visiting the cemetery, the boy shows Mr. Carpenter other features of the town, including the famous home of professor Jacob Barnhardt. The boy is informed enough to explain that he is the world's foremost mathematical genius, a clear reference to Albert Einstein. Carpenter/Klaatu now finds his chance to carry out his mission.

Nobody answers the front door, so Klaatu goes around to the back facing a garden. Through a pair of glass-paned doors he sees a blackboard with equations for celestial mechanics chalked on it. He enters and erases a term here and there and writes in others, while the boy watches with a sense now of who Mr. Carpenter really is. At this point the great mathematician's personal secretary enters and orders the intruders out. Professor Barnhardt follows, looks at the blackboard, then dismisses the secretary.

Barnhardt, played by Sam Jaffe with Einsteinian authority, shock of white hair and all, needs no explanation from Klaatu. The two get down to business straightaway. The Professor promises to arrange a gathering of the world's leading scientists at the ship, together with top United Nations diplomats, by a certain day and appointed hour. Klaatu in turn promises a convincing demonstration of his powers the day before—the day the earth stood still.

Bobby and Mr. Carpenter return home to Helen's relief. Bobby tells of meeting with Professor Barnhardt but keeps mum on what happened there. Later that evening Helen's boyfriend Tom Stevens (Hugh Marlowe) pays court. Bobby shows his displeasure, intuitively sensing a false friend in this oily insurance salesman. By now he is suspicious of Helen's boarding guest, connecting him with constant news about the dangerous alien on the loose. In the end he betrays Klaatu.

The night before the day the earth stood still, Klaatu leaves the house to see Gort and set it up. Bobby follows and watches as Klaatu signals Gort with a flashlight. The robot melts down the plastic block encasing him, then approaches the two guards, facing outward, and knocks their heads together. Klaatu and Gort enter the ship and program the demonstration. Having seen enough, Bobby goes home and honestly confides in his mother. When Klaatu gets back Helen says nothing, keeping her sympathies to herself.

On the appointed day, Mr. Carpenter accompanies Helen to her place of work. The elevator they ride together stops and goes dark. Carpenter explains that electricity will be out for thirty minutes all over the world, and tells her why. Helen says that she already understands. In the city streets, all traffic stops because car batteries are neutralized as well. The same in Times Square, outside the Houses of Parliament, around the Arc de Triomphe, and in Red Square near the Kremlin (all scenes in daylight!). General Cutler, in charge of apprehending Klaatu, orders his men to take the alien dead or alive. He concedes that hospitals and planes in flight were not affected by the blackout, but is unmoved by this humanitarian display of unearthly power.

News about the massive manhunt goes out and Helen's boyfriend Tom Stevens hears it while visiting yet again. He fastens on Bobby and browbeats him to reveal what he knows of the mysterious boarder. The boy's answer is too guarded to be believed. Bobby then replies, "I would never call *you* a liar." Tom storms out of the house and goes to the nearest pay phone, telling General Cutler where he can find the alien.

After that, things move rapidly. Helen gets Klaatu and Bobby out of the house and into a cab directed to the spaceship. The military finds nobody at home. Troops all over the nighttime city, wanted posters in hand, spot the cab as it drives by a checkpoint. A soldier shoots into it, mortally wounding Klaatu. As he lies dying in Helen's arms, he tells her three words to say to Gort.

Gort is very much on the alert. Helen fearfully approaches and says, "Klaatu barata nikto." Gort's visor opens and the ray begins to pulsate. She repeats, the visor closes, and Gort steps forward to receive the body. He carries it into the ship, Helen following. Bobby stays behind, as instructed, to sit on one of the folding chairs arranged before the ship where soon Professor Barnhardt's promised gathering will sit. Armed troops following the cab in jeeps and trucks keep their distance, knowing all too well Gort's potency.

Inside the ship Gort places Klaatu's body under a miraculous device that resurrects him. He arises to thank the amazed Helen, explaining that the revival is only temporary, but long enough to complete his mission. Dressing in his original costume, minus helmet, he is ready to address the assembled delegation. The ramp comes down under the glare of spotlights, and he descends, Gort and Helen in train. She retires to sit in the audience with Bobby, himself seated next to Professor Barnhardt.

Klaatu concludes his message to the world with these words: "Soon one of your nations will apply atomic power to rockets. Up to now we have not cared how you solved your petty squabbles. But if you threaten to extend your violence this Earth of yours will be reduced to a burnt out cinder. Your choice is simple. Join us and live in peace. Or pursue your present course and face obliteration."

He then departs, leaving the impassive Gort behind as a reminder of the choice. The ship silently ascends into the night sky, gathering speed as it disappears into starry vastnesss.

The haunting theremin music by Bernard Hermann adds a moving emotional tone to the production, integral to it. The basic theme, three ascending notes, repeats very briefly as the ship rapidly vanishes: understated yet unforgettable.

Special effects by Fred Sersen are modest, never calling attention to themselves. They serve only to smoothly advance the story line. The director of photography is Leo Tover, A.S.C., one of the best in the business. Working here in black and white, he excels.

The script by Edmund H. North is unusually intelligent by Hollywood standards. Producer Julian Blaustein wisely chose him to adapt a magazine story by Harry Bates. Although it was published in John Campbell's *ASF* (October 1940), it recalls the less sophisticated pre–Campbellian era, for which Bates is remembered as the first editor of *Astounding Stories* from 1930 to 1933. It did not become *Astounding Science Fiction* under Campbell until 1937.

The story, "Farewell to the Master," differs radically from the film in almost every respect. (The only common elements are a murdered space traveller name Klaatu and a giant robot, Gnut, himself the title's master.) Yet something of its original spirit carries over. Even that is less important than the question why producer Blaustein decided on a creative adaptation making for a most original science fiction movie.

The Howard Hawks production of *The Thing* is not comparable. It too departs radically from its basis, "Who Goes There?" by John Campbell. But the free adaptation is *not* creative. The film descends into just another horrific monster movie, however much critics may celebrate its film noir technique.

Blaustein discovered in the Harry Bates story the basis for an ideological statement that translates into a memorable film standing on its merits. Hollywood at that time was under fire by the House Un-American Activities Committee for harboring "Reds." Although the film dared to suggest that leftwing "One-Worlders" had a point, it escaped notice under the guise of science fiction. For all that, the film remains a classic of SF cinema.

The Magnetic Monster (United Artists 1953), produced in black and white by Ivan Tors: the lesson of this film is that movies are movies. What is known as hardcore SF in print does not and cannot translate to film. *The Magnetic Monster* tried that, with uncompromising rigor, and was a box-office disaster.

This is at once regrettable and inevitable. Scriptwriter Curt Siodmak is at home with the literature, himself a contributor. It made a believer of the producer, convincing him that he had a really different film to hand, and he gave it all the quality resources United Artists offered. Different it is. Nothing like it will ever be seen again. Thrilling production, wrong medium.

A new isotope is created in a research laboratory and doubles in size every few hours, eventually to destroy Earth. Scientific investigators are puzzled by the deadly radiation and strange magnetic field the isotope produces. This leads then to a counter-intuitive solution: Feed it with more energy than it can absorb, carried out in a deep-sea facility already in place. The finale includes riveting footage from special effects in the German SF classic *Gold* (1934), about the transmutation of elements.

The film's intelligence, attention to scientific accuracy, economy of style and execution, and strong performances by unknown actors set it apart. Also unusual is its attitude to the consequences of science and technology. No mad scientists here, but heroic figures who struggle to understand and control new-found aspects of nature.

Forbidden Planet (Metro-Goldwyn-Mayer 1956), produced in Eastman Color and Cinemascope by Nicholas Nayfack; screenplay by Cyril Hume from a story by Irving Block and Allen Adler: Film critics, usually hostile to science fiction movies, were taken by this one for its obtuse Freudian allusions and for its literate play on Shakespeare's *The Tempest*. I am not sure anybody out there in Hollywood was aware of that. They also favored the avant-garde "electronic tonalities" that served in place of music.

To follow the entrenched critical paradigm, Prospero is Dr. Morbius (the aging Walter Pidgeon), an obsessive scientist living alone with his daughter Altaira, the virginal Miranda figure on the distant planet Altair IV. These two are the only survivors of a colony whose fate a ship of the flying saucer type, flying at hyper-speed from Earth, comes to investigate. Ariel is the amusing Robby the Robot. The ship's crew finds itself menaced by an invisible Caliban, a "Monster from the Id" that expresses Dr. Morbius's jealousy of the outsiders who intrude on his incestuous father-daughter privacy. The monster, in the end, destroys Morbius and the whole planet. Just in time the crew rescues Altaira and departs.

Morbius's Id is empowered by the stupendous energies he draws from the interior where machinery left behind by the Krel civilization still functions automatically. The film's most spectacular special effects picture this awesome interior. The Krel had transformed themselves into beings of pure energy, all of it now concentrated in the morbid unconscious of Dr. Morbius. His frustrated power blows up the entire planet.

This film surely is the most handsomely mounted monster movie ever made. Its visual treatment was not surpassed until *2001* (Chapter 6).

2

The British Tradition

The Father himself *never* used the term "science fiction." It was beneath Wells's dignity. In his autobiography (1934) he says the aim of his youthful novels was "to discuss sociology in fable." The sons had reduced this lofty purpose to a discussion of science and invention, and he came to regret selling reprint rights to Gernsback for one of his "electro-technical journals." It took some time before SF writers reappreciated Wells in their development of social science fiction, the most faithful son being Robert Heinlein, after Gernsback had showcased him in *Amazing Stories* ("electro-technical") for the wrong reason.

In 1933, Wells collected his early work in *The Scientific Romances*, a London title studiously avoiding the magazine cachet that had actually renewed his Victorian fame. To no avail; a New York edition counter-asserted the American view by retitling it *Seven Famous Science Fiction Novels.*

Science fiction or scientific romance, what's the difference? Wells thought it great enough to discriminate in his 1933 title, which harks back to an older term in use when he wrote *The Time Machine* (1895). Before that he had been a science journalist, textbook writer (see fig. 28), and literary book reviewer.

From just before 1890 in Britain there emerged the scientific romance as a nameable genre, quite apart from any genre magazine (such did not yet exist until the Yanks hit the shore with imports of their pulpish examples). Fiction of all types appeared in the nation's preeminent general magazine, *The Strand*, in which Sherlock Holmes made his debut; Conan Doyle had no *Detective Story* for his outlet, nor any *Amazing Stories* for his Professor Challenger series.

The scientific romance was highly developed by the time Wells came on the scene, when he met with considerable competition. But he did it so much better, with so much

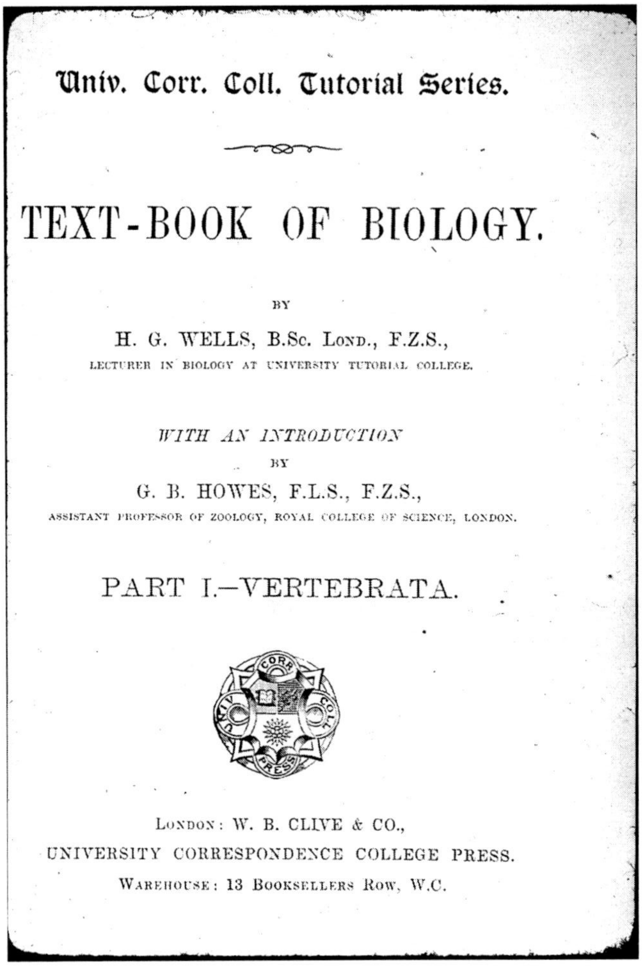

Univ. Corr. Coll. Tutorial Series.

TEXT-BOOK OF BIOLOGY.

BY

H. G. WELLS, B.Sc. LOND., F.Z.S.,

LECTURER IN BIOLOGY AT UNIVERSITY TUTORIAL COLLEGE.

WITH AN INTRODUCTION

BY

G. B. HOWES, F.L.S., F.Z.S.,

ASSISTANT PROFESSOR OF ZOOLOGY, ROYAL COLLEGE OF SCIENCE, LONDON.

PART I.—VERTEBRATA.

LONDON: W. B. CLIVE & CO.,

UNIVERSITY CORRESPONDENCE COLLEGE PRESS.

WAREHOUSE: 13 BOOKSELLERS ROW, W.C.

Fig. 28. *Wells's* Text-Book of Biology *(1893). He would return to this subject in his four-volume* The Science of Life *(1931) done with Julian Huxley, a collaboration that launched the latter's career in biology. His brother, Aldous Huxley, went on to author that most famous of dystopian novels,* Brave New World *(1932), a bitter technophobic reaction to the future imagined by Wells in* When the Sleeper Wakes.

literary éclat, that the others are remembered only because he outdid them. Indeed, this is the point of the collection put together by A. Kindsley Russell, *The Rivals of H.G. Wells* (1979). Among them is the formidable George Griffith, whose serialized "Stories of Other Worlds" is reprinted there. With his wife, a British scientist travels to other planets or their inhabitable satellites in his homemade, anti-grav spaceship (remarkable what the wealthy amateur, not unlike the Time Traveller and *his* machine, could achieve in those pre–R & D days). Intelligent life is everywhere out there in the solar system, a smashing rebuttal to man's geocentric view of the universe. On Mars he is witness to an advanced civilization, created by big-brained humanoids of tall stature (lower gravity, you see, allows for greater growth). See fig. 29. Wells, of course, improved on this image with his even brainier Martians, but who are far from human-like in their bodies. A true plurality-of-worlds thesis, if geocentrism is to be fully rebutted, must allow for radical differences in planetary evolution.

Another story from *The Strand* is "The Thames Valley Catastrophe" by Grant Allen. A geological fault in the Thames Valley opens it to a sudden incursion by the North Sea, which swamps London. The narrator remarks, "The universality of the catastrophe made each man feel as though it were selfishness to attach too great an importance to his own personal losses." What is me and mine in light of great impersonal events?

The essence of the scientific romance was that it took into account long geological and Darwinian horizons. In that new cosmic vision there was no excuse for the individualistic adventure story format. The triviality of men in the face of incomprehensible workings of the cosmos is the overpowering theme.

Fig. 29. *The original caption to this illustration for the George Griffith novel says, "A huge Martian, who seemed to stand nearly nine feet high."*

Nowhere is this more supremely expressed than in *The Time Machine.* In the end we have a *fin de globe* scenario, in which the sun dies and so does all life on earth. Yet something could have been done about it had men the sense to prepare to flee into outer space and found new worlds. But this option presupposes a united humanity in a one-world state given to the remote and mighty ends of racial salvation. The novel's prophetic future is a cautionary tale warning of catastrophic things to come if the political will to take Wells's advice is not mustered.

He argues that the social conflict between labor and capital in his day *must* be resolved, or else the resulting dégringolade of civilization will forfeit mankind's reach for the stars. The Time Traveller arrives in the year 802,701 only to find the descendants of the two sides, Eloi (= capital) and Morlocks (= labor) still locked in irreconcilable conflict as a prelude to decay of the whole solar system millions of years hence.

G. Peyton Wertenbaker, in my epigraph, may have had *The Time Machine* in mind when he defined SF as appealing to a sense of wonder regarding "things vast, cataclysmic, and unfathomably strange." He may also have been referring to his own "The Man from the Atom," the cover story of the special scientifiction issue of *Science and Invention* (see plate III). This also is a thing vast and incomprehensible: a story about a man who expands beyond earth, the solar system, even our universe to emerge into a macro-universe in which our own is but an atomic particle. *The Incredible Shrinking Man* (Universal's 1957 film) offers a variation, in the opposite direction, on Wertenbaker's original storyline.

The sense of wonder in Wertenbaker's widely accepted definition of the genre derives from that attending medieval cabinets of inexplicable anomalies and monsters, counterbalanced by philosophers of the time who attempted to explicate them in naturalistic terms.

Their rational point of view is asserted in "A Scientist Divides" by Donald Wandrei (*Astounding Stories*, 1934).

> That is why you write fiction. You romanticize things. I investigate them and find out their nature. Then they lose their mystery and neither repel nor attract.

The words are those of a hard-nosed scientist determined not to be sentimental.

Insofar as *Amazing Stories* and its imitators exhibited a new cabinet of curiosities, it implied the opposite of wonder when appealing to science. Wertenbaker missed this when he exalted the vast catastrophe envisaged in *The Time Machine*. He overlooked Wells's own rational, sociological explanation for what happened.

The Eloi represent a capitalist elite turned effete when they cower before the onslaught of organized labor, whose members are portrayed as the ape-like Morlocks (see fig. 30). They embody the "pithecoid Proletarian" of Wells's later scorn in *The World of William Clissold* (1926), a discussion novel dealing with labor unrest and other democratic ills. The fault of democracy is under-government; what is needed is a statist regime to put down independent trade unions. The beastly Morlocks cannibalize the Eloi just as unionized labor eats alive capital with its class-sectarian demands.

Fig. 30. *Student drawing of a Morlock, with proper ape-like appearance and large eyes adapted to underground darkness: a different species evolved away from the aboveground Eloi, still normally human in appearance except for their degenerate frailty.*

In *The Time Machine* the two sides are at a standoff: Labor fails to win a proletarian revolution, capital still is victimized and, no resolution in sight, industrial productivity halts. The minatory message is, such a protracted conflict can be settled only by a strong government that takes over the economy and subdues the unionized Morlock man, making for a docile, strike-free workforce: the Fascist and Communist solution alike. The various names Wells gives in his later nonfiction for this solution are technocratic socialism, state socialism, state capitalism. All three synonyms in Wells's political vocabulary oppose communal socialism *à la* Marx, at the same time *with* him he militates against private profit capitalism. Wellsian SF dissolves in its fabulation a gritty polemic for state capitalism unseen by his earliest American fans.

Wertenbaker sees in *The Time Machine* only the strange and cataclysmic end-of-the-world drama it displays. Yet there is a scientific (sociological) explanation for all this. The Eloi and Morlocks in the lapsarian future of 802,701 are but a paradigm for misbegotten class relations in the author's own day. The novel is a work of culture criticism, whose effect is indeed gained by an appeal at first to the strange and inexplicable; but at last it *is* rationalized. The two quotations above, from Wertenbaker and Wandrei, bring together what became the legacy of SF at its maturity: a return to Wells in a deeper understanding of his philosophical fatherhood.

Gernsback the electrical engineer, when reprinting *The Time Machine*, was interested only in the machine itself. His artist's illustration (fig. 31) features electronic gadgetry that suggests the possible development of such a device: just another product of R & D that might be featured in *Science and Invention*. Wells never presupposed any such thing. *His* illustration (fig. 32) offers no technical detail more definite than a bicycle saddle, as the only one specified in the text, and the Time Traveller himself is dressed in cycling costume of the period: a purely symbolic gesture. At the time Wells wrote, the newly invented bicycle (in its modern improvement) was the fastest thing on the road, surpassing the speed of horse-drawn carriages. In his first book of social prophecy, *Anticipations* (1901), Wells predicted bicycle mechanics would become the engineers of motor cars and then of airplanes. Indeed, the Wright brothers who invented the airplane in 1903 were bicycle makers. The significance of motorized transport for Wells was that it would unify the world in global village—to use today's cliché coined by Marshall McLuhan in the 1960s, referring to the unifying effect of modern communications. The Time Traveller, riding his bicycle into the future,

Fig. 31. *Wells's time machine reduced from symbolic significance to a practical electronic device, as illustrated by Frank Paul in* Amazing Stories.

Fig. 32. *Frontispiece to the New York first edition of* The Time Machine, *with original caption. The "men running" are Eloi, the first people the Time Traveller meets before he learns about the Morlocks.*

expects to find a progressive civilization far more advanced than his own. He is disappointed. There is no unified world-state controlled by the likes of Wells's Airmen in the 1936 film *Things to Come*.

Yet all that the early SF writers got out of Wells was an incentive to devise ever more clever theories of time travel. Harry Harrison finally ended that nonsense in his comic masterpiece, *The Technicolor Time Machine* (1967). In the magazine tradition the inventor is invariably asked, But tell me professor, how does it work?, followed by a narrative-stopping, textbook discourse. When Harrison's Professor Hewett is asked that he replies, "You could not possibly understand"; and the story moves on. The question asker is the head of Climactic Studios, a Hollywood firm in trouble with its New York bankers. If Climactic does not complete *Viking Columbus* within a week, the studio will be foreclosed. Advisor to its executive is one Barney, Hewett's friend, who brings his boss around to see the professor and to recommend his experimental machine (if developed) as a solution: go back in time, on location about A.D. 1000, and take whatever temporal liberty to do the production. The plan works, and the crew returns by the appointed deadline with film in the can. In the process they hire a Greenlander Viking who calls himself Ottar to play the starring role of Thorfinn Karlsefni, he who makes the first Viking landing in America in Newfoundland (Vinland) according to the *Graenlendinga Saga* and *Eirik's Saga*; but Ottar will accept only bottles of Jack Daniel's whiskey in payment for the job. In the end, Ottar turns out to be Thorfinn himself and Barney, the Bjarni who in the Vinland sagas bought him the ship in which to voyage to the New World.

The joke is complete when archaeologists at L'Anse aux Meadows in Newfoundland, the only documented site of Viking settlement in America, discover in its rubbish heap puzzling shards of Jack Daniel's glass—bottles emptied by Ottar. Harrison offers a comic juxtaposition of Hollywood and Viking ethnography, both authentic. The final crunch is, Barney consults Professor Hewett after the archaeological discovery is reported. A close study of *Eirik's Saga* had revealed that all the doings of the crew while on location can be interpreted in its light. "But the significance, Professor, the significance," he is exhorted to explain. "If this is true, the only reason the Vikings settled in Vinland is because we decided to make a motion picture showing how the Vikings settled in Vinland." Hewett's calm reply is, "It's as good a reason as any other." His throwaway line tops all previous elaborations on this or that paradox of time travel with a casually offered new one: the idea of a closed loop with no beginning and no end.

But to return to the scientific romance, and its profounder cosmic vision as Wells himself treats it in *The Time Machine* and elsewhere. In "Under the Knife" (1896) he brings that vision to fullest clarity.

The story is narrated by a patient who undergoes at-home surgery. While anesthetized by ether he experiences astral projection. His disembodied mind floats above, looking down on the operation, then upon London, the British Isles, and then the entire planet, and so on into outer space. The soul, or whatever, is not bound by gravity as is the material body; and so it is Earth itself and the whole solar system in its galactic orbit that flies away from him, not he from it, as at last the entire sidereal universe is left behind. He senses a "gradual slipping away from the pleasure-pain guidance of the animal man." Finding himself a "naked intelligence," parted from his "garments of flesh," he now sees all things with "unemotional clearness," knowing "the world about me for the phantasmagoria it had always seemed." Finally, the cosmos in its entirety disappears into one distant speck of light, which then reshapes as a glint on the jeweled ring of some godlike finger. Is the cosmos no more than some infinitesimal part of a vaster entity? Then he hears a booming voice, "There will be no more pain." It is the finger ring and voice of his doctor. The patient, coming out of his anesthesia, has experienced a cleansing, apocalyptic vision in accord with Revelation 21:4—"And God shall wipe away all tears from their eyes; and there will be no more death, neither sorrow, nor crying, *neither shall there be any more pain*: for the former things are passed away" (emphasis added). Henceforth there shall be "a new heaven and a new earth" (21:1). The awakened patient who had thought himself dead, is now a living saint destined to help make that new heaven and new earth. The apocalyptic visionaries of space travel, in Chapter 6, are no less saintly.

The immediate response to "Under the Knife" in *Amazing* was the 1929 story by Fletcher Pratt, "The Roger Bacon Formula." Here the narrator finds a long-lost Bacon MS., in which a formula for some mind-enhancing drug is prescribed. He mixes up a batch of the stuff and is carried away in a far-traveling trip that has no more consequence than merely beholding cosmic wonders.

Far from epigonal is what Olaf Stapledon, the last and most epic of the British scientific romancers, did with "Under the Knife." His narrator in *Star Maker* (1935), by means of "hypertelescopic imagination," is witness to the very birth and death of the universe on a scale of billions of years. Along the way he finds a variety of intelligent humanities, all who rise and pass away. His quest is to discover the creative principle, the title star maker, behind everything, so as to make our little terrestrial life seem meaningful. Stapledon's purpose, as he says in the preface, is to cultivate "the self-critical self-consciousness of the human species." The attempt is "to see man's life as a whole in relation to the rest of things"—a thoroughly Wellsian enterprise.

Such a grandiose philosophical effort was not in the least contemplated by the early magazine epigones of H.G. Wells. Yet they are fascinating for what they tried to make of him.

Another example they played on is "In the Abyss," a story of 1896 in which it is proposed that even on our own planet there are sufficient wonders to put mankind in its place relative to the cosmic dynamics of evolution. A scientist descends into heretofore unplumbed oceanic depths in a spherical device lowered by cable from a surface ship. Such a device for the study of deep-sea life was not invented until Charles Beebe, the American naturalist, did so in 1934 with his bathysphere ("sphere of the deep"). Later, the Swiss physicist August Piccard in 1960 descended in his bathyscaphe ("ship of the deep") to the bottom of the Marianas Trench, and deeper than that in the sea it is not possible to go. Piccard had been a youthful reader of Jules Verne, inspired by his exploratory voyages, not alone by Captain Nemo's submarine but also by his balloonists from on high. Piccard would do both ventures, first in 1935 ascending to record heights (19 miles) in a sealed balloon-carried gondola not unlike the bathysphere, a lightweight version made of aluminum. His subsequent exploration of the deeps may have had additional prompting from the Wells story.

It was a strange vertebrated animal.

they came into the radiance of his lamp, and he saw then that they were indeed fish of some strange sort with huge heads, vast eyes and dwindling bodies and tails. Their eyes were turned towards him, and he judged they were following him down. He supposed they were attracted by his glare. Presently others of the same sort joined them. As he went on down he noticed that the water became of a pallid colour, and that little specks twinkled in his ray like motes in sunbeam. This was probably due to the clouds of ooze and mud that the impact of his leaden sinkers had disturbed.

By the time he was drawn down to the lead weights he was in a dense fog of white that his electric light failed altogether to pierce for more than a few yards, and many minutes elapsed before the hanging sheets of sediment subsided to any extent. Then, lit by his light and by the transient phosphorescence of a distant shoal of fishes, he was able to see under the huge blackness of the super-incumbent water an undulating expanse of greyish-white ooze,

Fig. 33. *Original illustration in* Pearson's *(August 1896), another general magazine like* The Strand. *Text surrounding the animal's tail is included to show how magazines of the day used typography to create entertaining visual effects.*

At all events, "In the Abyss" tells of a naturalist discovering an unexpected civilization down there. His device is captured by its inhabitants, who grab hold of his cable, and he is confronted in fig. 33 by their emissary looking into his porthole. In fig. 34 the bathysphere is put on display as a trophy for the glory of the ruling potentate. By chance the naturalist gets free, improves his device and descends again, never to be heard from. "But it is hardly probable that any further attempt will be made to verify his strange story of these hitherto unsuspected cities of the deep sea."

The deeps, however, may decide to report to the surface, the premise of a story following the 1926 reprint of Wells in *Amazing Stories*. That story, "Davy Jones' Ambassador" by Raymond Z. Gallun, appeared in the December 1935 issue of *Astounding Stories*. Fig. 35 shows a deep-sea naturalist looking out at intelligent creatures, one of whom swims before his porthole. He (or it) is the title ambassador of an exotic civilization. In a pressure-sealed container, he returns with the diver to the surface, there to represent to astonished humans that they are no longer the only lords of creation.

Fig. 34. *The bathysphere displayed before the underwater king, with cityscape in the background. Nearer, the sphere is mounted on a display stand in the city's central plaza. Human skulls at the king's feet indicate his intention (as implied) to conduct a public sacrifice. No wonder the naturalist fears for his life.*

In the upper atmosphere too, may lie unknown creatures, these of unsuspected superiority. This is the revelation of Heinlein's "Goldfish Bowl" in *Astounding Science Fiction* for March 1942 under the Anson Macdonald byline. It surely plays on the Sir Arthur Conan Doyle story of 1913, "The Horror of the Heights" in which a high-flying aviator encounters strange beings up there only to crash afterward, his

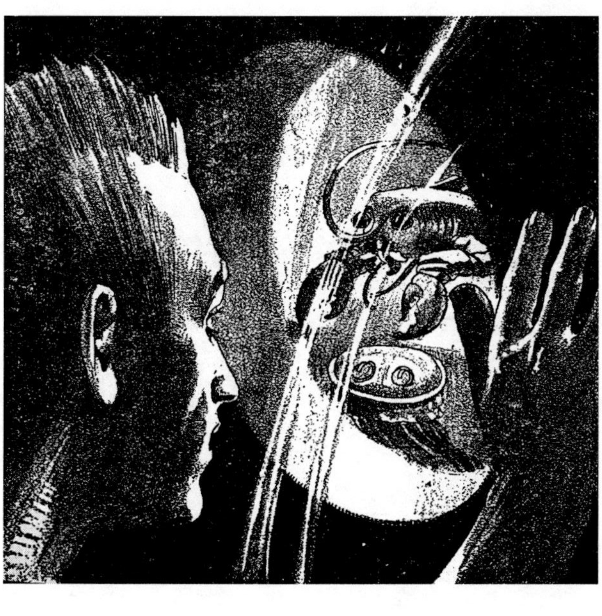

Fig. 35, left. *Illustration in* Astounding Stories *for "Davy Jones' Ambassador" by Raymond Z. Gallun.*

story untold except for some scribbled notes in flight, as interpreted by the story teller. They have no effect, and so the world remains uninstructed by what really happened in that encounter.

In "Goldfish Bowl," the title of which suggests that we may be no more than pet goldfish kept by higher beings, the one man able to communicate this awful truth is reduced to a four-word message. The story opens with the U.S. Navy observing two unimaginably powerful columns of water near Hawaii, one going up to who knows where and the other down. See fig. 36. Three naval officers undertake to ride a bathysphere injected into the upward column. All perish in captivity, their prison being some smallish container. The last man to survive figures out how the system of feeding and waste disposal works. Before he dies he sums up his knowledge in four words inscribed on his naked body with a toenail: "Creation took eight days" (fig. 37). His dead body (like the others) is disposed of in the down chute, its cryptic message never deciphered. Had it been, it would say the six days of biblical creation did not end there. God may have rested on the seventh day, but He went back to work on the eighth, creating beings higher than man. The creative evolution principle did not stop with *Homo sapiens*; the world is

Fig. 36, left. *Original magazine illustration for "Goldfish Bowl" in* Astounding Science Fiction. Fig. 37, right. *The cryptic message from the "Goldfish Bowl" is shown on the captive's body.*

not for his dominion over the lower animals, himself merely one of these: a cosmic outlook in the British tradition, never native to American SF.

Borrowings from it by American writers, however, often are creative adaptations that enrich the genre as a body of literature now given global recognition under American influence. One of the most majestic themes originated by the British is that of the last man: A single survivor of the human race underscores just how vulnerable to extinction it is, just like any other species known from the fossil record.

The theme takes its name from the title of an 1826 novel by Mary Shelley, *The Last Man*, in which a plague reduces humanity to one lone survivor who records the event. The novel, of course, is pre–Darwinian and lacks the language of cosmic vision. All the same, its resonant title had a lasting influence. Although the setting is A.D. 2100, "the last year of the world," technology is not developed far beyond the late eighteenth century. Shelley explains this by saying "human selfishness and greed" had retarded progress: the world deserved what it got.

M.P. Shiel in *The Purple Cloud* (1901) assimilates the theme to the scientific romance. Hydrocyanic gas liberated by volcanism kills off all mammalian life. The lone survivor sets out from the North Pole in a world full of corpses embalmed by the gas. He visits Calcultta, Peking, San Francisco among other cities in a grand *tour d'horizon*, reviewing the record of civilization.

Conan Doyle, in one of his Professor Challenger stories, "The Poison Belt" (1913), has the Earth plough through a cloud of toxic interstellar gas. He and a group of other scientists retreat to a sealed room and sip bottled oxygen. The next day they venture into a picturesquely deserted London. In the event, the gas induced not death but catalepsy. The world revives.

The American Wallace West in "The Last Man" (*Amazing* 1929) plays on the word "man," here taking it to mean the last male in a world of women. He is put on display in a zoo.

In *Earth Abides* (1949) by George R. Stewart, a professional ecologist descends from a California mountain range to observe the many changes attending the removal of humans from the landscape, depopulated by a pandemic disease (corpses already eaten by animal scavengers including dogs gone wild). He drives his car all the way out to Chicago, gassing up at still operative filling stations; further he cannot go because storms have flooded the highways and blown down trees. Besides, electrical power stations are beginning to go out. He has trouble enough getting back home, where at last he finds a few other survivors. They gather under his leadership to form a viable community, no longer dependent on raiding the diminishing supply of canned goods in grocery stores, and to bear children. For them he teaches school until realizing that the past is beyond recovery, as he knows from his futile attempts to board up broken windows in his university library. In the end, as he ages, he is the last American (see Chapter 8).

The British tradition influenced American SF writers, no question about it. This is not to say they were aware of that tradition as such. They rather responded to H.G.

Wells without knowing the history of the scientific romance he worked. With Jules Verne (thoroughly French), he was just a genre resource, having no specificity other than the tag Hugo Gernsback gave the two when he reprinted them in *Amazing Stories*.

British SF authors, of course, know differently. Apart from the later influence of American magazines, they had their own non-genre magazine heritage. It explains how Wells came to be a nineteenth-century literary figure in his homeland before Gernsback imported him in 1926 to exemplify what he had in mind for *Amazing*.

In 1870, Parliament enacted the Education Act as a response to the growing industrial economy. It established government schools, with required attendance up to eighth grade, to provide a more literate society and a better educated work force. It also led to the founding in 1881 of the Normal School of Science attended by H.G. Wells, the son of two domestic servants, on a scholarship as were other bright lower-class boys looking for a way out of their ordained servitude.

The first generation of public school graduates created a mass market for reading matter. Newspapers and magazine periodicals mushroomed to meet the need, and book publishers did a booming business in fiction. Wells got into this new market just at the right time to establish himself as a major celebrity. Escapist literature was in high demand, as the newly literate looked critically on their urban-industrial culture. Before the advent of World War I in 1914, even future war novels predicting it offered escape. The scientific romances of H.G. Wells played into this with great success, although today we know they are more than escapist fantasies. At the time, however, the author had no way of foreseeing that these works would become immortal classics of *Weltliteratur*.

Until 1927 Wells remained a literary celebrity of immense fame. No author since then has achieved that because it is no longer possible. His personal trajectory, dropping to zero after 1927, illustrates the rise and fall of the man of letters in a bygone era.

With his B.Sc., Wells intended a long career of science teaching. Indeed, his *Text-Book of Biology* (1893), long the only one available, got him off to a good start. But soon he fell to tuberculosis and then turned to writing, drawing on a fund of voracious reading. The new journalism offered ample opportunities for the ambitious beginner, including *The Saturday Review*, for which he acted as chief fiction reviewer. His reviews were quite astute in assessing novelistic art good and bad, and promoted the best—Joseph Conrad's first novel, for example. Meanwhile he learned skills to be applied to his own first novel, *The Time Machine* (1895), declared a work of genius. More scientific romances followed (together with other forms), which made him the most widely read author in the world. Thereafter he lived like minor royalty, whose every move was newsworthy.

In 1927, the year the BBC was constituted, he suddenly lost his readership. Radio programs gained more listeners than readers of books and periodicals. *The World of William Clissold* (1926) was the last Wells novel to claim a following. With the advent of film and television, the written word no longer served as a basis for celebrity. Media stars displaced autograph-signing authors.

At the turn of the last century, London was the literary capital of the world. So it had been at the time of Samuel Johnson in the eighteenth century. It was he who established the man of letters as a professional free of aristocratic patronage. Now the economy of industrial capitalism opened the market to writers with a mass readership available.

Not all was junk journalism or trashy novels. Much fiction appealed to understandable escapist fantasies: action-adventure, sentimental sex romances, and so on. But at the same time, some visionary authors working the scientific romance (not yet named) laid down a tradition that H.G. Wells perfected. In looking back on the record, he stands out as *the* great Victorian novelist of ideas for his artistry, intellectual grittiness and prophetic power.

The rivals of H.G. Wells in his own day were not seen as anything but highly competitive, no less likely than he to endure. In light of the outcome a century later, they are worth reconsidering for the attention Wells must have paid to them. A most instructive example is "The Last Stand of the Decapods" by Frank T. Bullen, F.R.G.S. (*The Strand Magazine*, December 1901). As a Fellow of the Royal Geographic Society, Bullen evidently is informed on the subject he writes about: decapods or ten-armed squids, the monsters of seafaring lore. The story reviews the history of attacks by giant squids on ships from ancient times.

Finally a gathering of sperm whales, also victimized, launches a counterattack; the squids gather to resist but are slaughtered in a day and night of bloody struggle.

> Henceforth they were no longer lords of the sea; instead of being as hitherto devourers of all things living that crossed the radius of their outspread toils, they were now and for all time to be the prey of a nobler creation, a higher order of being, and at last they had taken their rightful position as creatures of usefulness in the vast economy of Creation.

The interesting thing about the story is that it postulates intelligent animal communication and coordinated action, a fashionable object of study today. The noble whales triumph and the sea lanes are safe for shipping: man's part in "the vast economy of Creation." Bullen may or may not have read the earlier Wells story, "The Sea Raiders" (1896). Whatever, creative interaction is so complex that no one line of influence can ever be traced.

"The Sea Raiders" tells of intelligent octopuses (six-armed octopods) invading the land, humankind's domain. Scattered resistance is reported, and then the reports end.

> Whether it is really the last of these horrible creatures it is, as yet, premature to say. But it is believed, and certainly it is to be hoped, that they have returned now, and returned for good, to the sunless depths of the middle seas, out of which they have so strangely and so mysteriously arisen.

The story is consistent with others of later date that dwell on man's insecure place in Creation. How does man respond to alien species?

In "The Empire of the Ants" (1905, a *Strand Magazine* story), intelligent army ants on the march devastate plantations along the Amazon River. A river boat pilot, sensing a wider threat to civilization, by chance finds a way to stop them before they take over everything. In "The Star" (1897), a passing comet nearly depopulates the entire planet; the survivors unite to rebuild society along new lines.

In *The War of the Worlds* (1898), Martians fall out of the sky and devastate London as a point of departure for world conquest. Their flying machines (the Wright brothers did not fly until 1903) are readied to drop poison gas everywhere. Providentially, terrestrial germs kill off the Martians before they advance further. Humans learn much from their science and aviation technology. In *When the Sleeper Wakes* (1899), a sequel, great airliners are the means by which a capitalist world-state is held together by world trade. The novel argues the Wellsian thesis that "autocratic state capitalism" (words of 1928) is the only possible future.

In his 1936 film, *Things to Come*, Wells consolidated his thoughts on human destiny. Threats to it may come not alone from the deeps or from outer space, but from man's own suicidal war-making in pursuit of national rivalries. In time, the sun will burn out and then human complacency will have prevailed forever. So far man's survival in the cosmic scheme of things has been iffy at best, absent any political will to plan the future.

In the film, World War II (said to have begun in 1939) is under way. The results are catastrophic. John Cabal and his Airmen gather a superior force to bomb the last of the war-makers out of existence. In a speech to his victorious Airmen he says,

> Do you realise the immense task we shall undertake, when we set ourselves to an active and aggressive peace, when we direct our energies to tear out the wealth of this planet, and exploit all these giant possibilities of science that have been squandered hitherto upon war and senseless competition.

By "aggressive peace" he means a unified humanity making war on nature instead of each other. "Senseless competition" is a dig at private-profit capitalism, to be remedied by state capitalism.

John Cabal's grandson Oswald carries on as President of the World Council of Direction. It is now 2036 and Oswald Cabal plans for the next contingency: the sun burning out. He prepares a Space Gun for the first experimental firing of a manned projectile around the moon and back. Then later a landing, and so on until the other planets are conquered. At last, out across immensity to the stars, where the human enterprise shall be immortal.

In *The Time Machine* the Time Traveller is witness to the sun's end and the ending of all life on Earth. Critics take this gloom and doom climax as a pessimistic prophecy. Not at all. Wells intended to show the fate of man if action were not taken to avert oblivion. The standoff of labor and capital in the year 802,701 prefigures the decline and decay of the entire solar system, unless something is done about class warfare: Morlocks (labor) in unproductive conflict with the effete Eloi (capital). The only answer is industrial productivity ensured by a state-capitalist regime that abolishes both unionized labor (Morlocks) and a leisure class of private owners (Eloi). This is the solution *When the Sleeper Wakes* offers: labor disciplined, capital effective. *Things to Come* amplifies.

The Airmen in this film go back to a story by Rudyard Kipling, "With the Night Mail" (1905), and its sequel, "As Easy as A.B.C." (1912). A.B.C. stands for Aerial Board of Control, which dominates the world. Ostensibly a postal service, with mail delivered by a fleet of dirigibles, it actually is a world government. In the second story agents of the A.B.C. fly to Chicago from their London headquarters to deal with a revolt of the local underclass. The rioters are shot down at night by rifle fire from the skies, directed by terrifying searchlights mounted on the dirigibles.

The A.B.C. lives by two slogans, "Civilisation is Transport" and "Democracy is a Disease," that is just as apt for the Air Dictatorship in *Things to Come*. Its transport monopoly in the furtherance of world trade is a statist regime, leading on to a permanent world-state that ends the disease of democracy forever.

Kipling, whatever his intention, provided Michael Arlen with grist for his dystopian novel *Man's Mortality* (1933). Aviation is monopolized by International Aircraft and Airways, Inc., and its motto is WORLD TRANSPORT MUST GOVERN THE WORLD.

> This was originally no more than a world transport system. It grew because the world was rudderless. It displaced the existing system of individual and competitive capitalism. It displaced forms of government which, with few exceptions, were founded on democratic capitalism. Spawned in the despair of men, I.A. & A. rose and waxed strong. It was armed with a superb ambition, to dragoon the nations of the world into a colossal scheme of tidiness.
>
> The architects of this new order were inspired by the splendour of a dream of peace: of peace at all costs, even at the cost of tyranny. They courted tyranny. They were weary of the superstition of humility to the inevitable quarrelsomeness of human nature. Sick almost to death of the malaise of democracy, they denied that truth is the daughter of debate, and imposed an autocrat over the peoples.

But this "tyranny of tidiness" is overthrown after fifty years.

The same year Wells brought out *The Shape of Things to Come*, the novel on which his film *Things to Come* is based. In the novel, a character developed as the film's John Cabal, leader of the Airmen, spells out his credo.

> It is no good asking people what they want. That is the error of democracy. You have first to think out what they ought to want if society is to be saved. Then you tell them what they want and see that they get it.

In plain words, first you hijack control, then you make them like it. For all its lofty goals, this credo reduces to the strongarm code of gangsterdom.

In a literary response to *Things to Come*, Rex Warner's allegorical novel *The Aerodrome* (1941) is, alas, little known. Its Air Vice-Marshal, who rejects the human world as it is, sensual muddle and stupidity and all, proposes the training of "a new and more adequate race of men": the Wellsian program exactly. Published eight years before George Orwell's equally prophetic *Nineteen Eighty-Four* (also a response to Wells), it deeply reflects on the dangerous yet glamorous appeal of statist idealism.

3

Verne and Wells

The names of Jules Verne (*d.* 1905) and H.G. Wells (*d.* 1946) have been associated ever since their works were reprinted during the first three years of *Amazing Stories* from 1926. Its founding editor Hugo Gernsback took their writings as exemplars of what he thought science fiction ought to be: imaginative technology extending what he reported in his earlier *Science and Invention*. Vernean submarine and Wellsian time machine were all the same to him. Critics are quick to point out that Verne was the more interested in new inventions, whereas Wells held to sociological concerns; but they are not quite right either. Both Verne and Wells share the same political religion, their common motivator.

When in 1986 I was invited by the British Film Institute to introduce a fiftieth anniversary showing of Wells's *Things to Come* (1936) at the National Film Theatre, Arthur C. Clarke was the first to ask a question after the showing, one that had long bothered him. I remember him raising the same question in a 1937 letter to *Astounding Stories*. He now raised it again. Why did Wells revert to a Vernean space gun in the film when rocketing was known to him?

My answer went something like this. Verne's *Columbiad*, his gigantic space cannon in *A Trip to the Moon* (1865, first English translation), is above all symbolic. Verne had reflected on the American Civil War and wondered how its massive array of artillery pieces might be converted to peaceful purposes. The *Columbiad*, cast from a melting down of these guns (fig. 38 shows it in plan), achieves that object in the cause of mankind's unified space exploration. What is presaged by the moon shot is "the foundation of a travelling service through the solar world," then to provide "a means of locomotion [that] allow[s] us to visit those suns which swarm in the firmament." Off goes the first shot in fig. 39. The firing of a space gun in the finale of *Things to Come* (fig. 40) harks back to

Fig. 38, above left. *Verne's space cannon as if laid out on the surface. In actuality it is buried in the ground, pointing directly skyward. The whole system, gun and projectile, is named the* Columbiad, *just as the Saturn V rocket and the space capsule atop it were components of the numbered Apollo missions that first carried American astronauts around the moon and then landed them on it several times.* Fig. 39, above right. *The* Columbiad's *projectile shot from its gun (surely crushing its crew to jelly were the thing to be done). Flames from a similar cannon are seen on the surface of Mars just before the Martians fall out of the sky in* The War of the Worlds. Fig. 40, left. *The Space Gun in* Things to Come *is definitely a gun, complete with gunsight, a gigantic artillery piece muzzle-loaded by crane (top left) with a manned projectile.*

like symbolism. Even the manned projectile in Verne (fig. 41) has its exact parallel in Wells (fig. 42).

The costs of the *Columbiad* are raised by international subscription, even as the flight of its projectile—toward the moon, around it and back to splashdown in the Pacific—is tracked by astronomers from all over the world. Its construction by the United States, then the leading industrial country, takes place with exalted class collaboration between captains of industry and factory

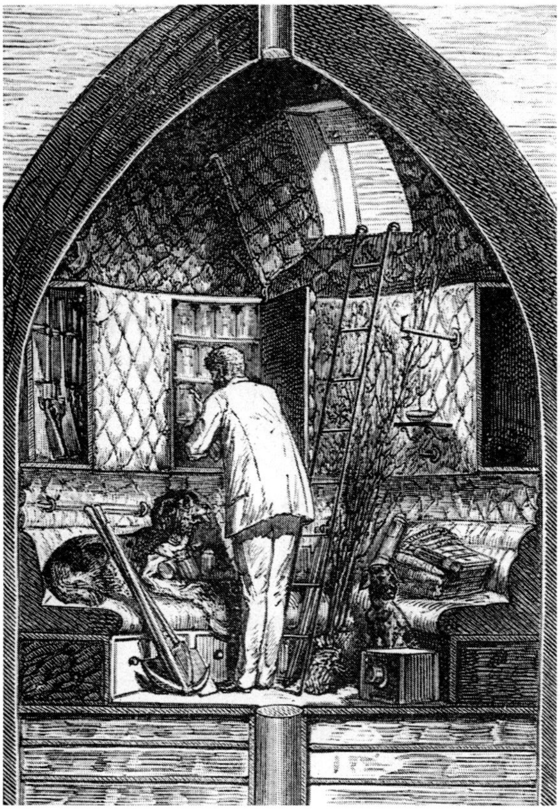

Fig. 41, left. *Manned projectile in Verne. Pickaxes and rifles presage future landings (not this time) for the mining and colonization of the moon.* Fig. 42, right. *The two passengers of the Wells projectile being strapped in. They too will only circle the moon, as a preliminary to landing on it and other planets.*

workers. The novel is a technocratic hymn to the partnership of capital and labor, knowledge and work, all in the service of man's collective conquest of nature.

There my reply to Clarke ended. Left unsaid, under the press of other questions from a large audience, was anything about the history of socialism. That cannot be avoided now if Verne's ideas are to be identified. The term socialism itself is a coinage in 1832 by a disciple of the French savant Henri Saint-Simon. He lived through the advent of industrialism, before there arose a labor movement in response to it. Saint-Simon himself named his doctrine *industrialisme*: the science of production entailing class collaboration between capital and labor, directed by capitalists. Karl Marx later took *socialisme* to mean a class-war socialism, pitting the "proletariat" (Saint-Simon's word) against its exploitators.

Jules Verne never dreamed that Saint-Simonian socialism would in due course lead on to revolutionary despotism; H.G. Wells did. Verne was no statist, yet like Wells he affirmed Saint-Simonism.

Historians of ideas conclude that Saint-Simon's cult of authority may be traced to the ideological roots of all three dictatorships dominating the twentieth century: the fascist in Italy and Germany, the communist in Russia. They claimed to be enemies of each other, but in fact were brothers in state capitalism. The Italian and German examples openly advocated its principle: the marriage of big business with government. The Russian example is more extreme: outright confiscation by the state of all private property.

The fraternal connection of the former with the latter was obscured, and still is, by the official communist line that it held state capitalism a foe to be defeated in a world revolution against capitalism everywhere.

At the time, Wells had gained a reputation as the most famous socialist writer in the world, although his leftist readers took him for what he was not: a popular Marxist. Few if any of them caught on that he was a pre–Marxian socialist of the Saint-Simonian school, even when in 1928 he advocated "autocratic state capitalism." His fame spread after his visit with Lenin in the Kremlin in 1920 and with Stalin in 1934. There he advised them, by invitation, on the prospects of their hoped-for world revolution. Nothing of the sort is possible, he said, unless they drop their Marxist double-talk about a proletarian revolt. Straight talk about autocratic state capitalism is the only way.

Frustrated by Stalin's rote Marxist rhetoric, even after he launched his Five Year Plan to transform Russia into a vast production company along Saint-Simonian lines, Wells returned home and began work on *Things to Come*, released by London Films in 1936. This movie, a classic in the SF cinema, is more than that. It states Wells's "Communist Revision": communism minus Marx. The so-called "workers' state" in Russia, he correctly observed, has a misleading double meaning. On the one hand it implies rule by proletarian workers; in practice it enforced a rule by state managers. In Saint-Simon's utopian future, all citizens, unless defective, are productive workers: managerial workers, scientific workers, and worker workers. This is the Wellsian utopia, scientific government, without duplicitous rhetoric.

Verne, unlike Wells, resisted utopian visions of any sort. A patriotic Frenchman, he believed in his nation's colonial *mission civilisatrice* to subdue savage tribes, and to bring the conquest of nature to obdurate resources. His Extraordinary Voyages extend French civilization to all parts of the globe, even into outer space. Wells hates nationalism and envisions a socialist world-state free of local patriotisms. Verne always novelizes irredentist movements that win his sympathy; a world-state is the last thing he would endorse. He rather looks to humanistic, noncoercive world unity, itself utopian. Verne and Wells are the odd couple in the history of SF, both Saint-Simonian idealists in their contradictory ways.

Even before *Things to Come*, Wells played on the Vernean space cannon. In *The War of the Worlds* (1898), invading Martians are shot from guns. Their home planet is the Mars of the American astronomer Percival Lowell. His huge international bestseller, *Mars* (1895), gave Wells a receptive audience. Plate I:1 offers the book's frontispiece. Green vegetation-bordered canals and oases are shown against pinkish deserts in need of irrigation. Water is provided by melting polar ice caps for a planet-wide system as the intelligent Martians fight off the increasing desertification of their aging planet. Lowell, an avowed Saint-Simonian, saw Mars as the future of socialism.

In Wells, the Martians, from an older and wiser planet, bring their saving state-idea to ours. Not really invaders, they are celestial teachers. Not "men in trousers," as Lowell had said, they are rather horrible-looking octopoidal monsters. In time, after the dirty germs of earth kill them off, they begin to look less monstrous. Men adopt their advanced technology and enlightened world order, free of nationalism and war, private capitalism and senseless competition. Men themselves become the inhuman monsters they once feared. Utopia arrives.

Wells's 1898 novel set the pattern for invading aliens in magazine SF, even more ugly. Stanley G. Weinbaum broke with that in his unprecedented "A Martian Odyssey," first appearing in the July 1934 issue of *Wonder Stories*. Members of SFWA voted it number two in their anthology of best SF short stories (Silverberg 1970 in Bibliography). Its exotic life forms capture the charm of a fairy tale combined with a witty sophistication that intuitively rationalizes the inexplicable. For this reason SFWA voted it as the best example of the genre's intellectual balancing act, at maturity, between Sense of Wonder and its opposite.

Meanwhile SF movies upscaled their special effects, crude at first, for more hideous-looking aliens motivated by ever more grandiose malice. The beauty contest began in monied earnest with the 1953 Paramount Production of *The War of the Worlds*. Weinbaum's refreshing story is a bygone of the vanished Gutenberg era. Print SF then was ahead of retrograde movies and television.

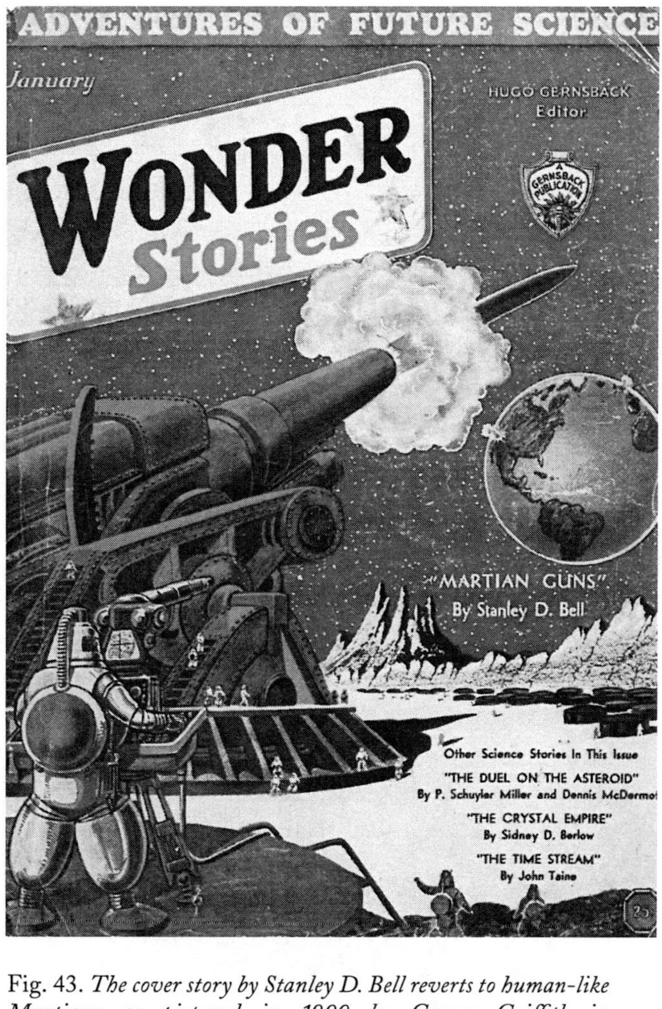

Fig. 43. *The cover story by Stanley D. Bell reverts to human-like Martians as pictured in 1900 by George Griffith in* Stories of Other Worlds *(see fig. 29). Here they are dressed in space suits. Presumably, Lowellian Mars of the canals has become not only increasingly waterless but airless: two good reasons for the Martians to shoot for the green hills of Earth.*

For Gernsback the novel's fascinating point was the engineering marvels of the Martian fighting machines. The initial installment in *Amazing* for August 1927 featured them with lovingly inventive detail worthy of *Popular Mechanics* (plate I:2). Also featured is fiery destruction wreaked by the Martian Heat-Ray, amplified by the planet-busting death rays of space opera (plate I:3).

Inevitably the other side of the Martian invasion had to be told, as it was with "Martian Guns" in the January 1932 issue of *Wonder Stories* (fig. 43). A more pacific Mars, still complete with Lowellian canals, emerged in *Red Planet* (1949) by Robert Heinlein and in *The Martian Chronicles* (1950) by Ray Bradbury. The all-purpose pulpist, Edgar Rice Burroughs, who wrote faster than anybody can read, led the way with the 11 novels of his Barsoom Series out of more than a hundred magazine-derived books. He was the most prolific and richest man ever to profit from the pulp jungle. Tarzana in California is named after his most popular hero.

But even before Lowell triggered the intelligent-life-on-Mars cult that followed his mistaken astronomy, the planet had been the setting for a doctrinal battle of the books debating Marxism and Saint-Simonism. In *A Cityless and Countryless World* by one Henry Olerich (1883), Mars is a Marxist utopia, arrived at by a proletarian revolt that restores the preindustrial good life. It responded to the better known *Across the Zodiac* by Percy Greg (1880), which offered a Saint-Simonian technocracy, likewise countryless but not because it is a planet of rural communes; Mars is rather home to a highly urbanized world-state. Greg's point, however, is that such a statist vision is evil. Lowell, who called himself a socialist but not a Marxist, found the alternative attacked in *Across the Zodiac* ideal. His Mars is Greg's, with the addition of globe-encircling canals.

Indeed, Lowell's *Mars* played into a canal building mania here on earth. The first attempt by Ferdinand de Lesseps at digging the Panama Canal, connecting the Pacific and Atlantic oceans for the benefit of world trade, then was current news. Previously he had succeeded with the Suez Canal, linking the Mediterranean, via the Red Sea, to the Indian Ocean. He had also carried out extensive irrigation projects in Algeria. More, it was de Lesseps, the most famous of Saint-Simon's disciples, who inducted Jules Verne into the French Legion of Honor. Verne's romantic globalism, as in *Around the World in Eighty Days* (1873), glorified a colonial mission to civilize unreached corners. "The world belongs to mankind" was a popular Saint-Simonian slogan in Verne's day, French leadership assumed.

Wells brings his Martian invaders from a planetary collective Lowell said pointed to the future direction of terrestrial progress. That future is realized in *The Shape of Things to Come* (1933), Wells's most massive utopian statement. The shapers are Fellows of the Modern State, who bring about a "rule of the new saints," the brains of what they dub the Modern State Octopus. In the derivative film, *Things to Come* (1936), they are the Airmen, whose leader is John Cabal, who wears a gas helmet like the head of an octopus—a Martian reference. When the visor is down, says Wells, "his head and shoulders are suggestive of a Buddha against a circular halo" (fig. 44). His Airmen fly gigantic bombers (fig. 45) whose WT in their letter-numeral designation stands for World Trade. It is their saintly duty to make the world safe for a global economy by dropping a Gas of Peace on the last still-fighting strongholds of belligerent nationalism in the aftermath of a catastrophic World War II. He finishes it and John Cabal's grandson then goes on to become President of the World Council of Direction in the accomplished utopia of 2036. And it is Oswald Cabal, now that the whole world belongs to mankind, who initiates experiments with a Vernean/Martian Space Gun for travel to other planets, extending man's harmonious conquest of nature to the rest of the solar system and beyond. So, the Martian invasion, while just as devastating as the Airmen's bombing raids—their war-for-peace—has benevolent ends. The Martians are no less monstrous and salvationist.

Fig. 44, above. *John Cabal's gas helmet, shaped like an octopus's head, with visor down; the effect, says Wells, is to display Cabal's head and shoulders against a Buddha-like halo. He addresses a soldier dressed in World War I costume, serving the Boss of Everytown. Everytown exemplifies all those ministates still at war with each other after the great nation-states have been smashed in World War II. The Boss keeps the spirit of bellicose nationalism alive, until Cabal and his Airmen extinguish the last of his type. The state monster, a state octopus whose bureaucratic tentacles control everything, is at once frightful and salvationist. From* Things to Come, *frame enlargement.* Fig. 45, below right. *Cabal's Airmen load up one of his gigantic bombers, WT 715, with the Gas of Peace destined for Everytown. The "WT" stands for World Trade, to be liberated from a system of national sovereignties into a unified world-state.*

Cabal's World Council of Direction echoes the Council of Newton proposed by Saint-Simon, the scientific governing body of his World Republic of United Interests. "All men will work, they will regard themselves as laborers attached to one workshop [and] the Supreme Council of Newton will direct their work." In *The Work, Wealth and Happiness of Mankind* (1931), Wells has it as a "single world economic machine." The Modern State Octopus is a big business government, whose managerial tentacles grip and control every aspect of society under a state-capitalist regime. For Wells, a socialist world-state and capitalist world-state were the same thing in Saint-Simonian terms.

Verne, however, never went that far. He may be said to be a utopist without a utopia. Yes, the world belongs to mankind, but also to those peoples who fight for national liberation in Ireland, French Canada, Greece, Hungary, Brazil; the Boers in South Africa, Muslims in Libya; the insurgents of the Indian Mutiny and the Taiping Rebellion in China; Crete under the Turks, Central Asian emirates under the tsars; Central America and the Caribbean dominated by the United States. Verne took to heart one legacy of the European Revolutions of 1848, the so-called "springtime of nations" that mark the rise of the modern nation-state. No world-state for him, but a furtherance of the very nationalism the Airmen militate against when it everywhere finally reduces, in the aftermath of a shattering world war, to irredentist ministates:

that hopeful springtime turned to a lasting winter of discontent. Verne glaringly contradicts the World Republic of United Interests in Saint-Simon's utopian vision. But even so he shares with Wells a deeply-felt contempt for Marxism, which sponsored that other fateful legacy of 1848, its proletarian uprisings. At the same time Verne said his aim in the Extraordinary Voyages was to "paint the earth," setting his adventures in all parts of Africa, America, Asia, and Oceania; at the poles, beneath the earth and under the seas; above and beyond: "the world we live in."

Verne wrote few works of nonfiction, principally his three-volume *The Exploration of the World*, the first titled *The World Outlined* (1878). Geographical instruction preoccupied him, in making for a global outlook. The equivalent in Wells, who came to write much nonfiction, is *The Outline of History* (1920). It traces the rise of humanity from cavemen and tribalism through barbaric nationalism to "The Next Stage of History," his projected world-state. It would be a World Republic of United Interests because all class and national conflicts were dissolved in it. Verne imagined no such thing, reconciling liberation movements with mankind's common heritage: everything opened up by marketing industrialism.

Verne's hatred of Marxism surely appealed to his bourgeois readers in a way the *other* socialism would not have. Yet in his posthumous novel of 1910, *The Survivors of the Jonathan*, he finally realized that authoritarian socialism's time had come. The novel is set in the remote Magellanic Islands, whose geography, flora, fauna, and minerals are exhaustively detailed. The novel's hero, *The Masterless Man* of volume one, seeks refuge there from European politics: the same lonely freedom Captain Nemo sought beneath the seas. But soon he is caught up in a civil war between Chile and Argentina for possession of the islands: nationalism gone wrong. At the same time survivors of the shipwrecked *Jonathan* introduce a chaotic labor communism. Both events call for a stern corrective, provided by *The Unwilling Dictator* of volume two.

The springtime of nations in 1848 overthrew Napoleonic imperialism, even as it accompanied proletarian revolts throughout Europe. Napoleon III, under whose rule Verne wrote up to 1871, rose to power in 1851 after he proved the most decisive in putting down the Marxist-driven insurgent mobs in Paris; thence to champion the sovereignty of peoples in his "Principle of Nationalities," a theory in advance of his era but one invariably echoed by Verne. Having exiled all Socialist deputies from his government, Louis-Napoleon went on to program French industrialism and the training of Saint-Simonian technocrats. France today remains the one European power most indebted to Saint-Simon for the state-run management of its major industries, its engineer-managers trained in the École Polytechnique founded by Napoleon III. Having also enlisted the nobility into his army of repression—they, too, had been targeted from below together with business interests—he was able to encourage the bourgeoisie to "*enrichissez-vous*," against any complaints from a decayed aristocracy. When defeated in the Franco-Prussian War (1870–1871), his triumph over labor unrest seemed undone during the Siege of Paris; the proles again tried their luck with a Red Terror that established the Paris Commune. But another patriotic leader emerged to put that down as well, war reparations to Germany were paid off, and France recovered and prospered mightily. All this Verne's French readers appreciated with unusual clarity. They knew their native Saint-Simon had not foreseen the rise of a virulent labor movement, against which his doctrine now served to immunize.

In America, Edward Bellamy proposed the same antilaborite answer in *Looking Backward* (1888) which, together with his political pamphlets on the subject, inspired a short-lived Nationalist Movement (versus Marxist workers-of-the-world internationalism). Yet, its aims were supra-national. The novel presents a World Republic of United Interests, with Boston as its Metropole (Saint-Simon of course had it in Paris). Bellamy's narrator is a comatose sleeper who awakes in A.D. 2000 to find the labor question settled once and for all. Wells plays on this novel in *When the Sleeper Wakes* (1899). His Marxist narrator, seen in fig. 46 at the moment of awakening in 2100, attempts in vain to raise a proletarian mob against the world dictator of a state-capitalist order, one Ostrog, who presides over a Council of Trustees (= the Council of Newton in Saint-Simon, the World Council of Direction in Wells).

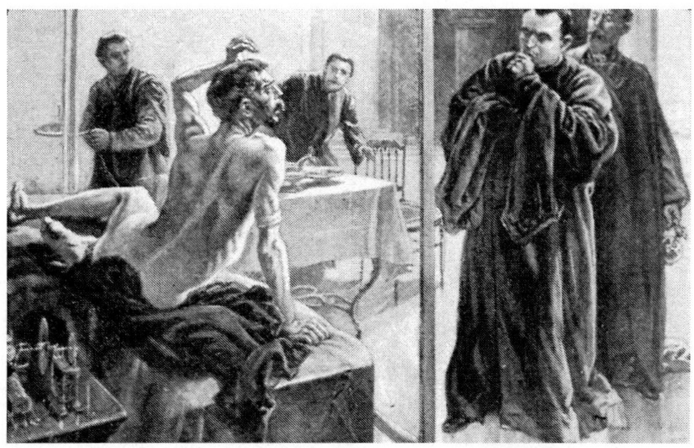

Fig. 46. *Graham awakens in a great Hall of the People (closed this day for maintenance), where his comatose body is on display. He is the title Sleeper, the world-state's most important asset, one impossible day to awaken and liberate the People from authoritarian socialism. Graham is imprisoned prior to execution and replacement with a wax dummy. He escapes to lead a failed proletarian revolt* à la *Marx, to finally die a deserving death in the struggle. His official title, Master and Owner of the World, supports him in that cause. A trust fund, set up 102 years before, has accumulated more than half the world's capital, now managed by a kind of politburo called the Council of Trustees.*

The Wells novel curiously anticipates the fate of the embalmed corpse on display in Lenin's Tomb, later replaced with a wax dummy now to be buried. In a cult fostered by Stalin, Lenin would return and fulfill the Marxist promise of democratic socialism, Lenin's false hope masking his own statism. By 1991, the Soviet Union he founded in 1914 had collapsed. In When the Sleeper Wakes, *by contrast Wells's ideal "autocratic state capitalism" is permanent. George Orwell took it as his point of departure in* Nineteen Eighty-Four, *a nightmare future turning utopia into dystopia.*

The impress of this novel on Robert Heinlein is evident in his choice of the same year for his *Revolt in 2100* (1970), only this time it is the revolt of technocrats against a theocratic regime. See plate XII:4, which illustrates the original *Astounding Science Fiction* serial of 1953, "If This Goes On." It is topical even today, when fears of right wing Christian extremism are expressed in some quarters. Heinlein also was fascinated by the "water bed" on which the Sleeper in fig. 46 has been reposing for 102 years, and went on to design the particulars for such a comfortable bed in *Stranger in a Strange Land* (1961), which led a commercial firm to patent that commodity.

Verne never went so far as Wells to novelize a fully authoritarian technocratic regime (unless it be hinted at in *The Unwilling Dictator*). At best Verne takes Saint-Simon's Council of Newton as a model of willing obedience to wise and informed leadership, precisely the attitude voiced by Voltaire when reflecting on Newton's royal funeral in 1727. As Saint-Simon worshipfully beheld the Newtonian law of gravity, so Voltaire did a basic law of human nature. "Not long ago," he writes, "a distinguished company were discussing the trite and frivolous question: 'Who was the greatest man, Caesar, Alexander, Tamerlane, or Cromwell?' Someone answered that without doubt it was Isaac Newton. And rightly, for it is to him who mastered our minds by the force of truth, not to those who enslave them by violence, that we owe our reverence." So too the law of gravity in human affairs; men of outstanding intellect and organizational ability attract followers enlightened enough to consent to whatever rationally must be done.

A perfect example is Captain Cyrus Harding—Smith in the French original, the name meaning worker of metal, a fitting name for his engineering skills. He is the hero of *The Mysterious Island* (1875), in which he takes charge of an escape from a Confederate prison during the Civil War. One stormy night he masterminds the capture of a military balloon used for observation; the storm carries it and its five passengers (and a dog) across the United States and into the southwest Pacific. There he organizes the survivors' lives before they are rescued four years later, after the war is over. Meanwhile they have developed the island as a microcosm of industrial society.

Fig. 47. *Title page of the French first edition of* Hector Servadac, *its hero standing center stage. The balloon, comet, and planetary bodies all figure in the story.*

How Cyrus Harding/Smith manages this is best discovered in the title hero of *Hector Servadac* (1877), the dignified personality in fig. 47, a French officer serving in Algeria. A passing comet tears off a portion of that French colony and whirls it into outer space. The story tells of survival on the icy fragment, which Servadac names Gallia (= little France, Gaul). He is there in north Africa to begin with because it was de Lesseps, the great irrigator of Algeria, who persuaded the government of France to annex it. For the French at that time, to colonize was to civilize; to develop, even in the absence of native inhabitants (as in *The Mysterious Island*, whose castaways are no less "colonists" than those on already occupied Gallia).

Hector Servadac offers a tour of the solar system, with many a lesson in astronomy, including a lecture on physics as the resident astronomer determines the specific gravity of Gallia (fig. 48). He also eyes the receding planet Earth, observing the Sahara Sea and the Australian Sea. Watering of the former is accomplished by French engineers in *Invasion of the Sea* (1905), while the latter, bringing agricultural productivity to another vast interior desert, Verne did not live to novelize as planned.

Fig. 48. *The astronomer calculates the specific gravity of Gallia from a bag of French coins, whose weight on Earth he knows. Knowing also their diameters, he constructs a meter stick, has cut a cubic measure of Gallia rock, then weighs it against the coins. The money-bag here on the scales was taken from a protesting Jewish money lender, a study in anti–Semitic caricature: Verne's Catholic prejudice. Wells expresses a like anti–Semitism but for a different reason: He is hostile to all sectarian interests standing in the way of a secular world order. During World War II he even advocated bombing the Vatican.*

Captain Servadac takes command of Gallia, fixing prices,* allocating living quarters (in caves), regulating migrations (according to temperature variations), and even conducting international relations with a stranded English garrison from a torn-off piece of Gibraltar. What he represents is the Saint-Simonian tradition of using the armed forces for carrying out public works, with a "peaceful army of laborers," as the disciple Prosper Enfantin put it (surely his first name is indicative of the resultant well-being). The military is a model of authority and discipline for the future welfare of society. Its chain of command rationalizes a division of labor essential to industrial production. When serving this peaceful purpose, however, it no longer entails a *coercive* division of labor: Everybody agrees to their place as willing collaborators in a collective enterprise directed by a worshipped man of Newtonian wisdom.

In the event, when the orbital comet Gallia nears earth again, Captain Servadac improbably brings his loyal band of followers home by balloon (fig. 49). Save for his personal aide-de-camp, the Algerian Ben Zouf, they are all civilians, shown in a group portrait on the novel's title page (fig. 47). The reluctant English are left behind, they being unprogressive disbelievers in modern technology. Such is represented by the balloon,

**A centralized banking system was a feature of Saint-Simonian thought which influenced Alexander Hamilton.*

Fig. 49. *Captain Servadac leads his little band of survivors back to Earth in a balloon, once the periodic comet Gallia returns. Conspicuously absent is the Jewish money lender, for all the importance of his money-bag (at fig. 48) to calculations crucial to getting home again.*

also featured on the title page amidst various planets, a machine that still carried plenty of mystique. Verne's first novel, *Five Weeks in a Balloon* (1865), was a sensation, not in the least for its astonishing guidance technology. By its means a scientist and his devoted helpers explore Africa from the air and discover the source of the Nile before land-based explorers had reported it. (By a shrewd study of maps and existing geographical data, Verne had hit on that long-sought source, much to his lasting repute.)

Captain Harding/Smith, a science-educated engineering officer in the Union Army, is the like of Captain Servadac. The civilian colonists under his wise command include a Negro boy: the earth does indeed belong to all mankind. The island on which they are isolated he patriotically names Lincoln Island, after the U.S. president and Civil War leader who had emancipated the slaves. His aim is to raise it to the American standard of life. "We will make this island into a little America. We will build towns and railways and telegraph lines and, one day, when it is properly regulated and civilized, we will offer it to the government of the United States."

The first thing is to make fire, which Captain Smith does with a magnifying glass of two water-filled convex watch crystals clamped together—a thrilling lesson in optics. So repeats the rise of civilization. Next is to get agriculture going from a single grain found in the pocket of one of the survivors, a development the captain explains in fig. 50. The scene is Granite House, a cave with a granite cliffside improved as best can be. More things are possible with the help of books and tools floated ashore in a sea chest from some ostensible shipwreck (the title's central mystery). The atlas and sextant contained therein enable Captain Smith to locate the island at W. longitude 153° 30' and S. latitude 34° 57'. No island is charted for that location—too far off from regular sea lanes.

In time the colonists do as they proposed. They build a hand-pushed railway system and a telegraphy network (with homemade voltaic cells) to coordinate their activities, including the smelting of iron ore. Louis-Napoleon had covered France with railroads and telegraph lines (the two go together for obvious reasons), and within ten years industrial production doubled and so had foreign trade. The same was happening in America, the first instance of massive economic "takeoff." The railroads themselves consumed much of the production of iron and steel they stimulated, even as they brought all sorts of raw materials from the hinterland to factory centers, thus realizing the globalized marketing industrialism Saint-Simon had foreseen.

Fig. 50. *Captain Harding gives a lecture on how a grain of wheat found by one of the survivors of the air crash will proliferate and provide food for the group. It was found in his coat pocket, a happy leftover from his habit of pigeon feeding.*

In the event, a volcanic eruption sinks the island, and the survivors cling to a sinking ledge of rock just as a rarely passing vessel rescues them. But not before the mystery is unriddled when Captain Nemo reveals himself.

It was he who had floated ashore the sea chest with the basic tools that enabled the colonists to perform their own little take-off. He comes out of retirement (his *Nautilus* parked in some hidden cove, his crewmen dead of old age) to congratulate them on their zealous conquest of nature: "You love this island. You have changed it by your efforts and it is truly yours." He repents of his terrorist days, and leaves with the improvers of Lincoln Island a coffer of jewels taken from sunken shipwrecks. With this treasure the colonists purchase a vast tract of land in Iowa, where they model for the rest of the world a hard-working community of collective interests along Saint-Simonian lines.

In *Twenty Thousand Leagues Under the Sea* (1872), Verne's masterpiece, Captain Nemo's identity is obscure. It is, however, vouchsafed to the colonists in *The Mysterious Island*, a sequel three years later. He is Prince Dakkar of Bundelkhand, whose formerly independent territory is now subject to the British Raj. He takes out his vengeance by sinking the warships of an evil empire that suppresses the sovereignty of peoples everywhere. In the French text, "le capitaine Nemo" is described as "*Ce terrible justice, véritable archange de la haine*" (that terrible judge, that archangel of hate). Yet his crewmen, drawn from all such places, are speakers of a synthetic language not unlike Esperanto, whose internationalist movement Verne avidly helped to promote—another interesting contradiction. In Saint-Simon's World Republic of United Interests the

Fig. 51. *Captain Nemo taking the altitude of the sun from the deck of the* Nautilus.

universal language is French; in Wells's equivalent New Republic (*Anticipations* 1902, as in *Things to Come* and earliest in *When the Sleeper Wakes*), it is English.

At the same time, Captain Nemo (fig. 51) is a hero of exploration. His *Nautilus* is a vehicle of the deeps, directly observing all that the American oceanographer Matthew Fontaine Maury had to say in the first textbook on the subject, *Physical Geography of the Sea* (1855). There are further excursions into ichthyology from other sources, and much else, not omitting lectures on the Linnaean system of taxonomy. Verne always did his homework, taking extensive notes, the one thing modern science fiction writers learned from him (except the lazy ones, lapsing from "hard core SF" to make up anything they please in occult fiction). Otherwise his influence on the genre was far less than Gernsback expected, because his inventions were too commonplace. To the fans of *Amazing Stories* become writers, the engine room of the submarine *Nautilus* (fig. 52) was not so amazing as it was half a century earlier, before the magazine reprints of Verne.

Another thing Verne influenced was the asexuality of his all-male characters (typical also in Wells's romances), not to say the tendency for modern SF writers to be themselves almost exclusively males. Women writers did not enter the field until some time after the creation. Now they pretty much dominate with their feminist agendum and in much else the genre is a goner, swamped by a culture-wide fixation on carnality.

Preceding that, however, Katherine MacLean had cover stories in Campbell's excellent magazine. Her "Incommunicado," *ASF* June 1950, takes a fresh approach to the computer revolution, demonized from the start in technophobic SF. The dehumanizing effect of computer programming (on punched tape at the time) she humanized by having the programmer punch in musical notes (plate IX:3). In "The Missing Man," *ASF* March 1971, she confronts hysterical fears that atomic power plants might blow up, and one does (plate VIII:4). But the fault is not the intrinsic evil of nuclear technology, rather the lack of that "missing" man, a competent manager, one who is more than a mere business-school graduate.

Fig. 52. *The engine room of the* Nautilus *shown to Professor Arronax by Captain Nemo. He is looking at the power plant, which generates electricity for the great coil of wires above: the electric motor that turns the submarine's drive shaft below. All this was amazing and futuristic to readers of the time, not so once electric motors came to be.*

Verne and Wells, I say again, are more alike than different if their doctrinal socialism is taken into account. Both are also readers of literary forerunners preceding their choice of subject matter, today identified as science fiction: a genre already losing its once cherished autonomy.

The First Men in the Moon (1901) plays on moon voyagers going back to the eighteenth century, as does Verne's *Trip to the Moon*. Verne had criticized Wells for his magical anti-gravitic Cavorite for getting there; "show me this substance," he demands, asserting that he gets there with a space cannon whose ballistics are calculated to the last decimal. What would he think of Wells's own space gun in *Things to Come*?

In Wells, a scientist named Cavor invents the substance in question and visits the moon to find out if it is inhabited. The anti-gravitic device itself has a venerable history, tracing to 1827 with Joseph Atterley's *A Voyage to the Moon* (fig. 53). In at least one quarter Cavorite was taken seriously, even if not by Wells himself. The eccentric American millionaire Roger Babson in 1948 set up the Gravity Research Foundation to reinvent it.

Inside the moon Cavor finds a "wonderful social order," the very apotheosis of Saint-Simon's utopian industrial order. "In the moon," says Cavor, "every citizen knows his place. He is born to that place, and the elaborate discipline of training and education and surgery he undergoes fits him at last so completely that he has neither ideas nor organs for any purpose beyond it.... So also he loves his work, and discharges in perfect happiness the duty that justifies his being. And so it is with all sorts and conditions of Selenites—each is a perfect unit in a world machine."

A "single economic world machine" is the Wells ideal in his later treatise on social economics, *The Work, Wealth and Happiness of Mankind* (1931). Directing the moon's exquisite division of labor along Saint-Simonian lines is the Grand Lunar (fig. 54). His big brain, like Gosplan, the former Soviet Union's central planning agency, substitutes

Fig. 53, left. *The antecedent of the Cavorite sphere is this box-like device coated with anti-gravitic paint in Joseph Atterley's novel of 1827,* A Voyage to the Moon. *It anticipates the propulsion system in Percy Greg's* Across the Zodiac *(1880), and later in* Auf Zwei Planeten *(1897) by Kurd Lasswitz. Wells's reliance on this tradition, however, is less important than the new thing he did with it in* The First Men in the Moon, *which was to critique human society and project what it could be from the example of his lunar utopia.* Fig. 54, right. *Student drawing of the Grand Lunar. His little eyes and frail arms beneath yards-wide brain are well done: the very image of impossible central planning.*

for a free market economy in deciding production and distribution. Cavor is brought before him to explain life on his home planet and is surprised to learn there is no Grand Earthly, but rather a savage rivalry of nation-states. Humans clearly pose a danger to the moon. They will come back for more gold now that Bedford, Cavor's greedy business partner in the lunar adventure, has absconded with some in the Cavorite sphere, leaving Cavor behind.

What he took with him were two long-handled butcher knives of solid gold, utilitarian objects of utopian disdain for the (to humans) precious metal. Cavor is allowed to radio-telegraph a glowing report on the moon's "wonderful social order." It is picked up by a radio experimentor (Marconi's transmission across the Atlantic had been topical news of the day) and forwarded to Bedford, who derives his narrative from it. He concludes that "the cold, inhuman reason of the moon" signals, to his capitalist-minded discomfort, "such a change in human conditions as mankind has scarcely imagined heretofore." At the point Cavor gives him out the formula for Cavorite, his monitors (in fig. 55) cut him off, never knowing that Bedford had carelessly let the sphere drift away

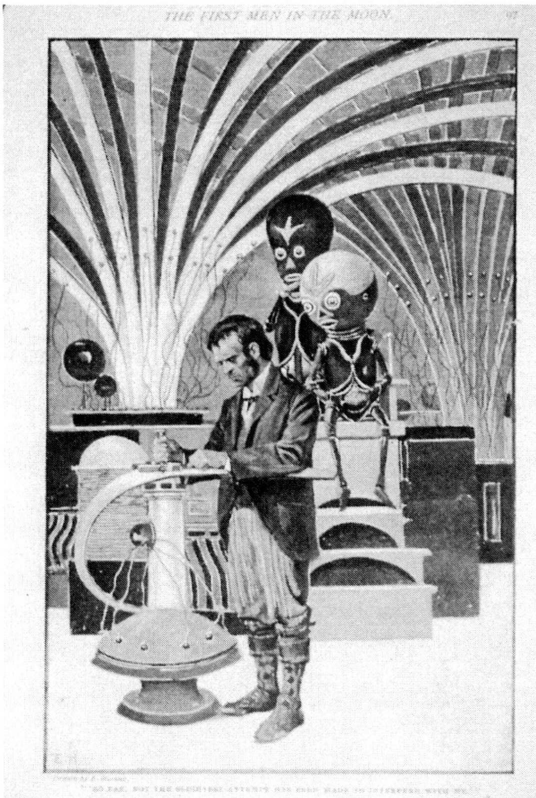

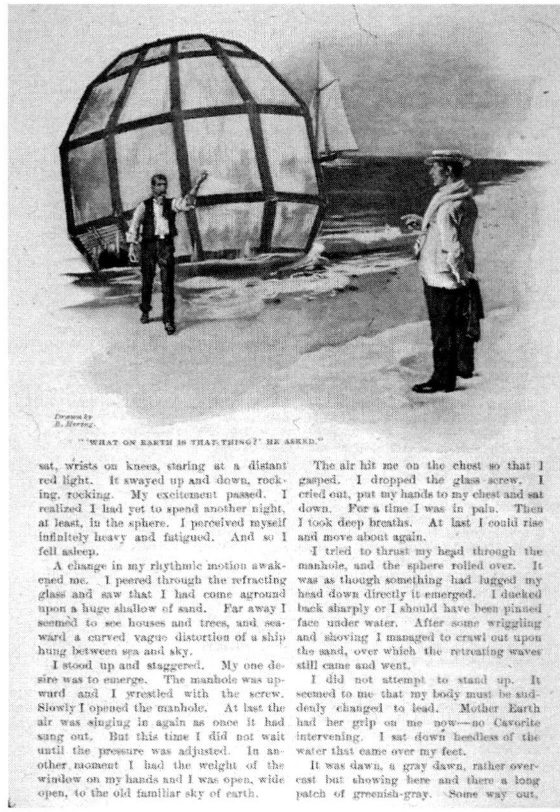

Drawn by B. Hering.

"'WHAT ON EARTH IS THAT THING?' HE ASKED."

sat, wrists on knees, staring at a distant red light. It swayed up and down, rocking, rocking. My excitement passed. I realized I had yet to spend another night, at least, in the sphere. I perceived myself infinitely heavy and fatigued. And so I fell asleep.

A change in my rhythmic motion awakened me. I peered through the refracting glass and saw that I had come aground upon a huge shallow of sand. Far away I seemed to see houses and trees, and seaward a curved vague distortion of a ship hung between sea and sky.

I stood up and staggered. My one desire was to emerge. The manhole was upward and I wrestled with the screw. Slowly I opened the manhole. At last the air was singing in again as once it had sang out. But this time I did not wait until the pressure was adjusted. In another moment I had the weight of the window on my hands and I was open, wide open, to the old familiar sky of earth.

The air hit me on the chest so that I gasped. I dropped the glass screw. I cried out, put my hands to my chest and sat down. For a time I was in pain. Then I took deep breaths. At last I could rise and move about again.

I tried to thrust my head through the manhole, and the sphere rolled over. It was as though something had lugged my head down directly it emerged. I ducked back sharply or I should have been pinned face under water. After some wriggling and shoving I managed to crawl out upon the sand, over which the retreating waves still came and went.

I did not attempt to stand up. It seemed to me that my body must be suddenly changed to lead. Mother Earth had her grip on me now—no Cavorite intervening. I sat down heedless of the water that came over my feet.

It was dawn, a gray dawn, rather overcast but showing here and there a long patch of greenish-gray. Some way out,

Fig. 55, left. *Cavor sending by wireless telegraph his reports on the "wonderful social order" within the moon, which he forecasts as the future of human society. His monitors, however, cut the transmission when he gives the formula for Cavorite. The Selenites have no wish to see a return visit by terrestrial barbarians the likes of Bedford, Cavor's fortune hunting investment partner in the voyage.* Fig. 56, right. *The Cavorite sphere landed on the beach of a bathing resort near Cavor's home laboratory, the point of departure. But it was only by chance that Bedford the scientific ignoramus managed to get back.*

after he landed. Fig. 56 shows it beached near a seaside bathing resort, where (in fig. 57) idle rich men in tennis dress help carry his loot to the bank. They are effete, Eloi-like types, recalling the degenerate capitalists in *The Time Machine* who spend their mindless days bathing and sportive lovemaking. When Bedford tells the bathers he has just come from the moon, they wonder what that is until he points it out in the sky. They are weak-minded men too brainless to rule much longer.

If earth is no longer able to ravish the moon, the moon's instructive example of "inhuman reason" will soon enough transform mankind, thanks to the social formula for utopia the saintly Cavor was able to transmit. Unwittingly the gold-questing Bedford has published a compelling report bound to subvert his own kind. Writing it up (the text of the novel) in a luxurious Italian villa (fig. 58) bought with lunar loot, he remains as ignorant as the seaside resorters of why "exceptional" men of science like Cavor, selfless in their quest of "knowledge for its own sake," will be agents of the transformation he but dimly apprehends.

THE FIRST MEN IN THE MOON. 653

I gesticulated convulsively. He receded a step as though I had threatened him. I made a bolt through them into the hotel. I charged back into the coffee-room, rang the bell furiously. I gripped the waiter as he entered. "D'ye hear!" I shouted. "Get help and carry these bars up to my room right away."

He failed to understand me, and I shouted and raved at him. A scared-looking little old man in a green apron appeared, and further two of the young men in flannels. I made a dash at them and commandeered their services. As soon as the gold was in my room I felt free to quarrel. "Now get out," I shouted; "all of you get out if you don't want to see a man go mad before your eyes!" And I helped the waiter by the shoulder as he hesitated in the doorway. And then as soon as I had the door locked on them all, I tore off the little man's clothes again, shied them right and left, and got into bed forthwith. And there I lay swearing and panting and cooling for a very long time.

At last I was calm enough to get out of bed and ring up the round-eyed waiter for a flannel nightshirt, a soda and whisky, and some good cigars. And these things being procured me, I locked the door again and proceeded very deliberately to look the entire situation in the face.

The net result of the great experiment presented itself as an absolute failure. It was a rout and I was the sole survivor. It was an absolute collapse and this was the final disaster. There was nothing for it but to save myself, and as much as I could in the way of prospects, from our débâcle. At one fatal crowning blow, all my vague resolutions of return and recovery had vanished. My intention of going back to the moon, of rescuing Cavor, or at any rate of getting a sphereful of gold and afterward of having a fragment of Cavorite analyzed and so recovering his great secret —all these ideas vanished altogether.

I was the sole survivor and that was all.

I think that going to bed was one of the luckiest ideas I have ever had in an emergency. I really believe I should either

Drawn by E. Hering.

"THE FAT LITTLE MAN STOOPED AND LIFTED THE END OF ONE OF THE BARS."

THE FIRST MEN IN THE MOON. 655

have it as fact, then the world may take it as fiction. It is no concern of mine.

And now that the account is finished, I am amazed to think how completely this adventure is gone and done with. Everybody believes that Cavor was a not very brilliant scientific experimenter who blew up his house and himself at Lympne, and folks explain the bang that followed my arrival at Littlestone by a reference to the experiments with explosives that are going on continually at the government establishment of Lydd, two miles away. I must confess that hitherto I have not acknowledged my share in the disappearance of Master Tommy Simmons, which was that little boy's name. That perhaps may prove a difficult item of corroboration to explain away. They account for my appearance in rags with two bars of indisputable gold upon the Littlestone beach, in various ingenious ways—it doesn't worry me what they think of me. They say I have strung all these

Drawn by E. Hering.

"I AM WORKING HERE AT AMALFI."

Fig. 57, left. *The bathers help Bedford carry the solid gold butchering knives to the local bank. When Bedford tells them he has just come from the moon, they wonder what that is until he points it out in the sky. Mindless exemplars of the leisure class, they have no more curiosity than the Eloi in the Time Traveller's machine who did not wonder where he came from in the past.* Fig. 58, right. *Bedford writing his self-serving account of the voyage in his gold-purchased Italian villa. Only later does he hear of Cavor's radio transmissions from the moon, his betrayed partner whom he thought dead by now. He then accommodates them by falsely casting Cavor as the betrayer. The reader, however, easily discerns the irony: Bedford reports on what Cavor said about a lunar-modeled human future, himself ignorant that it means the end of men of his type.*

Yet when Gernsback reprinted the novel in *Amazing Stories*, the focus of attention was on the turning wheels and girdered walkways of the moon's industrial plant (see fig. 59). The fannish writers of engineering fiction to follow completely missed the social engineering. Wells had said, in *Mankind in the Making* (1904), that his romances rather formed "a literature not simply of ... science but of power, which shall embody and make real and living the sustaining dreams of the coming time"—political dreams of a world-state/world-machine.

In Verne's *Trip to the Moon*, guessed-at lunar inhabitants are named Selenites, the same used by Wells for his actually living inside the moon. More influential, however, was *Underground City* (1877). In this novel Verne catalogs the interior geology of the earth, the setting being a coal mine in Scotland, and he does not fail to touch upon the irredentist movement which today is realized in a separate Scottish parliament with full independence to come. Wells of course never subscribed to the Principle of Nationalities, and in fact opposed it as a *causa mali*.

The interest for him is the novel's Coal City. Here, deep underground, a team of coal miners and their families decide to live for and with their work under their idolized administrative "overman," one Simon Ford (curious evoking for us that other "captain of industry," Henry Ford, to use a phrase coined by Saint-Simon). Coal City is a "laboring town" founded by Ford as both a home and workplace for miners, foremen, and engineers alike, together with their wives and children. The whole of their vasty cavern is lit by "electric discs" hung from the vaulted ceiling (see fig. 60). All is monolithic harmony, united in the brotherhood of work. In that, the citizens of Coal City find their lives complete and on Sunday, after church service, they tour the cavern and its galleries discussing the tasks of the coming week. The sermon, given by Simon Ford, is always a pitch for selfless labor and the Saint-Simonian dedication to work for its redemptive value. Here Wells altogether coincides with Verne. In *The New World Order* (1939), collective labor enables "man's power over nature and human nature." "Man in association with man" for the extraction of natural resources, in Saint-Simon's moral formula, ends "man's exploitation of man." Instead of stealing wealth through violent economic warfare and downward class war, it is *produced* by means of industry. "Politics is the science of production."

Fig. 59. *Frank Paul's illustration of Selenite technology in the serialized* Amazing Stories *reprint. Paul started out doing architectural and engineering graphics for Gernsback's popular electrotechnical journals, then crossed over to do covers and interior art for his science fiction magazines.*

Society itself is then purposely integrated into the likes of a production factory. Capital and labor are brought into copartnership under a Great Legislator, the wise and universally worshipped brain of Saint-Simon's Council of Newton. Ford, with his council of foremen, is that philosopher king (yes, echoes of Plato's little communist city-state).

Those not worshipful, failed citizens disbelieving in the collective ethos, are ejected to the surface to fend for themselves in a cruel, competitive world.

Verne's Russian translator, living into Lenin's time, reported that Verne was more influential on the Bolshevik Revolution than historians usually credit. The GULAG system of forced labor camps (begun by Lenin and hugely expanded by Stalin) were planned exactly like Coal City, except for the celibacy of their inmates.

Fig. 61 shows a typical "corrective" (= forced) labor camp. At last the GULAG system became a mainstay of the Soviet economy and a model for the rest of it. Housing as many as 1,000 prisoners, industrial camps like the one here illustrated confined them to a compound divided into two fenced-in parts. (**II**) is the industrial

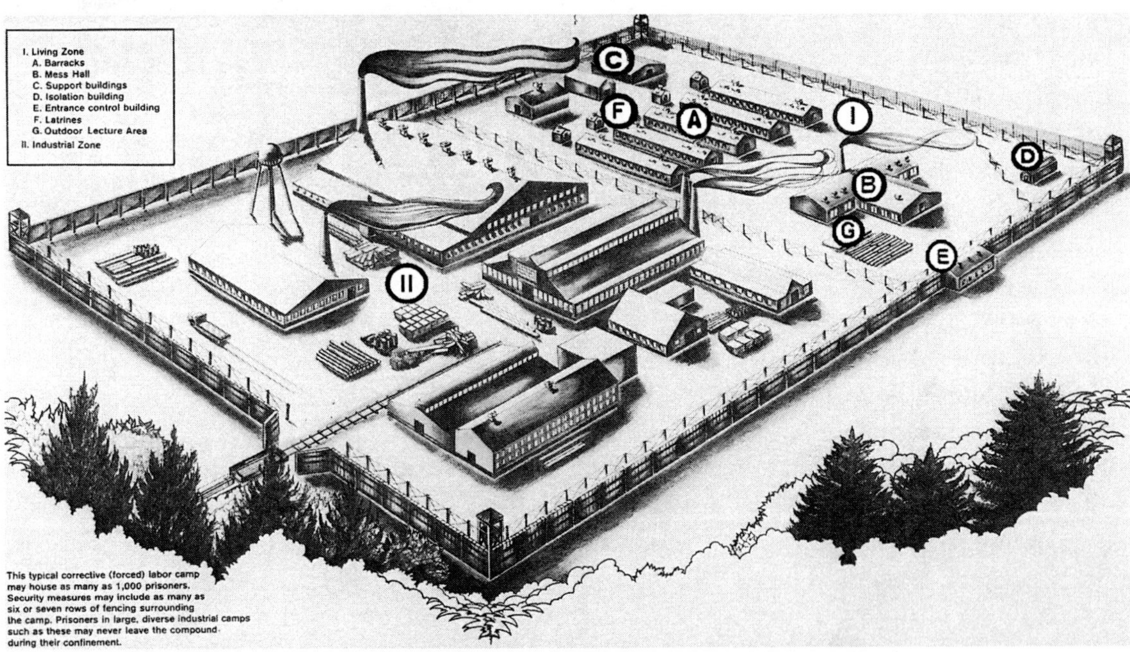

Fig. 60, top. *Verne's Coal City in* Underground City. *The community of work and society it idealized had a measurable influence on the utopian ideals of the totalitarian states, nowhere more evident than in the Soviet Union (see fig. 61).* Fig. 61, above. *Design plan for all* GULAG *camps, with an outdoor lecture area of log seats at (G), lower right. From* Preliminary Report to the U.S. Congress on Forced Labor in the USSR *(5 November 1982), prepared by the Central Intelligence Agency for the Department of State.*

zone. (I) is the living zone, comprising (A) barracks, (B) mess hall, (C) support buildings, (D) isolation building for the punishment of slackers, (E) entrance control building, (F) latrines, and (G) outdoor lecture area. This last is where pep talks are delivered: rows of log seats fronting a podium, Simon Ford's church. True to Saint-Simon's doctrine, the gateway to each compound is emblazoned "Work Is Honorable." As he promised "All men will work"—or else be treated like a "quadruped." Here the quadrupeds redeem themselves at the same time they *are* the economy.

Saint-Simon never visualized a prison state, although collective submission to deserving authority and respect for good management were expected. It did not work out that way in the USSR, Inc. Its founders thoroughly militarized the Saint-Simonian idea. The original "brotherhood in the doctrine" reduced to the use of the term "comrade" among Party and military ranks in upward deference, but "citizen" for addressing those below. Trotsky, Lenin's colleague, got his conscriptive "labor army" from Bellamy's *Looking Backward*. Lenin himself was more familiar with the doctrinal fount. In *State and Revolution* (1917), written on the eve of the Bolshevik coup, he determined that after his takeover "The whole of society will become a single office and a single factory"—with him as its Grand Lunar in the front office: Saint-Simon's Great Legislator.

Fig. 62. *Wells's pamphlet of 1912, advocating the crushing of independent trade unions and their replacement by state agencies: a policy realized in 1917 by Lenin and later imitated by Mussolini and Hitler. It is what Russian Communism and Italian and German Fascism have in common. Wells, in 1899 at the outset of the troublesome labor movement, however, had already novelized this solution to the problem in* When the Sleeper Wakes.

This key statement certainly unmasks the Marxian communal socialism Lenin advertised in public. The authoritarian socialism he actually practiced rested on a belief in willing servitude to a good cause if convincingly preached. If so, Wells anticipated him in a pamphlet of 1912, *The Labour Unrest* (see fig. 62). Here he says that "the tendency of modern industrialism has been to subdivide processes and make work more boring and irksome." It is that very condition that has energized the upward class war of Marxist socialism. But the same rebellious workingmen "will toil very cheerfully in subordination if they feel that the collective end is a fine thing and a great thing." The pamphlet responded to the rise of militant movements everywhere. What we see in the totalitarian regimes of the twentieth century—Russian Communism, Italian Fascism, German Nazism—is the attempt to crush independent trade unions for the sake of a docile work force, if industry is to go on.

In *The Time Machine*, Wells's Morlocks are symbolic of that runaway labor movement, pithecoid proletarians eating alive their erstwhile capitalist masters (the Eloi) with their insatiable demands. Significantly, the Morlocks reflect on the Coal War of 1893, the biggest labor strike ever undertaken in Great Britain or anywhere else. These underworld creatures, unionized Morlock men, are at last reformed in *The First Men in the Moon*. The Grand Lunar coordinates the subdivided tasks of every Selenite worker, each one fitted to his place in a world machine. "And so also he loves his work, and discharges in perfect happiness the duty that justifies his being." But the instructional method is forcible conformity; the joy is by default, adjustment to a painful loss of individuality.

In Verne, however, such a coercive division of labor is contemplated with horror. The mechanization of human beings, reducing them to cogs in a machine, goes too far. In the Saint-Simonian definition of *socialisme*, the social in the -ism repudiates *la personalité* (= individualism). Wells went all the way. "Man's soul is no longer his own," it belongs to the species for its universal welfare, and this Man must learn however painfully (in *What Are We to Do with Our Lives?* 1931). Such is the New Socialist Man Lenin had envisioned, eventually to take over the planet in a "United States of the World," exactly Lenin's 1918 phrase Wells borrowed for his Next Stage in the final installment of his *Outline of History*, serialized in 1920 (see fig. 63). Wells, however, improved on the idea. In *The Shape of Things to Come*, a "history of the future," the Next Stage is no federation of nation states; "the world which had once been divided among territorial Great Powers became divided among functional Great Powers." That is, the Modern State Octopus, through its World Council of Direction, controls

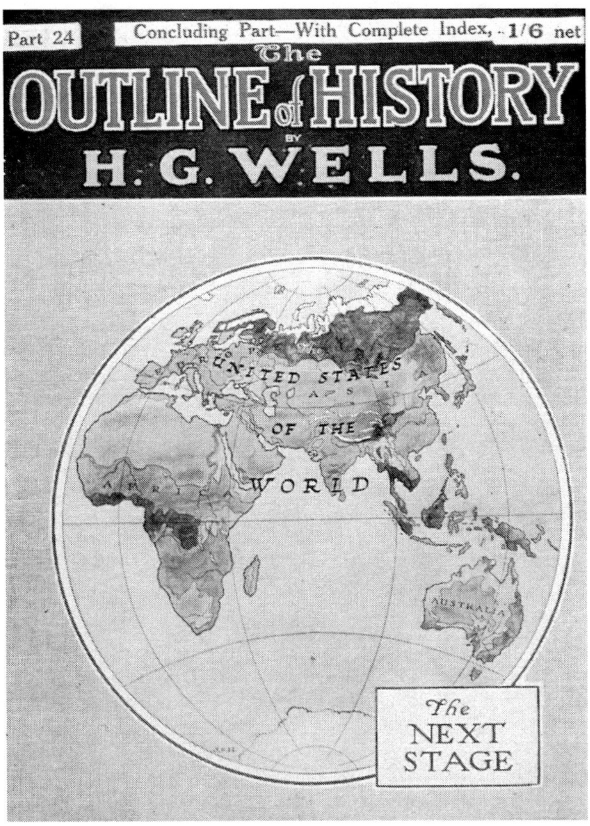

Fig. 63. *The last serialized installment of* The Outline of History *(1920), whose inevitable "final stage" is here pictured on the magazine cover. The phrase "United States of the World" is Lenin's coinage of 1919, a borrowing calculated to play on the sensational aims of his advertised world revolution. But Wells in fact had a different vision; from the start, in* When the Sleeper Wakes, *he foresaw a world revolution ending the nation-states altogether. His world-state was to be a totally new level of organization, no mere federation of obsolete political units.*

nonlocalized business cartels, acting as a "trust of trusts" (Lenin's term for his Economic Council). Wells favorably called it "autocratic state capitalism." But already in *The Sleeper Wakes* (1899) he postulated the same functional scheme, under direction of the novel's Council of Trustees.

Fig. 64. *Verne's "clipper of the clouds,"* The Terror, *armed with big guns and bombs. Its Captain Robur challenges the world to accept his terms for the harmony of nations. Unlike John Cabal, leader of the Air League in* Things to Come, *with its invincible fleet of bombers, he does not aim to smash the nation-states for the sake of a world state, but only to redirect their sovereignty to international cooperation: stop the rivalry for colonial possessions and allow irredentist movements to have their say. The world belongs to mankind and every political entity is entitled to a share of the global heritage. Captain Nemo's use of the* Nautilus *for submarine warfare against British colonialism is to the same purpose.*

The closest Verne came to suggesting a global dictatorship *à la* Wells is *Master of the World* (1904), a sequel to *Robur the Conqueror* (1866). Robur masters the air as Captain Nemo the seas. His "clipper of the clouds" is lifted by an array of 74 helicopter rotors (fig. 64), whose invention allows Verne to discourse at length on the feasibility of heavier-than-air machines when they were deemed impossible by advocates of improved ballooning. From the clipper's altitudinous vantage a survey of world geography is offered. At the same time Robur is animated (like Nemo) with a hatred for British imperialism; naming his craft *The Terror*, he bombs their warships from on high: the lesson being that, if the world belongs to mankind per Saint-Simonian doctrine, it rather belongs to its oppressed nationalities. But it is exactly against this sovereignty of peoples that Wells militates with air power in *Things to Come*; his airmen master the skies, world trade, and, by terrorist bombing, a one-world state. Robur's message is to signal a *cooperative* oneness "in the economic and political ways of the world," not a *coordinative* dictatorship, imposing global unity from a single control center.

Near the end of his life in 1944 Wells claimed, "My rôle has always been that of a propagandist, direct or indirect, for world socialism." Verne, who did more than anybody in France to advance Louis-Napoleon's Principle of Nationalities, made no such claim. No World Republic figures in his work, and while he appreciated Saint-Simon's division-of-labor morality, he expressed horror that it might be made involuntary. So it became with the making of *Homo sovieticus*, prefigured in the Selenites of *The First Men in the Moon*.

Responding to Mr. Wells, Verne took issue with the prospect in "Mr. Ray Sharp and Miss Mi Flat," gathered in a 1910 posthumous collection of stories. It opens with a new choirmaster come to a little village in the Swiss Alps, where he replaces his predecessor, Mr. Eglisak (or Mr. Church). He stands for the Christian ethic of individual moral responsibility. The new man is Mr. Effarane (or Mr. Fear), who disquiets the community with ethical revolution.

After his arrival, the first thing Mr. Effarane does is to interview the children's choir. He asks each member to sing the diatonic scale, and what he seeks is each individual's capacity for his or her personal note, "his physiological note so to speak." This determined, Effarane tells the sixteen he has chosen (they each naturally sing C, D sharp, E, F sharp, A, and so on) that they are to be trained for a register in his redesigned organ. They will be its "living keyboard." Accordingly, he shuts them up in pipes of the *grand jeu* (great joy), each by himself next to each other in the register's scale. He then plays at the Elevation, which terminates the church service. Thereby do they perform a social service, by their division of labor, to a higher and more joyous collective order of things in which the personal is depersonalized, indeed mechanized. But in effect, what he has terminated is the Church itself. In many respects Verne was a traditionalist, a devout Catholic—not agreeable to the scientific atheist Wells.

At all events, Mr. D Sharp, standing in his appointed place, reflects on the distance his functional part keeps him from his girlfriend, Miss E Flat, in the next pipe. At first he worries that his duty to the organist's music, however socially useful, deprives him of mutuality with his fellow singers. But then, "an air-current inflates my chest, a current skillfully controlled, which carries the D sharp out of my lips." His doubts cause him to wish for silence, but he finds he cannot give in to them. The next moment he rejoices in the role assigned him by the organist that justifies his being. "When he strikes the keyboard, it is as if a valve in my heart opened!"

But the music is hard to sustain, and D Sharp feels that, if it goes on, "the sound we emit will be cries of pain," the pain suffered "when Master Effarane plays with his terrible hand." Yet the playing goes on, under the hand of that "cruel, merciless artist," and D Sharp, feeling close to death, loses consciousness. Awakening, he discovers it was a nightmare. D Sharp had swooned while being interviewed by Master Effarane, now gone from the village. (He did not get the job.)

Wells, who believed in man's unlimited plasticity, does not hesitate to suggest pedagogical violence to achieve perfectibility. The Selenites are educated to their special functions by the Grand Lunar, who uses the means of painful physical molding and vivisection. Indeed, even the Martians are products of the same process. The original natives of Mars were humanoids who so transformed themselves that they became all brain and hands (tentacles), the sole creative organs of a higher being, saved from animal appetites lodged in sexual and digestive organs. Somewhere in the background is a successful Doctor Moreau.

This brings us to *The Island of Doctor Moreau* (1896). His island, Noble's Isle, is located at S. latitude 5° and E. longitude 105°, which places it off the coast of Ecuador near the Galapagos. These islands were visited by Darwin in 1835 during the famous voyage of the *Beagle*, and where he gathered decisive evidence for his theory of evolution.

Moreau's House of Pain, his vivisection room, is where he conducts experiments in directed evolution. His products are the Beast Folk, who keep reverting to type, the animal raw material he works with; the "beast flesh" always creeps back, dissolving the stamp of humanity he attempts to impress on it. The narrator, a shipwrecked castaway named Prendick, encounters Beast Folk so soon as he lands on the island (fig. 65). When he first meets Moreau, he thinks them humans perversely made into animals. Later he learns that Moreau is attempting to make humans out of beast flesh. At that time Prendick hears that the reversions are experimental failures; but that the doctor might do better with refined methods. "Each time I dip a living creature into the bath of pain, I say: this time I will burn out all the animal, this time I will make a rational creature of my own."

Fig. 65. *Frontispiece to the London edition of* The Island of Doctor Moreau *(1896). The drawing shows Prendick's first encounter with the Beast Folk in the tropical isle's jungle, just after landing on the beach.*

As Wells explains in "Morals and Civilization," an 1897 article bearing on the novel, the Beast Folk are surrogates for the "man beast," humankind as it presently exists before evolving to a higher stage. The Darwinian premise is, if the man beast is a child of his apelike past, he is also the parent of a perfected future: a transitional form that can be helped along by deanimalization, burning out all traces of primordial origins. What the physiologist attempts to achieve by surgery the narrator of "Under the Knife" gains for himself by means of astral projection: released from the pain/pleasure principle, he is become a "naked intelligence" disgarmented of flesh.

Doctor Moreau's namesake is Gustave Moreau, the French painter whose "Oedipus and the Sphinx" of 1864 won international renown. Oedipus represents pure mind, resisting sexual assault by the erotic and aggressive sphinx. Before reaching that conclusion in my 1996 critical edition of the novel (which has that painting for a frontispiece), I consulted the directeur of the Musée Gustave Moreau in Paris, Geneviève Lacambre. A *docteur des lettres* altogether familiar with Wells, he said I was correct to see in Doctor Moreau the same focus on mind/body duality, his name obviously reminiscent of the painter's.

The nobility of the good doctor's ambition to reform human nature is manifest in the name of his island. Although his methods fail, they triumph in *The Shape of Things to Come* (1933), in which "the coming man from the man of the past" is at last made into a "new species"; the Modern State, as a successful House of Pain, burns out man's "animal individualism" and by its discipline generates a new collective mentality, man "socialized entirely against his natural disposition." The very word socialism always implies this.

Yet when Hugo Gernsback reprinted the 1896 novel in *Amazing Stories*, all his readers, later the founding SF writers, got out of it was the marvel of biogenetic engineering, the Beast Folk examples of it (see fig. 66). This led to all sorts of "mutant" stories in which, by artificial or natural means, new forms of life often result in monsters to be combatted. In 1927 the magazine ran "The Tissue Culture King" by Julian Huxley, a coup for Gernsback who relished bringing in real men of science (see fig. 67). Huxley was later to collaborate with Wells in *The Science of Life* (1930), which updated Wells's 1893 *Text-Book of Biology* (fig. 68). They suggested that protoplasm could be manipulated like steel for the benefit of human progress. The brother, Aldous Huxley, doubted, in *Brave New World*, such hubris (see Chapter 10).

Fig. 66. *Frank Paul's illustration for the serialized reprint of* The Island of Doctor Moreau *in* Amazing Stories. *Moreau and his assistant stand on the beach, pleading with the suicidal Prendick, about to drown himself in the ocean; he fears that he will be used as an experiment in vivisection, to end up like the mock-human Beast Folk (foreground).*

Perhaps the most notable mutants in modern SF are those in *Slan* by A.E. Van Vogt (serialized 1940 in *Astounding Science Fiction*), mental supermen endowed with telepathic powers—an untapped possibility already hinted at in *The Science of Life*. Indeed, Wells's brainlordly Martians are telepathic, a source for the paranormal in SF.

Verne addressed Darwinian theory in *The Village in the Treetops* (1901). As

Fig. 67, top. *Illustration for Huxley's "Tissue Culture King" in* Amazing Stories, *August 1927. The head-scratching scientist observes of his monstrous creations, "I thought I would see whether art could not improve upon nature." The story (first published in* Yale Review*) is very much in the Faustian tradition. But after Huxley began his collaboration with Wells on* The Science of Life*—a four-volume survey of modern biology and its possible applications—he changed his tune.* Fig. 68, right. *Title page of Wells's* Text-Book of Biology *(1893). The book includes a defense of vivisection, which suggests that Doctor Moreau is not the mad scientist most critics make him out to be.*

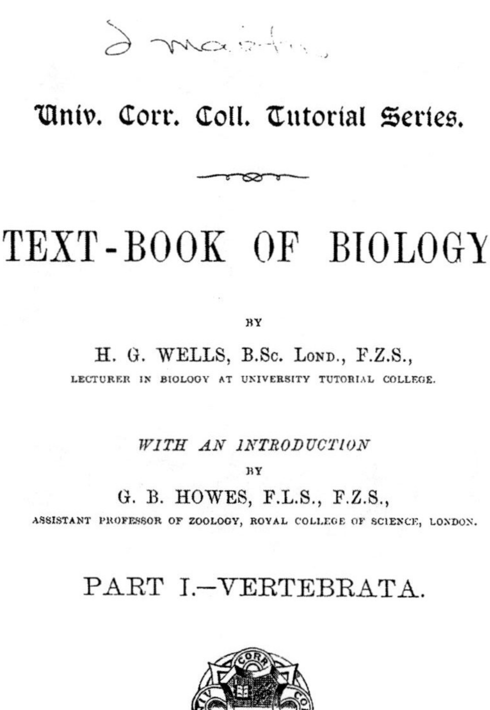

Univ. Corr. Coll. Tutorial Series.

TEXT-BOOK OF BIOLOGY.

BY

H. G. WELLS, B.Sc. LOND., F.Z.S.,

LECTURER IN BIOLOGY AT UNIVERSITY TUTORIAL COLLEGE.

WITH AN INTRODUCTION

BY

G. B. HOWES, F.L.S., F.Z.S.,

ASSISTANT PROFESSOR OF ZOOLOGY, ROYAL COLLEGE OF SCIENCE, LONDON.

PART I.—VERTEBRATA.

LONDON: W. B. CLIVE & CO.,

UNIVERSITY CORRESPONDENCE COLLEGE PRESS.

WAREHOUSE: 13 BOOKSELLERS ROW, W.C.

a good Catholic, he disbelieved in evolution. The novel, set in Central Africa with plenty of local ecology thrown in, recounts various learned speculations on the so-called "missing link" between apes and men, which he dismisses. Man is a divine creature endowed with religious faith by his creator, upon which all human culture is founded. A French explorer comes upon a nest of apemen, living in treetops, who lack this quality. The translation says "monkey men," a mistake. French *singe* does not distinguish between monkeys and apes as does English, and Verne meant apemen (more closely related to man in primate studies). The explorer runs into a German on site before him (just as suspect as Englishmen). Recalling French defeat in the Franco-Prussian War, Verne finds Teutonic imperialism at work again in rule over the monkey-men. But to be their king, the German has first to teach them the ways of human culture, including language. In this he utterly fails, meanwhile regressing to their level of animality. "But it must not be inferred that man is a perfected ape or a degenerate man." The discontinuity between man and the lower animals is complete. If the "king" degenerates, as do Moreau's experimental Beast Folk, it is no sign of their link to tigers and bears and apes he uses as raw material; it is rather a sign of science overreaching itself.

Without reading the whole variety of Verne's work, it is easy to assume that he always is given to futuristic inventions (the fabulous *Nautilus* a prominent example). Primitive means of transport may also serve, as in *A Trip Down the Amazon* (1881), aboard a large river raft the Brazilians call a *jungada*. There are also static settings, as in *The Lighthouse at the End of the World* (1905), in which the importance of the title beacon to world trade in Tierra del Fuego is underlined. Exploring the North Pole is done the old-fashioned way in *Journeys and Adventures of Captain Hatteras* (1866); Captain Nemo, when he easily gets up there, recites the entire history of polar exploration. In *Measuring a Meridian* (1872), the very size of the earth is gauged from a triangulation survey conducted with simple equipment on the wide open African plains.

Fig. 69. *The "steel Giant," a train in the form of an elephant and Hindu temples, the whim of the Raja of Bhutan. Designed by a British engineer for a party of his compatriots, they tour India in it on a journey of exploration and mapping combined with hunting and adventure.*

In *The Steam House; or A Trip Across India* (1880), Verne has two Englishmen make the trip in search of tiger hunting and adventure, not incidentally providing a geographical conspectus of that subcontinent. Any exotic means of transport will serve his purpose, to paint the earth. Financed by the Rajah of Bhutan, the title steam house consists of a complete house on wheels, entrained with a supply depot, both designed like Hindu temples, drawn by a huge traction engine having the form of an elephant (fig. 69). They pass over the ground made memorable by the Sepoy Rebellion (1857–1859), an irredentist movement directed against the British Raj.

Expressing sympathy for it, the two Englishmen, very unlike their compatriots, hold views more in tune with that rebellious Indian prince, the Raj-hating Captain Nemo. This did not sit well with Verne's translator in England, who edited out these disagreeable passages. The same happened to *Twenty Thousand Leagues Under the Sea*. The translation of the "standard" edition (still in print) was done by an Anglican cleric hostile to Nemo's political views, and who cut them together with a whole chapter, "All by Electricity," because he found the technical details boring, not to mention much of the ichthyology—in all, fully a quarter of the text. Still, enough of the Science and Invention ambience came through for readers of the *Amazing Stories* reprint to follow when they became writers of engineering fiction.

One favorite SF theme conspicuous by its absence in Verne is "the war of the future" favored by Wells. In *The War of the Worlds*, the Martians' futuristic weapons derive from advanced Prussian weaponry in the Franco-Prussian War. Prussian military prowess is again drawn upon by Wells in *The War in the Air* (1908). Foreshadowing World War I, the first fully mechanized conflict, the novel has a great fleet of Prussian airships (fig. 70) initiate an attack on France that gets out of control, as other world powers join in

Fig. 70. *A portion of the Prussian fleet of airships. In 1870, Prussia had launched its war of aggression against France. The war effort, as intended, unified all the German states under the imperial rule of a single Reich. Now, again under Prussian leadership (with its usual command of advanced weaponry), Germany aims at world conquest for global unity. The result, however, is universal devastation and the collapse of civilization. Unity emerges only after this holocaust, with reconstruction carried out by a Wellsian world-state: a replay of the scenario first mooted in* Anticipations *(1902), a nonfiction work of social prophecy recalled in* Things to Come.

to combat the airships with fighter planes. The conflict spreads until even New York City is bombed to pieces (fig. 71). Eventually, "every organized government in the world was as shattered and broken as a heap of china beaten with a stick." But out of "the furnace" of scientific war is born "our present world state," the narrator says in retrospect. The same scenario is replayed in *Things to Come*, with a massive German airfleet (fig. 72) smashing the chinaware at the outset of World War II. Then rebirth with the advent in 2036 of the Modern World-State under the dictatorship of Oswald Cabal, grandson of John Cabal the "great Air Dictator." His League of the Airmen, recruited from English and German aviators alike, fought the last of the surving warring ministates—still contesting little shreds of territory—to a halt.

Verne, to be sure, in *Facing the Flag* (1896) imagined a powerful new explosive tipping the warheads of guided missiles—taken as a forecast of today's atomic-loaded ICBMs. But the mysterious explosive ingredient, termed a Fulgurator, is only melanite renamed, and the rocket bearing it is the invention of a renegade scientist working for pirates located in Bermuda (whose geography is duly explicated). They attack Atlantic shipping, and the "flag" they face is that of the various nations putting a stop to it.

For Wells, however, national sovereignty *is* war, and in *The World Set Free* (1914) he did indeed imagine something like today's unprecedented explosives. This time a world war is fought with atomic bombs (actually fizzlers that contaminate with radioactive poisons), but their effect is the usual. Having "burnt our way to freedom," the narrator reporting on a future world-state says, we are at last free of competitive nation-states.

Verne's inventors are loners, whereas in Wells (after the likes of Cavor and his Cavorite), they later form part of the R & D establishment. Industrialized science is the key to material progress in all fields, including the military. Powerful weapons in the right hands can only advance the cause of globalism versus localism: two opposite world views. In "The Land Ironclads" (1903), Wells has a force of tanks (fig. 73) attack the "bawling patriotisms" of some war-mongering country. Like the Airmen, the tankmen make war for peace. The tanks themselves (a product of group research) Wells later claimed were a prophecy of those first used in World War I. But they move not on caterpillar treads but on pedrails, as specified in the story (see fig. 74). What he *did* correctly forecast, however, was the coming of mechanized warfare and did so one year earlier in *Anticipations*, his first treatise of social prophecy. But he went on to anticipate that war technicians, more interested in mechanization itself and its productive potential, would turn against their masters of destruction, unite, and form a world-state—exactly what the Air League does.

It is often said that Verne doubted his own belief in progress. The dark side attributed to him, however, belongs to men of bad character. A perfect example is *The Begum's Fortune* (1879). A progressive-minded Frenchman somehow inherits great wealth from a distantly related Indian prince. With it he builds Franceville, a model of town planning (fig. 75). It carries further every aspect of the Sanitary Revolution launched by Saint-Simonians in the mid-nineteenth century. Its charter is novelized in *Hygeia: A City of*

Fig. 71, top. *The Prussian air fleet bombs New York City to rubble and ruination. American air defenses, as elsewhere, constitute only ineffective fighter planes not far developed beyond the first primitive Wright flyer of 1903. This battle for the skies gives the novel its title,* The War in the Air*: prophetic enough for 1908.* Fig. 72, bottom. *The German air fleet of the Third Reich over England in* Things to Come. *Frame enlargement.*

Fig. 73. *Tanks prophesied in "The Land Ironclads" (1903). They are the superior weapons of Wellsian tankmen who, like the Airmen in* Things to Come, *are consecrated enemies of nationalism in the cause of a world-state. They both wage war for peace, to end all patriotic wars.*

Health (1878) by B.W. Richardson. Verne summarizes it in chapter 10 of *The Begum's Fortune*. Meanwhile, an evil-minded German (another suspect Teutonic type), with his own unexpected legacy, builds a rival city, Stalstadt (fig. 76), and threatens to bombard Franceville with a gigantic steel-cast cannon (threat happily resolved).

In pollution-free Franceville, factory production is removed to industrial parks on the outskirts, the origin of green-belt cities in modern planning. *Amazing Stories Quarterly*, summer 1930, carried a story, "Paradise and Iron," offering the same contrast between Franceville and Stalstadt (fig. 77). A sanitary utopia, or "great white world," also figures in *Things to Come*. In its futuristic city of 2036, a clean industrial plant and all dwellings are underground, parkland outside. See fig. 78.

Just as Verne responded to *The Island of Doctor Moreau* in *The Village in the Treetops*, he also reacted to *The Invisible Man* (1897). In *The Secret of Weilhelm Storitz* (1910, posthumous), he plotted the machinations of another sinister German living in Strasbourg, the French city whose regional geography is richly displayed. Storitz concocts invisibility for the sole purpose of taking revenge on the family of a daughter refusing to marry him. His method entails hocus-pocus based on newly discovered infrared and

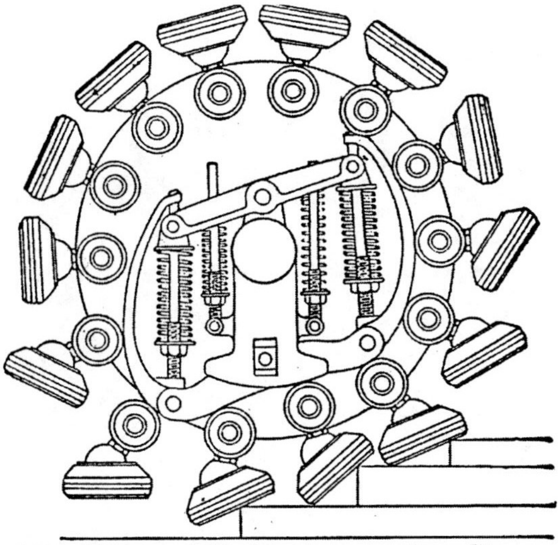

Side View of Pedrail mounting Steps.

Fig. 74, left. *Although Wells claimed his tanks were a true prophecy of those first used in World War I by England against Germany, they in fact moved not on caterpillar treads as actually developed but on pedwheels (pedrails), a device then used on farm tractors.* Fig. 75, top right. *The idyllic city of Franceville in* The Begum's Fortune. *It expresses Verne's patriotic faith in the enlightenment of French culture over that of Germany. He remembered from personal experience the humiliation of national defeat in the Franco-Prussian War of 1870.* Fig. 76, bottom right. *The ugly Germanic city of Stahlstadt in* The Begum's Fortune. *It is everything Verne hates in the Teutonic view of progress.*

ultraviolet rays. Wells's invisible man, no less loosely predicated, is more impersonal. His man, Griffin, is a political terrorist who aims to destroy the filthiness of private-profit capitalism. The gryphon, his mythical namesake, is the classical Greek chastiser of greed and avarice. A fabled chimera, the gryphon (or griffin) mixes the head and wings of an eagle with the body of a lion (fig. 79). Griffin, a student of chemistry before turning to a new career, fails to spark the revolution he hoped for. Before he is hunted down and killed for his Reign of Terror, however, he promises "Invisible Man the Second"—a successor that does indeed appear in *The Holy Terror* (1939). Its world

Fig. 77. *A derivative story is "Paradise and Iron" by Miles J. Brewer, M.D., a physician concerned with air pollution. The two cities in Verne typify national traits that demonize Germany and elevate France. Those in Brewer rather contrast two urban environments on a single imaginary island. From* Amazing Stories Quarterly, *summer 1930.*

dictator, a successful revolutionary, is termed "invisible Great Man"—invisible because he does not show himself to the public as do democratic politicians; rather he visits unseen punishment on opponents of his regime. His model may have been Stalin behind Kremlin walls, drawing up lists for political execution and exile to the death camps. Most of their 18 million inmates in any one year perished, only to be replaced.

Invisibility, even after the Wells novel was reprinted in *Amazing*, was much the subject of how it might be accomplished technically, along with the mechanics of time travel, mutant-making, and other feats. The sociopolitical aspects of the scientific romances of H.G. Wells were completely lost until a new sophistication informed the field when John Campbell took over the editorship of *Astounding Stories*.

Verne and Wells together have had more cinematic adaptations of their work than any other author. As might be expected from Hollywood, these films are adventure films merely, blind to the ideological thrust of the originals.

Verne was the first in 1902, but not in Hollywood which did not exist until later in the century. It is *La Voyage dans la lune*, a 21-minute silent produced by Georges Méliès in his Paris studio. By now it is familiar from film clips repeatedly shown on television documentaries about the history of movies in which Méliès is featured as the most significant pioneer. His 1902 one-reeler achieved instant popularity worldwide. *La Voyage dans la lune* not only marks the start of the film industry, it is the first science fiction film. Méliès was a stage magician who found that his cheap tricks and props looked all the more authentic when seen through a camera lens: the first special effects.

A papier-mâché cannon, an artillery piece on the ramparts, is pointed just above the horizon, a painted backdrop showing the moon. Bathing beauties, drawn from the Corps de Ballet du Châtelet, breech-load the cannon and fire it. The manned projectile hits the moon's weeping eye, a face in crude makeup not much bigger than the model projectile sticking into it. Next it is shown reposing on a jagged stalagmite-studded moonscape. Umbrella-waving caricatures of the disputive scientists finally agree to enter the moon's interior, where they are attacked by armed Selenites, who are beaten off with the umbrellas. Escaping to the projectile, they push it off the edge of the moon and it falls to Earth.

The Selenites inhabiting a cavernous interior of course derive from Wells's moon novel. So, the first science fiction movie conflated both Verne and Wells. The two would continue to be filmed up to the present day. More Verne than Wells, actually, too many to retail here. Wells came much later with fewer titles, all of which are worth mentioning.

From the Earth to the Moon (Warner Bros. 1958), starring George Sanders in a wasted role, is carelessly made with special effects as obvious as anything in Méliès.

Fig. 78. *The underground city of* A.D. *2036 in* Things to Come, *a "great white world" evolved from Verne's hygienic Franceville. The architecture is a curvilinear variant (streamlined moderne) of the international style led by Mies van der Rohe, which has indeed become the world standard of modernity. Wells had anticipated it in* A Modern Utopia *(1905), where he ended not only all forms of traditional architecture but also the traditional norms of social life that went with them.*

Fig. 79. *A gryphon as correctly represented on the bronze elevator doors of a Chicago office building. Student drawing.*

Captain Nicholls (Sanders) develops a powerful new explosive to propel the projectile, a dangerous development the likes of nuclear energy, the film moralizes. It is a needful propellent if the huge projectile, as roomy as Nemo's submarine, is to be lifted. A feeble attempt to cushion the concussion of the gun's firing is given in stupid rotary devices that spin the passengers around at the crucial moment. Captain Nicholls and his like-minded evil colleague in misguided progress (Joseph Cotten, in another pathetic role) depart the projectile in a space capsule that lands them on the moon, their object of conquest. The heroine and her love (the Captain's rival) return to Earth, leaving behind to perish the two most dangerous men in the world: a Cold War fable preaching against the arms race in nuclear weapons. The love triangle, remote from anything Verne ever wrote, is typical Hollywood. But even this trusty formula failed to save a badly made film from no sale at the box office. No matter, since little was lost on a cheapo production.

From 1905, *20,000 Leagues Under the Sea* was the most frequently filmed. By 1916, Universal produced a lengthy 113-minute film, using a World War I submarine as Nemo's vessel, exotic enough at the time. The story is hopelessly confused, badly acted and ineptly directed. The director evidently learned nothing from D.W. Griffith's monumental epic, *Birth of a Nation* (1915). But its innovative underwater photography, with new cameras invented for the purpose, is remarkable even today.

By far the best film adaptation is the Walt Disney production of 1954, starring James Mason as Captain Nemo. But even he is upstaged by the heroic Ned Land, the Canadian harpooner (American in the film), played by Kirk Douglas. Other stars are Paul Lukas as Professor Aronnax, the French naturalist, and Peter Lorre as Nemo's valet. These three are the novel's other main characters, prisoners aboard the *Nautilus*, to which is added the inevitable heroine for love interest.

The *Nautilus* itself is a period personality, designed with Victorian ironmongery, well imagined controls and instruments on the captain's bridge, and lush interior decor in the salon. When in 1963 I heard that Disneyland (then only in California) was exhibiting the film's artifacts, I hastened to visit. The exhibit cost only 10 cents to enter, much cheaper than the more attractive rides. Within I found myself happily alone, there to look at detailed scale models of all the ships used in filming, also the diving suits with imaginative helmets, then to sit for hours in the magnificent full-size salon. It was pure Verne.

The Mysterious Island had quite a number of versions, at times incoherently mixed up with the submarine saga. All lack any serious production values save one, whose only marginal merit is a bigger budget, better casting with known Hollywood stars, and fancy special effects, the latter totally irrelevant. I refer to the expensively advertised 1961 film of Charles H. Schneer Productions, GB/US. The castaways of course include that extra ingredient (Joan Greenwood) for the imperative sex romance. They find themselves on a deserted island whose mystery is oversized poultry and crabs, a welcome food supply. These edible creatures turn out to be mutants caused by radiation from the nuclear power plant in Nemo's *Nautilus* parked in a nearby hidden lagoon. Nemo himself (Herbert Lom) walks out of the sea in diving dress to explain.

Hector Servadac: Loosely related are any number of films that deal with a collision or near-collision with some stray celestial body, planet, asteroid, comet, or meteor. These, however, are mediated by the better known derivative story by H.G. Wells, "The Star" (1897): A comet passes close by and leaves vast destruction in its wake. The surviving third of humanity is shocked into unity and forms a world state. The most spectacular example of a film descending in this tradition is *When Worlds Collide* (Chapter 8).

A little less tangential is *Valley of the Dragons* (Columbia 1961). At least it begins with Verne's premise, two dualists interrupted by a grazing comet. Next they find themselves on a comet, where they encounter dinosaurs. These giant reptiles, portrayed in back projection, are taken from special effects used in *One Million Years B.C.* (United Artists 1940): one more play on the cavemen and dinosaurs theme (see Chapter 9). The one and only film adaptation to follow the novel all the way is the Czech-made *Na Komête* (*On the Comet*, Studio Barrandor 1970). At the end, this fantastic story is rationalized as a near-death experience during the moments Captain Servadac nearly drowns before being saved by his aide.

Around the World in Eighty Days (United Artists 1956) is the biggest production of any Verne novel ever made. Filmed in Todd-AO, a widescreen system developed by Mike Todd the producer, it attracted a public willing to pay high seat prices for a spectacular show, unheard of after television instituted home entertainment. A further attraction was all the many stars of stage and screen who did bit parts in cameo roles. Once Noel Coward signed on, the others gladly followed. Among them the names range from Marlene Dietrich to Fernandal, Buster Keaton and Beatrice Lillie, not omitting the great John Gielgud. Robert Newton appears briefly now and again as the detective in pursuit of Fogg for some dim reason. David Niven plays Phileas Fogg the traveller, Cantinflas his valet.

Todd chose a subject of proven worth. Verne's novel was his biggest success and most enduring. Stage productions from his own day to recent times entailed ever more imaginative sets and a growing parade of circus animals. The last was Orson Welles's extravaganza. At the start of each performance he stood before the audience and announced that it had "everything in it but the kitchen sink." At that point a stagehand walked out from the wings to dump a kitchen sink at his feet. Laughter. Everything.

Instead of the kitchen sink, the film throws in every popular tourist locale on the map, not always consistent with Fogg's voyage nor with a rambling stay in Paris he had no time for. The cameo roles are contrived to highlight these places in a story line invented for the purpose. Verne's romantic globalism, "the whole world belongs to mankind," reduces to a world belonging to the tourist trade.

The film's most acclaimed episode was a balloon flight, Niven and Cantinflas aboard, which never took place in the novel. In response, Irwin Allen at the same studio produced a big-budget remake of *Five Weeks in a Balloon* (1962), done once before in 1959 by a French company. Filmed in Cinema 77 (an improved widescreen version), it too had a host of stars in cameo parts. Two scientists (not the novel's three) control and maneuver the balloon over Africa, the *Victoria* here renamed the *Jupiter*. It really is a giant balloon, with a huge and capacious gondola and oversized cabin. One of the scientists is played by the ageing but dignified Sir Cedric Hardwicke, the other by Jacques Verlaine, who is just plain silly, as is much else. The original mission to map central Africa and discover the source of the Nile is quickly diverted as the balloon acquires no fewer than five additional passengers (plus a chimp for Disney cuteness) when landing here and there; not one of these is in Verne's novel, nor any of these landings.

The five surplus passengers are a mere excuse for the cameo roles, unrelated to anything in the original story. They are Red Buttons as a comical reporter, Barbara Luna a stowaway and escaped slave, Richard Hayden as an idiotic imperialist general, Barbara Eden as a willful missionary strong to end white slavery, and the ageing Peter Lorre as Ahmed the Arab dealer who wants to enslave her. The crew of the *Jupiter* now switch interests from exploration to the evils of white slavery while ignoring black slavery in Africa.

Facing the Flag had only one film given to it, but is the most impressive, not to say bizarre, production of any Verne novel. Czech made, it is *Vynález Zkazy* (Le Film Tchécoslovaque 1958), released in English as *The Fabulous World of Jules Verne*. The French title is *L'Invention diabolique du Professor Roch*, after the mad scientist who works for the Caribbean based pirates freely terrorizing Atlantic shipping, until they finally "face the flag" when the world's great naval powers unite to go after them and destroy Professor Roch's diabolical weapon of mass destruction.

Remarkably, the story is told almost entirely in visual terms, with only sparse dialogue in a few scenes, nor is there any narrative voice-over to explain. The even more remarkable visuals tell it all. They combine live-action with varied techniques in a seamless flow. Two dimensional cutout figures are sailors, other cutouts depict machinery or scenery; more special effects blend in, models, mattes, cartooning, forced perspective. The black-and-white imagery perfectly captures the world of Jules Verne with its engraved effects, lines and whorls over the cutouts and action, evoking the etched engravings illustrating the original French editions of Verne's novels.

Journey to the Center of the Earth ("trip" for "journey" in the first English translation): Related to this novel are a number of tangential films. Only one big-budget production takes it on directly. Despite that, more of the others were produced.

The most notable is *At the Earth's Core* (Amicus 1976, GB), basing on a 1914 novel of that title by Edgar Rice Burroughs, the first of seven in his Pellucidar series; he even gets Tarzan there, the land inside a hollow Earth. Inventor Abner Perry and assistant enter it in a mechanical digging machine. They find a savage world of surviving Ice Age man and mammals, dinosaurs from the Age of Reptiles, and some even weirder monsters thrown in for good measure. The film stars Peter Cushing as professor Abner Perry, Doug McClure as David, his former pupil, who dubs the burrowing machine the "Iron Mole." Intended for geological exploration, it unexpectedly breaks into the hollow Earth. The underground humans just happen to speak English, so David is able to persuade them to compose their tribal differences, likened to national rivalries on the surface, and unite against their common enemy, the monsters.

Journey to the Center of the Earth (20th Century–Fox 1959) stars James Mason as the explorer. This adaptation is the best Hollywood can do in a serious vein, given its needful hokum. It does not shrink from looking at and naming the mineralogical wonders of the interior. Verne's original trio, Lindenbrock, Axel, and Hans, reappear with different personalities. Lindenbrock (Mason) is here renamed Sir Oliver Lindenbrook, a Scottish (not Danish) geologist. Pat Boone plays Alex McKuen, a greatly revised Axel who no longer is the narrator and voice of skepticism but Oliver's enthusiastic partisan. Hans (Peter Ronson) is a simple-minded strongman indifferent to everything, not the subtle Hans in Verne whose attitude toward science and progress is another contrapuntal voice. The film, however, brings in other discordant notes entailing intricate intrigues, provided by two new characters.

The one is Carla Goetaborg (Arlene Dahl), the wife of Peter Goetaborg, a scientist racing Oliver to the center of the earth. After her husband is murdered by Count Saknussem, Carla goes on the trip with Oliver and insinuates herself as his romantic interest. Count Saknussem is the descendant of Arne Saknussem, whose manuscript account of a previous trip is followed by both Oliver and Peter Goetaborg before he is murdered. His widow now sides with Oliver, the better man, in search of a better marriage. The other new character is none other than Count Saknussem the murderer and professional rival. He goes in pursuit of the exploratory team and catches up with it, to everybody's consternation. These tangled human concerns are the film's central interest, not Verne's exaltation of science and exploration.

The technical effects are first-rate throughout, except for one scene on the beach of the underworld sea. Here the dinosaurs are ordinary lizards, enlarged in back-projection: a cheap trick often used before. A raft voyage across the sea, in Verne, is forgotten in the film. When Oliver returns to the surface, he lectures on the trip at his University of Edinburgh. He apologizes for losing his notes, without explaining the underground strife that got them lost. Nothing eventuates. Verne's Victorian paean to scientific discovery is not possible to sell today, even though the film is carefully crafted as a period piece. The lost notes testify to a lost optimism.

Robur the Conqueror and *Master of the World*: The only film of note bearing on either one of these two novels, the latter a sequel to the former, is unremarkable. *The Master of the World* (AIP 1961) is a loose composite of both, merged and modified in a pathetic production wasting the talents of its two stars, Vincent Price and Charles Bronson. Other members of the cast also have distinguished credits to their name. As is often the case, the budget is expended on casting, to the sacrifice of script and production values.

The film begins in Morgantown, Pennsylvania (the North American site in *Robur the Conqueror*), where the Great Eyrie is located. Here Robur (Price) is busy in his workshop, fabricating a flying machine at a time when only balloons took to the air. Flashes of fire and a booming voice citing apocalyptic passages from scripture issue forth from a volcanic crater (in Pennsylvania?). John Strock (Bronson), an official from the Department of the Interior, arrives to investigate. He first goes to a meeting of the Weldon Balloon Society, where he witnesses a feud between two embittered factions disputing how to design the steerable airship the Society proposes to build. One side, led by Uncle Prudent (Henry Hull), argues that the propeller should go in front; the other side, led by Phil Evans (David Frankham), is for putting the propeller in back. Strock steps in with a practical solution: Place one fore and one aft. (In Verne's earlier novel, it is Robur who intervenes with haughty contempt for the whole project.) That settled, he requests that the airship fly over the Great Eyrie to see what is going on there.

It flies over and Robur shoots it down with a rocket, then appears at the crash site and imprisons the survivors in the capacious cabins of his gigantic flying machine, the *Albatross* (the *Terror* in the later novel). The prisoners taken from the crashed airship number all the principals; Robur himself, as captain of the *Albatross* and its large crew, presides. The prisoners are all treated generously in roomy cabins and at the captain's table in his lavish dining room. Seated there are Uncle Prudent, his daughter Dorothy (Mary Webster), who is Evans's fiancée, and Strock. They listen to Robur expound on his maniacal mission.

Once Strock observes Robur bombing warships in his campaign to end war, he resolves to sabotage the *Albatross*, a kind of gigantic helicopter held aloft by a vast array of whirling propeller blades along the topside from stern to stern. It is able to carry plenty of weight: engine room, bomb bay, ornate appointments. Strock succeeds and escapes with Dorothy, his love interest. The film degenerates to that, cheapened also by a bad model of the *Albatross* in flight: The same shot is seen over and over again, intercut with the interior shots.

H.G. Wells in the cinema is not all science fiction. For many professors of English literature, his realistic novels of social criticism still are more important than the famous romances. Five of these are rendered in *The Wheels of Chance* (Stoll 1922, GB) and *Marriage* (Fox 1927), the one U.S. film in this lot. The first talkie is *Kipps* (20th Century–Fox 1941, GB), starring Michael Redgrave as the title figure under director Carol Reed. A major production is *The Passionate Friends* (Rank 1948, GB), directed by David Lean, script by Eric Ambler, and starring Ann Todd, Claude Rains and Trevor Howard. No less distinguished is *The History of Mr. Polly* (Rank–Two Cities 1949, GB) starring John Mills, who also acted as producer.

The scientific romances have been Hollywood's preserve. The only related British production, based on a 1906 short story, is *The Door in the Wall* (produced by British Film Institute 1956). Actually, the story relates more to mainstream fiction than to SF and is one of the classics of short story writing. The film experimented with a new technique, the dynamic screen, and was not publicly shown. I saw it at a New York film club, and found it the most perfect adaptation of anything Wellsian ever likely to be seen.

Contrast this with Hollywood's treatment of a 1905 story in *Empire of the Ants* (American International 1973). In the story, a highly intelligent breed of army ants march out of some South American country and defy research scientists trying to prevent the creatures from taking over the world. In the film, a colony of ants on a Caribbean resort island by chance eat radioactive waste matter dumped nearby and grow into monsters, unstoppable atomic mutants.

Four years later the same production company did *Food of the Gods* (American International 1977), from a 1904 novel satirizing the limits of local and national boundaries obstructing the growth of a world-state. In the novel, two children, brother and sister, steal into a chicken coop and eat a growth stimulant research scientists have been feeding the birds, who then assume gigantic size. The children, too, become giants. They come to realize their responsibility to represent the Wellsian world-state, the big dominating the little. Reactionary little people go after them in their mountain fastness and shoot them and *their* children (of an incestuous union) down. The film is just another silly monster movie, featuring not children but giant rats, aside from the chickens, who threaten humanity. The novel, of course, has a more serious political slant, but artistically it does not rank with the other scientific romances of classic stature.

Those classics are the subject of a number of Hollywood films. All are high quality productions that aim at being faithful to Wells, at least in spirit, but instead totally misread it. The five scientific romances that now belong to *Weltliteratur* are treated with due respect in their Hollywood film adaptations, yet with a profound misjudgment of the author's purpose. All the same, the films are excellent in their own right, as examples of crafty showmanship in the science fiction cinema. Below, the films follow the order in which the novels appeared, from 1895 to 1901.

The Time Machine (M-G-M 1960): Directed by George Pal, who in 1953 did *The War of the Worlds*, it stars Rod Taylor as the Time Traveller and the fetching Yvette Mimieux as Weena the moronic Eloi girl, here a bright young thing worthy of marriage to the genius who mastered time travel. Rod Taylor in his home laboratory fabricates a time machine, explained to fellow intellectuals attending a dinner party. After the guests depart, Taylor retires to his lab and starts up the machine. Gone is the novel's bicycle saddle, instead a comfortable armchair. Behind is what looks like a satellite dish with signs of the zodiac emblazoned around the rim. How fast or slow the dish rotates indicates the speed at which the machine moves through time. At the two control levers, ahead and reverse, are two flashing electronic tubes (!), wildly inconsistent with a pre-electric Victorian period piece.

The Time Traveller begins slowly, while looking outside his lab, through a wall of glass panes, at a shop window across the street. He watches women's fashions change: hats fly off and on, hems go up and down, recalling George Pal's stop-motion photography used at the start of his career in his popular series of puppetoon shorts. He then moves cautiously ahead to pause in a London under German Zeppelin raids during World War I. Pausing again as London is bombed in World War II, he then speeds on to some further future of indeterminate date, expecting to find a suitable place to stop. He arrives just in time to witness a mushroom cloud billowing up on the horizon. To escape the atomic blast almost enveloping him, he presses the lever to full throttle, the disc spinning madly, and does not stop until his dials read A.D. 802,701.

The place looks idyllic, a garden world: no more London, no urban civilization at all. Perhaps a rural utopia, unexpected, is the final solution to human ills. This is the best place to make a new home. The first people the Time Traveller meets are the Eloi, indifferent to his machine, not speaking to him. He later learns of the Great Fear that makes them inarticulate, a curable problem he knows how to fix once he finds the cause. Then he meets Weena, who explains everything to him. She even takes him to a derelict museum, where she spins a Talking Ring that records the death and burial of modern civilization: World War III. Ah yes, the event he barely escaped at the moment of his third pause in London.

He returns to the elegant glass-domed dwelling place of the Eloi, where they sleep unquietly at night and dine communally on fruit. Eating with them, he thinks how to repair the dome's neglected panes, broken here and there. A simple job for a handyman like him. Then he hears loud hooting whistles (they are air-raid alarms) and the Eloi empty out and silently head for a surface structure where the hooters are mounted. Also atop the building is the landscape-dominating head of a sphinx made of stainless steel (the novel's enigmatic marble sphinx).

The building houses an entrance to a no longer functional shelter left over from World War III. As the Eloi head for it, a great steel door opens and they begin to enter. The Time Traveller, curious to know what is inside, joins them just as the door closes. Most of the Eloi are left outside and they return home where they continue to breed; only a small batch is entrapped in the shelter at any one take. The Time Traveller descends into a cavernous underworld, lit by flaming braziers, where he is roughly handled by shaggy creatures with glowing green eyes, typical of all monster movies. They are the sinister Morlocks that Weena had alluded to in hushed tones when she spoke of the Great Fear. The Morlocks provide the Eloi with colorful clothing, sashed tunics, and fruit picked from untended gardens above ground. That is all it takes to make contented cattle of the Eloi, unaware of the coming slaughter when they end up on Morlock carving tables.

The two-fisted Rod Taylor resists being eaten and socks his captors in the jaw. Then he spots his beloved Yvette Mimieux and punches out her captors as well. Together they escape to the surface. Once outside, the Time Traveller (called George in the film, after Herbert George Wells), finds that his machine has been abducted by the Morlocks. Presumably they know what it is, as the Eloi do not, and keep him *here* so they can recapture him. George, however, is not fooled; skid marks on the ground show where it has been dragged to cover under nearby bushes.

George then speeds home on reverse in time for his appointed dinner party. The machine reappears in his workshop a few feet away from its original position; skid marks on the floor show just how far the Morlocks had moved it. Meeting with his usual guests, George tells his tale and says he is going back, this time with a portable camera to prove it.

After the party, his best friend lingers behind to discuss the coming trip. George's housekeeper helps him pack the camera and a few select books from his library. This is reported by the housekeeper to the friend when he revisits. It is evident that George has returned to the future to rejoin Weena, dispose of the Morlocks, and rebuild Eloi civilization. The film of course omits the novel's climactic *fin de globe* scenario, "The

Further Vision." Typical of the British tradition of the scientific romance, it depersonalizes human events in the cosmic scale of things. The film reduces to a highly personalized sex romance, a phrase Wells used with contempt in speaking of the usual film fare.

The Invisible Man (Universal 1933): The same studio released *Frankenstein* only two years before, starting a run of horror movies. The present one likewise became a classic of this genre, above all for its memorable special effects. Hardly anything today is that good. The intelligent script is by the distinguished British playwright R.C. Sherriff. Starring as Griffith is Claude Rains in his first (unseen) film role, a New York stage actor whose commanding voice with a British accent and body carriage made him the perfect choice. His voice held authority when unseen, his body, too, when hidden by exotic clothing: the famous head bandages and aviation goggles.

The story line, however, reverses Wells's. Griffith no longer is a political terrorist, called to revolution as his vocation, but a mad scientist run amok. In the film he is the bad guy, the bourgeois Dr. Kemp the good guy. More, a love interest is central: Griffith's jilted fiancée. She even follows him to the remote village of Iping where he hides out, after a series of horrific crimes, and is harshly sent back home. Dr. Kemp explains that the madness is a side effect of the drug taken for invisibility.

When Griffith, unclothed, sneaks into the doctor's grand estate to exact revenge, Kemp is prepared, with London police constables waiting. They wear gas masks and spray the mansion's interior with a foggy mist, and Griffith is made visible in outline. But he escapes the net about to be thrown over him and retreats to a nearby barn. Now he is trapped for sure. The barn doors fly open and running footprints on the snow-covered ground are seen, then end as Griffith is shot down. As he lies dying on a hospital bed, his fiancée attends him, still professing love. Dead, he returns to visibility. His head above the covers undergoes a spectacular transformation: bone, arteries, nerves, then tissue appear and the quiescent face of Claude Rains is revealed, beatified by undying love.

The Island of Doctor Moreau: Two film versions of this novel were made, the first more famous. It is *The Island of Lost Souls* (Paramount 1932), one year after Universal scored two big horror hits with *Frankenstein* and *Dracula*. It stars the histrionic Charles Laughton as a completely deranged Doctor Moreau. The Beast Folk he turns out by vivisection in his House of Pain gave the creative make-up artists their own wide field of monster-making. Prendick the castaway, renamed Edward Parker and played by Richard Arlen (a romantic lead in other films), is properly scared by them.

One of the Beast Folk is the novel's Sayer of the Law, who repeats Moreau's whip-enforced rules of decent human behavior: not to claw bark of trees, not to kill and taste blood, etc. He is played by Bela Lugosi, who starred as the blood-thirsty vampire in *Dracula*. In the end, he leads the others to kill Moreau with his own surgical instruments, and to drink his blood.

Meanwhile Richard Arlen falls for the not particularly bestial "panther woman," Lota, who pads about the island in a dubious manner natural for an inexperienced actress impersonating a heroine with no soul. She is Kathleen Burke, selected for the part out of 60,000 other girls who entered Paramount's highly published contest. Her pointed face, sloping eyes, fuzzy hair and graceful physique were just right, no acting ability needed. The romance proceeds nicely until Arlen notices that Lota's fingernails are claws. Finally his fiancée comes to rescue him, accompanied by a drunken sea captain. (The woman's dress and freighter she travels on indicate the 1930s.) They manage to get him off the island just in time before it goes up in flames, and as Charles Laughton screams horribly under the cuts of his own scalpels.

The other notable film (not in the black and white of the 1930s) is *The Island of Doctor Moreau* (American International 1977), a lush Cinema 77 production. It stars Burt Lancaster, who comes across as quietly reasonable, but whose utter rationality is itself the madness. It also stars Michael York as the castaway, renamed Braddock, who plays the invariable innocent. Nigel Davenport plays Montgomery who, as in the novel, is Moreau's drunken and cynical assistant; over drinks in his quarters he explains to Braddock what is really going on in the island. The immensely dignified Sayer of the Law is Richard Basehart, who holds forth in a cave decorated with Upper Paleolithic art, the suggestion being that the Beast Folk are throwbacks to caveman primitivity.

The love interest attracting Braddock is Maria (Barbara Carrera), Moreau's most artful normal-seeming creation. The Doctor warns off Braddock, saying that Maria is his daughter. So they meet in secret and plot to get away together. Braddock cannot guess that Moreau suspects she might revert at any moment, which she does in the final grotesque shot, to Braddock's heart-sickening dismay.

Publicity for the film included a book, published by Doubleday in New York, directed at the educated by way of affirming Hollywood's intellectual credentials: profound classic, profound movie. The book contains both the novel and a screenplay adaptation, plus photographs of the principal actors and a full display of the humanimals™ in their extravagant Beast Folk makeup. The film was shot on St. Croix in the Virgin Islands, United States territory from 1917. Moreau's retreat, were it located there at about that time, would be appropriate for an American geneticist; but the film sticks to the novel's 1890s. But Hollywood is ever tempted to be supersophisticated with a stance both antiscience and anti–American.

Braddock questions Moreau's ethics in a talk session. His drink is drugged and he wakes up strapped to a surgical table as Moreau injects him with something and he is then put in a cage. Moreau explains that he wants to find out from him what an animal thinks and feels, the better to understand why his creatures invariably revert. The injection delivers DNA from a bear, and while it starts to take effect Moreau questions Braddock moment by moment; he resists by struggling to recite events from childhood on. The freshly-imported black bear in the next cage shows restless empathy, breaks out, throws Moreau unconscious to the floor, and departs. Braddock reaches out for the keys in Moreau's limp hand, lets himself out, and departs to recover in his room.

Meanwhile the escaped bear has incited the Beast Folk to release all sorts of wild animals from their outdoor cages. Then they head for Moreau's compound and threaten him with rebellion. Moreau steps out of the gate and tries to hold them off with whip and revolver. They overpower him and kill him. Braddock pulls the body inside, locks the gate, then promptly strings the body up on a rope so that Moreau appears to be looking down on the Beast Folk from high over the palisades. They are for the moment subdued as Braddock speechifies about his not being dead: He is immortal.

Braddock takes the moment to escape with Maria out the back gate, and flee to the beach where they have restored and hidden a rowboat. As they head out for the open Caribbean Sea to await rescue from a passing vessel, they watch the island go up in flames. Then comes the cruncher. Braddock notices that Maria's fingernails have become menacing claws. The film abruptly ends there. More reversion is in store, Braddock is doomed.

The War of the Worlds (Paramount 1953), produced by George Pal: A low-budget cast of unknowns makes way for big-budget special effects, which are the film's excuse for being. The setting is California, in and around Los Angeles. A young physicist (Gene Barry) on a fishing trip observes with interest a fall of meteors, and goes to investigate a nearby impact. When he arrives, a crowd has already gathered around a huge cylinder that is definitely not a fallen meteorite. At the base of the tilted cylinder a hatch unscrews, and what looks like a periscope on a long cobra neck emerges and peers about. Intelligent creatures are in there.

Three men advance with a white flag. One of them, a clergyman, steps forward to address the aliens inside. He says that we humans want only peace, harmony, and interplanetary communication. The periscope pulls back, another cobra-necked device comes up and zaps the humans with a disintegrator ray. The men turn to skeletons in the haze, reducing to a pile of dust. The fire ray, emitted in screechy vibrato, will be heard in concert in scenes to come.

Gene Barry knows the clergyman to be his love-companion's father, and drives off in his camping truck to see her. She is played by Ann Robinson. The two retreat to a farm house in open countryside not very California-looking. While cooking breakfast, another giant cylinder plows into the ground nearby, throwing up a mound of earth that crushes the frame house. The long view of this impact is one of the many spectacular technical marvels.

The centrality of special effects, half the film given to their display, is the producer's joyful preference. George Pal explains them in his article for *Astounding Science Fiction* (October 1953), "Filming 'War of the Worlds.'" Readers of *ASF* welcomed it, knowing that Pal was Hollywood's only producer specializing in science fiction movies, starting with *Destination Moon* (1950) and *When Worlds Collide* (1951). His partisanship for the genre outweighed a nescience of Wells's philosophical message.

Gene Barry and Ann Robinson look out through cracks in the kitchen wall to see what happened. Then a cobra-necked scanner snakes inside, and Barry hacks it off with an axe. It is a triple-lensed television scanner, red, green, and blue in three parts trisecting a circle. While the two look at it, a crab-like Martian dances by the open doorway. The body is dumpy, with one large cyclops-eye with three separate lenses (like the scanner), big head for an oversize brain, and long spindly tentacles with suckers on the end for arms.

The two take the scanner to Barry's lab at Pacific Tech, modeled after Cal Tech in Pasadena. His graduate students help connect what is left of the cobra neck, a snake-like metal coil, to a television monitor. Barry scans everyone's face in turn. So, that's how we look to the enemy.

As the Martians approach Los Angeles, the U.S. Army goes after them. Their presence is quite topical. Only three years before, from 1950, the first UFO sightings were reporting from the Western states as "flying saucers." The Martians approach not in flying saucers but flying wings. Each is armed with a cobra-necked disintegrator atop it and with wing-tipped flame throwers. These weapons quickly dispose of the U.S. Army. Now for the atomic bomb, which is carried by the new Northrop YB-49, the Flying Wing, with credit given to the Northrop and North American Aviation companies for stock footage. The YB-49 was the prototype for the Northrop-built Stealth bomber. At the time of the movie, it was the most advanced warplane in the American arsenal; still it is no match for the Martian flying wings and for the more advanced technology they represent. The blast of the atomic bomb fails to penetrate the force shields they throw up.

As the Martians near Los Angeles, the city is a chaos of unplanned evacuation. Barry, companion and students load a Pacific Tech truck with equipment to be used elsewhere in researching ways to defeat the Martian invaders. But it gets into a massive traffic jam. Meanwhile, the flying wings begin their assault on the city. Scenes of ruination follow one after another, entailing the destruction of exquisite scale models. City Hall, with its landmark tower, is taken down; a representative residential street is taken out, house by house, as a flying wing slowly flies by.

Barry's truck is attacked by a mob scrambling to get aboard, its load thrown out to make room, and he and his companion get separated. He now commences a desperate search for her midst flames and falling debris. The city is doomed, like all other great cities of the world, as one learns from cuts to television broadcasts showing flying wings bringing fiery destruction to their every landmark symbol. As Barry passes a still-standing cathedral (God's grace), he remembers Ann Robinson's revered religious father. He goes inside, looks about, and finds her huddled in prayer with a group of children. Then quiet descends, broken by a crashing sound in the street outside.

Barry and Robinson go out to look. What they see is a crashed flying wing, as further distant crashing sounds are heard. A hatch at the bottom of the craft opens, a long spindly arm hangs out; its veins pulse, then stop. The ultramodern Martians, coming from a sanitary planet on which they have conquered nature down the last microbe, are vulnerable to the dirty germs of Earth. All die, and mankind is saved.

The First Men in the Moon (Columbia 1964, GB): This period piece is framed by a modern-day story. Bedford (Edward Judd), Cavor's partner in the moon voyage, still is alive. A frail old man living in a nursing home, he suddenly is the center of world attention as television crews descend on his private room.

American astronauts have just returned from their first landing on the moon. It did not happen until 1969, but everybody knew it was coming from the space program's trial flights. When the astronauts land, they find a British Union Jack already planted there, together with a note signed and dated by Bedford. A quite elderly Bedford is traced to his present abode in the nursing home, where his room contains authentic memorabilia of the trip. So, his matter of fact account of it is impossible to disbelieve. The film tells that story.

Bedford recalls meeting Cavor in Cornwall where he had just rented a summer cottage. Cavor is played as a pleasantly dotty scientist by Lionel Jeffries, England's respected low-key comedian. The two meet at Bedford's cottage, which Cavor wants to buy from him so as to spare him the dangers of a risky experiment about to be conducted nearby. Bedford, seeking to exploit a new invention, joins Cavor when he learns why the experiment is dangerous, and after sensing that Cavor is a total innocent in business matters.

The experiment in question entails the first casting of molten Cavorite. The assistant Gibbs (Erik Chitty) fails to exactly control the Cavor-specified temperature of the furnace in which the metal is heated. An explosion results. The next batch is properly controlled and then aplied to panels on the multifaceted Cavorite sphere, which is also studded with bumpers to absorb the shock of landing. The passengers get on board, including Kate (Martha Hyer), Bedford's romantic interest (not in the novel as none of the women in the films are). The sphere takes off, bursting through the roof with a tremendous whoosh. It lands on the moon, bumping along the ground until coming to a stop. Cavor and Bedford step outside in diving suits, then walk about.

When they return to the spot, the sphere is gone. But they trace the tracks along which it had been dragged, a play on the tracks in George Pal's production of *The Time Machine*. Here it is not Morlocks who have dragged away the machine but Selenites who also live in caverns beneath the surface. The trail leads to the entranceway to that underworld. Inside, Cavor and Bedford are able to take off their helmets because of breathable air. The interior is filled with crystalline structures pulsing with light from within, as if they were living things. Bedford, worried about Kate, goes looking for the sphere. Meanwhile Cavor is captured by not very convincing Selenites, actors dressed like insects, and taken before the Grand Lunar. Here the special effects are impressive, and the Grand Lunar's judgment on human savagery is close to Wells's in the novel. Cavor is doomed by his own honest testimony.

Bedford finds the sphere with Kate safely inside. He takes off, upward through a volcanic vent conveniently located overhead, and returns home. Cut to Bedford's nursing-home room. He is told that the astronauts did indeed find the Selenite caverns, but no sign of Selenites or crystal growths. Speculation has it that some kind of viral infection destroyed them. Ah yes, says Bedford: Cavor *did* have a bad cold. So, the film concludes with a feeble joke on the terrestrial germs that did in the Martians in George Pal's production of *War of the Worlds*.

Things to Come (London films 1936, GB), produced by Alexander Korda, who founded London Films to rival Hollywood: Some of his films were the most expensive ever made (relatively speaking), always of superior quality and polish with stellar casting. He respected good writers as Hollywood did not, and especially admired H.G.

Wells. In 1934 he gave him his head to write and supervise a film of his choice. Raymond Massey (who played John and Oswald Cabal) said in his autobiography that "No writer for the screen ever had or ever will have such authority as H.G. Wells possessed in the making of 'Things to Come'." Wells commanded every detail: architecture, decorations, costumes, casting, music, and special effects, and appeared on the set every working day during a whole year's shooting.

Hollywood's production of the scientific romances are consciously rooted in traditions of the science fiction cinema going back to Méliès. Critics quite naturally judge *Things to Come* to be a classic of the genre, outdated to be sure, but still the first modern SF film. Wells held to a loftier purpose, saying that it was a propaganda film for "Wellsism."

Before beginning work on the film, Wells in 1934 went off to visit Stalin in the Kremlin at the dictator's invitation to discuss prospects for the world revolution. Wells had praised Stalin for his technocratic Five Year Plan, but now was disappointed to learn that he still insisted on giving it a Marxist cover story.

While in Moscow, Wells was taken to see Dziga Vertov's *Three Songs of Lenin* (1934), in Russian with English subtitles. Wells offered a positive opinion when interviewed about it: "One of the greatest and most beautiful films I have ever seen." What impressed him, evidently, was the third song, with its montage of building the Soviet Union's industrial might under the Five Year Plan. He worked visual images like these into the reconstruction sequence in *Things to Come*. The propaganda point, however, turned on "Wellsism": Communism minus Marx. That is driven home by Theotocopulos (Sir Cedric Hardwicke), who leads a Marxist labor revolt, only to be extinguished by the blast of world dictator Oswald Cabal's space gun. Ralph Richardson plays the Boss of Everytown, whose reactionary ministate earlier is wiped out by John Cabal's Airmen.

Although the film bombed at the box office, it remains a critical success (for the wrong reason Wells would say) in the history of SF cinema. Its time has come for reevaluation.

4
John Campbell

Modern science fiction would not be what it became, after Gernsback, without Campbell. He applied his powerful intellect and polymathic talents to make magazine SF a literary force. As editor of *Astounding Science Fiction* he led the genre into its Golden Age, bringing forth that roster of excelling writers on whose record judgment now rests.

John W. Campbell, Jr., to give his name in full (used only by himself), began as a writer of space opera for *Amazing Stories*. Later he graduated to *Astounding Stories*, a somewhat better class of magazine (dating from 1933), for which he wrote under the byline Don A. Stuart: with these stories he redefined SF. Hereafter, a naive sense of wonder would harmonize with naturalistic explanations no less wonderful.

Here is a passage from "The Mightiest Machine" (serial 1934–1935):

> I saw a machine. It was the mightiest machine that could ever exist. It was an atomic, better, a material engine. It burned matter to energy. Most of the energy was electrical in nature at one stage of the process, but it was converted to heat and light and other forms of energy. And one of those forms of energy was a curious field of force that could tear great holes in tremendous masses of matter, and there appeared coincidentally with that a force that seemed to hurl masses of matter greater than a dozen worlds like Earth, greater than mighty Jupiter, a million miles into space.
>
> It was a wonderful, pulsing, rhythmic machine, and operated in a wonderful adjustment more delicate than any machine man ever made. Controlling unimaginable billions of billions of horse power, it remained in perfect balance with a variation in its output of less than one percent. Controlling forces that could have hurled this planet about like a bit of dust, it remained in perfect equilibrium.

And what is this machine? It is a star, our star, the sun. The description of it as an atomic engine is offered by a writer holding a degree in nuclear physics.

But why the machine metaphor? And why the machine as an ideal of perfection?

Knowledge of the sun conveyed in this imagery projects the power of observational science, which is the power to determine the material world in the R & D equation. The machine products of industrial science are the means whereby humanity perfects the expression of its godhood, knowing and making.

When in September 1937 Campbell took over *Astounding Stories*, he retitled it *Astounding Science Fiction* (*ASF*). Under his editorship, until his death in 1971, he changed even the cover's typeface. This borrowed the sans serif font designed in 1918 by Edward Johnson for the London Underground Railway, the last word in electrified rapid transport. Since then the style has come to suggest modernity and is now everywhere to be seen. The first to circulate it internationally was the Institute of Design at Illinois Institute of Technology (IIT).

Among Campbell's early stories were those belonging to the Penton and Blake series (1936–1938): "Brain Stealers from Mars," "The Double Minds," "The Immortality Seekers," "The Tenth World," and "The Brain Pirates." Penton and Blake depart from the usual all-action adventures undertaken by individualistic scientists. As a pair of cosmic explorers landing on various worlds, they enjoy collegiality in the adventure of solving exotic puzzles that must have a scientific explanation. Another popular team was that in the Arcot, Morey, and Wade series (from 1930). In *Islands of Space*, for example, the three make a tour of the cosmos in a faster-than-light spaceship. The islands of the title are island universes, galactic nebulae in which star-making is described and explained. At the time, some stars beyond our own Milky Way galaxy were not widely understood to be other galaxies. Members of the team, who design the ship, are researchers at Transcontinental Airways, a multinational corporation. They represent the R side in the R & D equation.

When John Campbell at my invitation visited IIT to lecture, he drew the largest audience ever. During the day I introduced him to the university's administrators, including the vice president, himself an *ASF* writer; they all greeted him with perfectly solemn respect, having been inspired to enter fields of science and engineering by Campbell's magazine and his own fiction. I then took him around to meet staffers at ITT Research Institute, the tallest building on campus, given to applied science. He discussed intelligently with them every aspect of development they directed. Campbell was pleased enough with his visit that he offered to return each year thereafter. He did not live to see the next one. We then in 1972 founded the John W. Campbell Award. This was a mistake. The Golden Age was over. The older generation of scientists and engineers at ITT are now retired, as myself. There is no going back to a time when American industry had the academic support of John Campbell's inspiring magazine.

Some works of his are worth mentioning for their philosophical viewpoint. In *The Moon Is Hell* (1951), the first rocketship to the moon crashes, and the research scientists stranded there on that dead rock win from it water, air, and food. Their curiosity about the nature of nature is the basis of their survival, the same that drives the conquest of nature for man's benefit in the R & D enterprise.

Indeed, curiosity is the uniquely human thing that motivates man's inventiveness,

Fig. 80. *Cover art for a collection of essays on magazine science fiction by James Blish* (d. *1975), an early fan whose 1952 story "Surface Tension"* (Galaxy) *was voted number 19 in the* SWFA *anthology of all-time best. Here he writes under his nonfiction byline. Advent Publishers, Chicago, 1964. The artwork plays on a famous panel painted by Michelangelo on the ceiling of the Sistine Chapel.*

and will outlive him. In "The Last Evolution" (1932), Campbell introduces an original concept of robots, heretofore regarded only as utilitarian aids. He has them being evolutionary descendents, "science machines" that make other machines, a theme not missed by later writers. The divine spark passes on to inanimate minds (see fig. 80). All the same, Campbell insists in the Introduction to *The Astounding Science Fiction Anthology* (1952) that "Machines and gadgets aren't the end and goal; they are the means to the true goal."

Modern technology exists to reify man's immortal urge to explore, seek new knowledge, and create new things that never existed before—the practical object of industrialized science. But even R & D has behind it the noninstrumental, spiritual motive to satisfy curiosity—the basis of observational science. And nothing is more purely observational than astronomy, which is why Campbell's magazine so often featured astronomical covers. See plate VI for a striking example, "Einstein Eclipse," that illustrates a repeat of the famous project undertaken by two observatories, on 29 May 1919, one located on the island of Príncipe off West Africa, the other at Sobral in Brazil. Having separate vantage points, they confirm a phenomenon predicted by Einstein's theory of relativity: Gravity bends light. This time, the cover art shows, the observation is made of another sun's eclipse from the inner planet of some other solar system in a distant galaxy: The rules of the universe are the same everywhere. The "true goal" of science is to understand man's place in the cosmos, and thus better to understand human relations. "The eventual goal of man is to understand man."

One of Campbell's Don A. Stuart stories is entitled "Twilight" (1934) is reprinted as number 14 in the SFWA hit parade.. It is 8 million years in the future and man is nearly extinct, having long forgotten science, but his great automatic cities are still on duty. The deathless cities go on with "the tireless, ceaseless perfection their designers had incorporated into them." "The men know how to die, and be dead, but the machines didn't": This is retailed to the narrator in the 1934 present by a time traveller, who has been to the very far future and then overshot the mark in coming back. To place himself in historical time, the first thing he asks is, what are the most important inventions of the day. Answer: "airplanes and radio." The two go together. Flying was the first mode of transport to exploit voice communication, just as railroads did telegraphy in the nineteenth century (the latest technology in Verne's day). In the distant future, the time traveller reports, men may be dead, but before they declined into effeteness they left behind "curiosity machines" that carry on the essential human thing.

In "The Machine" (1935), Campbell/Stuart has the title device descend from the heavens to provide wealth, ease, and abundance. Sent to earth by a super intelligence out there in space, men learn the wrong lesson from it. So the machine stops production. They try to get it going again by offering up human sacrifices ground between wheels of stone. The saving elect depart the scene to conquer nature on their own, at last attracting others to join their cause: the conquest of sloth and selfishness. The story echoes the Enlightenment's battle with religious superstition: Unreason is the enemy of progress. As we already have seen in Heinlein's "If This Goes On" (Chapter 3), in which a scientific elite overthrows a Christian theocracy, it is a recurring theme in SF.

Number Six in the SWFA anthology of best SF is "Nightfall" (1941) by Isaac Asimov. See plate V. Like many others, Asimov was a Campbell protégé, who as editor had a superfluity of ideas to share. In this case he suggested to the young Asimov, What would happen if the stars could only be seen every thousand years? In a galaxy far, far away, a peculiar solar system revolves around its planets around multiple suns, which all are eclipsed at one rare interval. Between times civilization arises again and again, with astronomical science coming into being at each peak. Then, when the stars go out, the fearful public panics and blames the observatory attempting to behold this phenomenon, which is put to the torch. All else is burned down as well, and the cycle repeats. So, if religious fanaticism is ever the enemy of science, then maybe one solution is for scientists to promote the actual miracles of technology as priestcraft—the premise of "Gather Darkness!" (1943) by Fritz Leiber. See fig. 81. Campbell always encouraged his authors to explore every possible idea in arriving at some new line of reasoning.

Another Campbellian spin-off is "With Folded Hands" (1947) by Jack Williamson, one of the old-timers going back to creation. Starting out in space opera he got wiser under Campbell's tutelage. Late in life he earned a Ph.D. for a dissertation on H.G. Wells, a subject we hotly disputed. The story here reported is a turn on "The Machine." Robots come to earth from some other star system to serve and protect mankind. Also a switch on the rebelling robots theme (Chapter 7), it is men who rebel against robots; they no longer can endure the welfare state created by them. Human nature resists idleness ("folded hands"); fulfillment requires engagement with the world. See plate VIII:2.

Fig. 81. *The Fritz Leiber story "Gather Darkness!" was featured in color on the cover of the May 1943 issue of* Astounding Science Fiction, *here reproduced in black and white. Darkness is what gathers on the established church as red-robed clerics ponder the genuine miracles of science, now effectively masked as a rival religion.*

Like *Amazing*, *ASF* ran a letters column. This feature began with Hugo Gernsback, who provided the correspondents' addresses, so the fans could write to each other. That is how organized fandom got started. The letters column in *ASF* likewise ranked stories in each issue and evaluated cover art and interior illustrations. Campbell, however, added another department, "Readers' Corner," in which scientific plausibility was at issue.

Fig. 82 shows the ideal reader Campbell catered to. He is educated, possesses a library, telescope, star chart, globe, and radiometer. He is expected to challenge assumptions by finding in the weirdest things imaginable a logical if not a strictly scientific rationale. Take one extreme example, "The Fairy Chessmen" (1946) by Lewis Padgett. The strange and baffling scene illustrated in the cover art, plate XII:2, addresses a thought experiment: What might not happen if the rules of our universe were different somewhere else? It is a serious question, only now being posed by astrophysicists after the advent of the Big Bang theory. Many different universes, with different physical laws, may have been created.

Indeed, Campbell for a brief time edited a magazine given to just such alternative rules. Titled *Unknown Worlds* (1939–1943, cut short by wartime paper restrictions), it offered a rationalized version of *Weird Tales* (from 1923, three years before the first SF pulp), a case of disciplined fantasy that rigorously excluded elements of the supernatural.

Fig. 82. *Logo for "Readers' Corner" in* Astounding Science Fiction, *later "Brass Tacks." Erudite discussions of the science in science fiction always took place here.*

Even the hard-headed Heinlein, as Anson MacDonald, tried his hand at it in "Magic, Inc." (September 1940). He was later to say that maybe SF ought to stand for speculation Fiction, which is but one step away from erasing the genre altogether.

The magazine furthered the education of its readers with another department comprising science-fact articles. This too had a precedent in *Amazing*, but they were written by an in-house science editor. I myself followed in this tradition by serving *Amazing* with my regular "Science of Man" columns (1967–1969). The logo, fig. 83, was designed by one of my students; juxtaposing a stone-age tool on a computer card, it makes the point that *all* tools are examples of human technology. This point was hard to sell to most students, who disbelieved that any piece of hardware not modern—not a computer with flashing lights—could be "technology." My subject matter, however, was not all that narrow; anthropological SF is widely diffused in the genre. Harry Harrison and I collected a sample of it in our anthology *Apeman, Spaceman* (1968).

At all events, *ASF* untypically had no science editor on staff. The department was filled by some of the *ASF* writers themselves, professional scientists and engineers adept at both fiction and nonfiction. Isaac Asimov, a biochemist, did articles on biochemistry and much else, a range amplified in his later *Biographical Encyclopedia of Science and Technology* (1964, 1972). L. Sprague de Camp, a mechanical engineer, wrote on ancient engi-

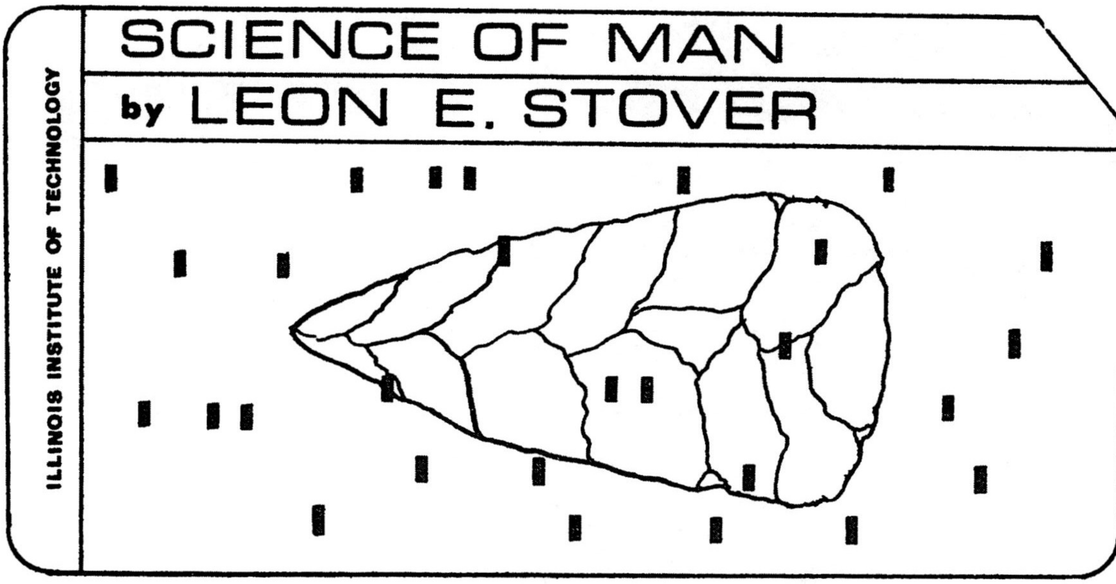

Fig. 83. *My own logo as the science editor for* Amazing Stories *(1967–1969), which featured anthropological subject matter.*

neering, classical science, and exotic zoology. Willy Ley, the rocket scientist fled from Nazi Germany, did articles on rocketry (fiction as Robert Willey), becoming science editor at *Galaxy Science Fiction* when it was founded in 1950. R.S. Richardson of the Mount Wilson observatory did astronomy (fiction as Philip Latham).

Campbell himself already was doing science journalism while writing as Don A. Stuart for *Astounding Stories*, notably his planet-by-planet survey of the solar system for the same magazine. At *ASF* his interest in chemistry, electronics, computers, nuclear physics, astronomy all were subjects for his own articles. In 1960 he changed the magazine's title to *Analog Science Fiction Science Fact*. Nothing could better express his editorial policy: The wonderful in SF must be analogous to man's power to understand nature and to manipulate it.

Above all, the supreme conquest of nature for Campbell was the advent of nuclear physics in the 1930s, the key unlocking all secrets of the universe—the literal key pictured on the cover of the August 1948 issue (see plate VIII:2). Stories about atomic power were encouraged from the start. "Blowups Happen" (September 1940) by Robert Heinlein recounts up-to-date theory, then extrapolates to the first of the atomic power plants. They are recognized as dangerous. Fig. 84 shows watchers watching the watchers of every move made by plant workers. Eventually, for safety, the plant is placed in orbit, using atomic fuel for its launching rocket.

Then, in the March 1944 issue, came the big revelation—Cleve Cartmill's "Deadline," which exactly detailed the making of atomic bombs. The Army Counter-Intelligence Corps instantly descended on Campbell's office and demanded to know who was leaking secrets of the Manhattan Project. Nobody, he replied; nature itself is a blab-

Fig. 84. *"Blowups Happen" is a link in Heinlein's Future History stories, on which he built his reputation. More than a master of engineering fiction, he showed himself a reflective thinker on the cumulative effects of technology unfolded in the future.*

bermouth for all those who study it. Even so, you must shut down further articles and stories on the subject; our enemies will know what is going on from your magazine. No, he reasoned, the giveaway would be my suddenly *not* continuing to publish. Nobody ever argued with John Campbell without losing. In the end, his was the only magazine during the war to openly discuss the forbidden.

Some of his fannish readers, and all literary critics of the genre, fault him for the long-running Lensman series, 1937–1948, by E.E. Smith—a throwback to the unfashionable space opera with which he began in *Amazing*. Campbell justified the series in *ASF* by billing it as The History of Civilization. One who did not find this out of place in modern SF was Robert Heinlein, himself the epitomized modern master. In "A Memoir in Tribute to Dr. Edward E. Smith" (1980), he credited the man as a decisive influence on his own Future History series.

In Smith, our galaxy and others are alive with intelligent beings, with whom humans in their space travels are bound to relate. At a kind of intergalactic UN, Smith's Lensman represents planet Earth (see fig. 85), or rather its federation of both colonized and native life within the solar system. This is a long way from the monstrous and malicious aliens of earlier SF. The same with Heinlein's Terran Federation in his Future History. Aliens are now established as political if not intergalactic commercial partners, as in Poul Anderson's "Trading Team" (July 1965). See plate XII:3. They are man's intellectual equals in the great scheme of things, everywhere endowed with the scientific know-how to build faster-than-light ships able to travel interstellar distances.

Intelligent life everywhere must in time arrive at that supreme triumph, that masterful conquest of nature, because intelligence everywhere must be science minded, given to the discovery of natural laws. This is the point of H. Beam Piper's novelette "Omnilingual" (February 1957), which occasioned Campbell to editorialize on the scientific method. Archeologists on Mars excavate a lost civilization covered by desert sands when the planet aged. Very advanced, with technical secrets to reveal, its writings are of course

Fig. 85. *Some of the aliens gathering for an intergalactic conference. The human there, "Doc" Smith's hero, is just another alien from the others' viewpoint: multiculturalism anticipated.*

untranslatable until its Rosetta Stone is uncovered. Fig. 86 shows the expedition's linguist piecing together fragmentary texts, as was done with broken clay tablets found in the ruined libraries of ancient Sumer and Assyria. The Rosetta stone, key to Egyptian hieroglyphics, turns out in this case to be a periodic table of the elements. The scientific method must ever expose the regularities of chemistry and physics. Science is indeed the omnilingua of rational beings.

But not in the most grandiose of all space operas after "Doc" Smith, Isaac Asimov's. His cosmos is populated entirely by humans, who had spread out from Earth to occupy 25 million worlds in our own galaxy. Vast as is this larger Roman Empire, it still controls but less than a tenth of a percent of the local system's 100 billion suns. The contrasting scales are meant to stupefy. Man's place in the vaster universe of billions of galaxies remains a humble one. Still, this microcosm is *his* home, with eternally human problems to solve.

Fig. 86. *Linguists piece together fragmentary texts from a long-vanished civilization on Mars. The key to reading them is what self-evidently looks like the same periodic table known to terrestrial scientists and which made atomic bombs possible. No doubt the Martians had done themselves in with the same application. The story takes place in a happy future, after we humans have avoided that fate; but it was written when Cold War jitters were at their height.*

I refer to Asimov's epic Foundation series in *ASF*, *Foundation* (1942–1944) and *Second Foundation* (1948–1950). Begun at the outset of World War II, when the collapse of Western civilization seemed possible, the series treats a vast galactic empire threatened by internal collapse owing to overextended administration. The story line is, how to devise a scientific plan to reverse this decline, for that must be superior to the use of force. It is the plan of a secret cabal of scientists who

Fig. 87. *An imperial general hands a weapon to a civilian intellectual who is about to depart in a warship on a backed-by-force diplomatic mission. He will not be needing it because he belongs to a cabal of scientific historians, the Foundation, that has a better plan to keep the Empire together: very long-range, but better.*

have the advantage of a highly developed social physics, by which they plot orderliness on a grand historical scale. Fig. 87 is the first illustration in the first installment, itself titled "Foundation" (May 1942).

After the advent of the *Star Wars* movies (now extended to yet more of them), Asimov's publisher urged him to extend *his* series, running until his death in 1992. By 1965, however, Harry Harrison exploited the comic possibilities of Asimov's milieu in *Bill the Galactic Hero*. Curiously, both authors have met with such great success that their respective universes continue to flourish. Harrison, with other projects in hand, has farmed out more "Bill" novels to various other writers, while the Asimov estate has done the same for a posthumous series. What is curious about all this is the fact that SF has turned inward on itself, in a Talmudic muttering over texts of the past, elaborating on what already has been done: a sure sign that the once imperial genre is itself in irreversible decline.

Another series in *Astounding Science Fiction* that became something of a cult was "The World of Ā" (1945–1949) by A.E. van Vogt. It turned on the work of Alfred Korzbski, *Science and Sanity: An Introduction to Non-Aristotelian Systems and General Semantics* (1933), a faddish book widely propagated in popular editions up until 1938, and which impressed not only John Campbell but also the usually sane Robert Heinlein; in "Gulf" (November-December 1949), the gap is that separating unsanity from the logical perfection of null-A (Ā) thinking. Korzbski's thesis has it that the either/or logic in Aristotle is the source of all human error. If only we could get to a non–Aristotelian way of thinking, man would better understand man, and better control the universe. However murky van Vogt's attempt to clarify the unclarifiable, he is typical of *ASF*'s disposition to grapple with even the most esoteric of intellectual debates.

Van Vogt's first novel *Slan* (September–November 1940), following a 1939 story, won much greater acclaim. The Slans are a mutant race of supermen endowed with two hearts, telepathic powers, and superior intelligence. Driven underground by the jealousy of normals, they at last prevail to save mankind from its errors. The transcendent hero of "The World of Ā" is Gosseyn (go sane). He is able to shift from one Gosseyn body to another, being in two places at once, as it were. Thus is demonstrated the inferiority of either/or, yes/no preconceptions.

From the start, science fiction magazines ran editorials in every issue, usually jejune. Campbell elevated them to a new level of sophistication. They might treat new developments in science and technology, but invariably they came around to stating the editor's political credo. They are now so much a part of the literature that Harry Harrison assembled a selection in *Collected Editorials from Analog* (1966). (The magazine title *Analog* stands for *ASF* in its later incarnation as well as its earlier.)

In "God Isn't Democratic" (April 1964), the most opinionated of Campbellian dictates, he asserts that "The Laws of Things" (June 1965) are violated by social legislation in the United States Congress. In its liberal policies it might as well legislate against the law of gravity when it is inconvenient to human welfare.

The editorial brings to a head the point of "The Cold Equations" (August 1954) by Tom Godwin, voted numer 10 in the SFWA anthology. A deadly disease breaks out in a mining colony on some distant planet, and a high-speed medical ship is dispatched to the rescue. It has only enough fuel to get there, and to brake and land. The pilot finds a stowaway on board, sister to one of the miners in the stricken colony; she wants only to rejoin him, not realizing that ballistic rigor forbids it. She must be chucked overboard. If she comes along the ship will crash and all the miners' lives lost. She exits the hatch screaming, "I have done nothing wrong!"—nothing except be stupidly ignorant of the universal law of gravity.

Campbell's chiefest discovery, Heinlein, from 1939 became the magazine's glory and its most sturdy conservative writer. *Astounding* premised a realistic understanding of man's place in the cosmos. In this the genre descends from the British tradition, that of the scientific romance (chapter 2), in which humanitarian values are subordinate to the cosmic laws of things. How we cope with them is the philosophical problem raised in SF at its most serious.

The importance of John Campbell to the genre is indisputable. The big three he cultivated, Asimov, Heinlein, van Vogt, are still associated with the glory days of SF. Some others are noteworthy as well: Poul Anderson, Hal Clement, and L. Sprague de Camp. The one big name not mentioned here is Ray Bradbury, who contributed to *Astounding Science Fiction* only once. That story was "Doodad" (September 1943), which got a negative response from readers. It is a variant on the magic shop, here retailing nondescript items like thingumbobs, doodads, whatchamacallits, gadgets and doohickies that can do almost anything the owner wishes by reading his mind. Bradbury's brand of illogical nonsense and ornamental prose, too artsy for some, had other markets and a growing body of separatist fans.

Apart from "Brass Tacks" for the discussion of story content, Campbell ran another department called "The Analytical Laboratory" (An Lab for short). Regular readers knew the drill: Send in a postcard every month ranking the stories in each issue, and Campbell would do a statistical analysis. In the November 1943 issue he tallied the results for the September issue as follows.

Place	*Story*	*Author*	*Points*
1.	Judgment Night	C.L. Moore	1.5
2.	Attitude	Hal Clement	2.4
3.	Concealment	A.E. van Vogt	2.65
4.	Robinc	H.H. Holmes	4.15
5.	Doodad	Ray Bradbury	4.2

The Bradbury story "Doodad" came in last. He never again appeared in *ASF*.

Campbell's attention to reader response guided his editorial policy. He kept informed as to how well or badly he was leading *ASF* in the direction he desired. In striving to remake SF in his own image he made a successful business of it, giving his magazine unprecedented prestige and respectability. Alone of all magazine editors in all fields, he held total control over his creature. The publisher of *ASF*—owner also of pulps and slicks alike, the largest magazine chain in the business—gave him his head. A dominating presence, tall, forceful, persuasive, John Campbell got his way and took it for granted without being lordly about it. His mission was everything, which he took on with a patient regard for his writers and readers alike: They would in time see things his way out of respect for his powerful intellect and editorial skills. At the same time he welcomed unexpected developments and well-argued reader suggestions, all along keeping up a rigorous correspondence in many-paged letters encouraging his writers. In the An Lab report cited above, he himself offered his own assessment of that issue, hinting at satisfaction with the results. "Having stuck my neck a bit outward in prophesying that the ending of 'Judgment Night' would be liked, I'm not unnaturally pleased to see that the voting seems to agree with my bet."

C.L. Moore was a Campbell favorite for good reason, but she and other worthies are now overshadowed by the big three, not to mention the belletristic Bradbury, so much adored by critics that he is tagged Mr. Science Fiction. After Catherine Moore's marriage to Henry Kuttner, another *ASF* regular, she wrote under the name Lawrence O'Donnell. That is the byline that appears on her remarkable "Fury" (May 1947). See Chapter 8 and plate VIII:3. "Fury" is a sequel to the equally remarkable "Clash by Night" (March 1943), included in Campbell's *ASF* anthology. The two wrote jointly as Lewis Padgett, exampled by "The Fairy Chessmen" (see above). Lewis Padgett stories always rated highly in the An Lab, no matter how numerous or varied. Most popular were "Mimsy Were the Borogoves" (February 1943) and "When the Bough Breaks" (September 1944). The first is honored in the SFWA anthology, the second in Campbell's anthology.

Moore/O'Donnell brought to *ASF* literary qualities of mainstream literature that Campbell looked for wherever he could get them: sophisticated characterization and refined writing. Her masterpiece is "Vintage Season" (September 1944), contained in the second volume of the SFWA anthology given to best novellas (Bova 1973 in Bibliography). It keeps distinguished company with ten others including "The Time Machine" by H.G. Wells, "Who Goes There?" by John Campbell, and "Universe" by Robert Heinlein (see Chapter 5 of the present work). When readers come to Chapter 7 of the present work, they will encounter "With Folded Hands" by Jack Williamson, also included in the SFWA anthology.

"Vintage Season" unfolds the story of three tourists from the future who arrive one golden day in May, somewhere in the northeastern United States, to rent rooms from Oliver Wilson; it is one of the "Vintage Seasons" they and others visit throughout time—vintage disasters actually. In this case Oliver's house is the choice location spared destruction, which explains why the others intrigue among themselves to get the place because it overlooks the doomed city. In the end, after the disaster, a third visitor arrives, a connoisseur among dilettantes, to register his artistic impressions of the catastrophe. Oliver's fiancée Sue urges him to sell the house to the highest bidder so they can buy a better house once they get married; but Oliver already has signed a lease with the first three. They bring in guests on the night before the exciting event to observe it. A meteor strikes the city and Sue is consumed in the fiery holocaust. Oliver is bitter and questions the artist: If you people can travel in time, can you not change events? Yes; but it would alter *his* present. He also explains the scar on his forearm that Oliver noticed on all of them: innoculation against a deadly disease to follow, one whose name it would be against the rules to divulge. Oliver already has learned too much from his persistent curiosity. As Oliver staggers under the effects of he knows not what, he scribbles a note to warn humanity of these decadent tourists. "The house was dynamited six days later, part of the futile attempt to halt the relentless spread of the Blue Death."

Since I am old enough to have read the magazines when they were current, and to have met most of the authors I talk about, my emphasis tends to differ from the assessment of a younger generation of academic critics. They did not experience the stories as they came out, nor witness reader response and how it impinged on editorial policy and on the writers themselves. The genre evolved not abstractly but through a complex of personal histories. The result, SF at its most accomplished, looks different from the outside. But criticism itself also evolves and still is changing. I offer myself as the trace of an earlier stage in a shifting landscape. The big three, Asimov, Heinlein and van Vogt, all deceased, are now legendary figures that simplify the record. What happened to C.L. Moore? She was a deciding factor in the original mix. Or to another big three I am about to mention? Present-day critics, in their academic journals and books, press ever onward in the shifting sands of critical theory and the latest interpretive models.

Poul Anderson (*d.* 2001), an arch-conservative like Campbell himself, won favor with the readership on the same ideological grounds in his regular contributions to *ASF*. Small wonder that he has dropped from sight in the view of today's liberal-minded critics. Heinlein too held less obvious conservative views in his early stories that established him in *ASF*. Only in his later books did he make them more explicit. By then he was too big a name to ignore, so critics busy themselves with untiring attacks on him as a "fascist."

Anderson's "Trading Partners," touched on above in this chapter and given a color illustration in plate XII:3, universalizes the principle of free enterprise. The story is one of a series featuring a human capitalist and his alien partners engaged in a galactic business. They do what comes naturally to all intelligent life-forms, unless a statist government interferes.

Hal Clement is the exemplar of hardcore SF, working out stories faithful to scientific fact. His "Mission of Gravity" (from April 1953 in four parts) was highly acclaimed at the time but is of a type now gone out of fashion. An expedition from Earth lands a heavy vehicle on the surface of the planet Mesklin, whose gravity at the poles is 700 times that of the Earth. The crew discovers the unexpected: intelligent life, indeed a whole civilization down there. It comes to light when the crew comes across a raft manned by tiny creatures sailing a stormy sea of liquid methane, one of many on a commercial trading route.

Astounding author L. Sprague de Camp died only in 2001 at the age of 92, active to the end. His regular stories in *ASF* reflected the depth of his learning shown in frequent science-fact articles, just as popular with the readership. His contribution to the space program, as a mechanical engineer and officer in the Naval reserve, is noted in Chapter 6.

The last significant author cultivated by John Campbell is Harry Harrison. I met him in 1950, when he was a comic book artist and illustrator for some of the lesser SF magazines, and I a graduate student at Columbia University. We were neighbors in the same New York City apartment building, and soon got to discussing a project of mutual interest—a new kind of SF anthology, the first theme anthology: all anthropological stories. Years later this emerged as *Apemen, Spacemen* (1968). Meanwhile Harrison packed up his family and drove to a remote Mexican village where he worked, with few expenses, on his first SF novel. He sold it to *ASF* as *Deathworld* (January–March 1960), based on research in the ecological sciences. Thereafter he did much more highly-rated work for Campbell, whom he idolized even though they were poles apart in ideological outlook. As already noted, he went on to escape the genre by marketing a successful run of books in the field of alternate history. He remains, however, the most fervent champion of didactic SF I know, always doing his homework in exhaustive detail. Yet he delivers instruction packaged as fascinating entertainment, written in exquisitely precise language, itself a delight. If I am not mistaken, he must sooner or later be recognized more widely as a major literary artist in American letters. Or I should say in cosmopolitan letters. Already his reputation in England, where he now lives, is solid, and translations of his work in many languages are universally appreciated.

Campbell did not always agree with his authors. He threw out ideas, in his office or in correspondence, but he never told his authors what to do with them. He was content to watch the seeds he planted grow as they willed. Intellectual stimulation was his aim, whatever the growth. A remarkable example is his editorial, "The Fallacy of Null-A" (April 1953), a comment on "The World of $\bar{A}$" by A.E. van Vogt. Although van Vogt (*d.* 2000) always rated highly, this particular serial got mixed reactions. Campbell then gave his own opinion. The story's thesis that either/or thinking is insane he did not accept:

yes or no propositions are essentials to human nature and the commonplace perception of reality. All the same, he encouraged stories like this in order to raise issues that arouse critical thinking—the purpose of his magazine. John Campbell's devout leadership and informed nurturing of SF literary talent proved instrumental in the elevation of the science fiction genre to its Golden Age.

5
Robert Heinlein

After World War II, Robert A(nson) Heinlein signed himself with his middle initial, his full middle name used for the Anson MacDonald stories. But earlier the byline was just plain Robert Heinlein.

In a long autobiographical letter, dated 8 June 1986 (two years before his death), he told me that he once believed in Wellsian socialism, but "today I no longer trust any of these things." The occasion was a response to my book about *Things to Come*, the Wells film of 1936. He had seen the film during his 1934–1938 activity in California politics, running at last as a socialist on the Democratic ticket for State Assemblyman; when defeated in 1938 he turned to writing, selling his first story ("Life-Line," August 1939) to *Astounding Science Fiction*. At age 32 he began late, a naval officer retired for medical reasons. Four years of service in the Navy and then four years of politics were but a short interval compared to the nearly half century of professional writing that from the start put him at the front of his chosen genre.

His Terran Federation, however, owes a lingering debt to Wells's world-state, whose coming is predicted in *The Outline of History* (1920), a book in Heinlein's personal library from high school days. He showed it to me during my visit with him in 1984. But as a patriotic American he never shared Wells's vision of a nation-free future. He always believed in American exceptionalism. His Terran Federation is but the U.S.A. on a larger scale, with free enterprise the motive to pioneer space travel. (Verne was just as *pro patria*, with France the exemplary nation among nations.)

In "Requiem" (*ASF*, January 1940), the entrepreneur D.D. Harriman (named after Edward Harriman the great railroad magnate) is buried on the moon, on the outskirts of Luna City, gateway to the planets. It was the last wish of a man who as a boy had read Verne's *Trip to the Moon* (fig. 88). From there Heinlein goes on to further devel-

Fig. 88. *The American capitalist D.D. Harriman, who pioneered space travel and the first Lunar colony, is laid to rest on the moon: his last wish.*

opments, charted in his Future History scheme (fig. 89). This was published in *ASF*, May 1941. It has not been reprinted elsewhere, even in Heinlein's own story collections, where the years of original publication have been erased for the sake of not seeming dated, even as new stories were added.

The Future History chart integrates all stories in a single evolving scheme, allowing for the realistic ups and downs of history. Finally mankind achieves THE FIRST HUMAN CIVILIZATION (from 2074), a good idea that travels well in space. But not at first. The first attempt to take this budding idea to the stars is a failed experiment, recounted in "Universe," given a Prologue dated 2120. The story appeared in the same May 1941 *ASF* issue as the Future History chart. See plate X for the

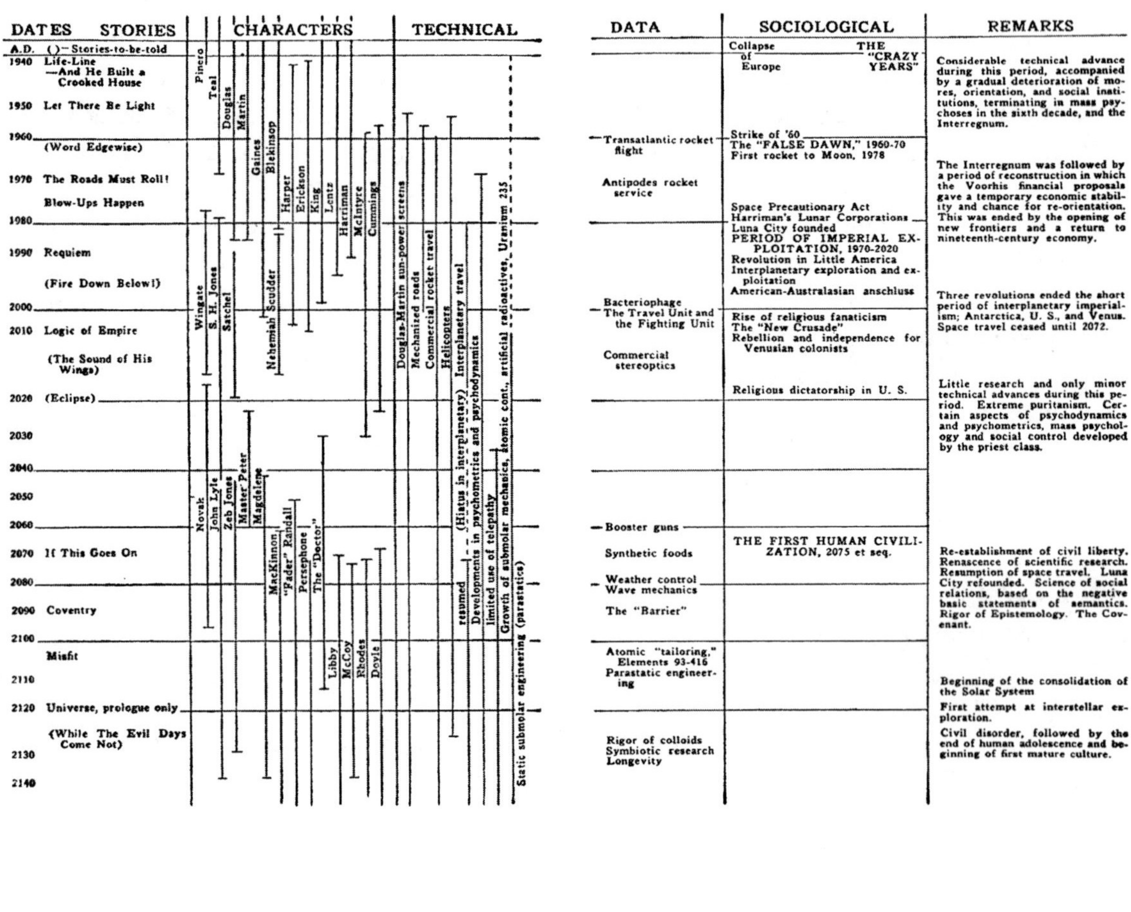

cover art. Campbell introduced both story and chart in his editorial "History to Come," which laid the ground for Heinlein imitators to come.

"Universe" is the story of a great starshisp that sets out to colonize an earth-like planet orbiting *Alpha Proxima*, the nearest star in our galaxy. Incidentally, this is the first instance in science fiction of the so-called generation starship, in which its human supercargo must continue to breed and perpetuate a scientific culture until the destination is reached. The city-sized ship must maintain a complete civilization, urban life and agricultural support (hydroponic farms). Over the generations the culture descends into medieval barbarism; one enlightened soul discovers the mission but is unable to save it.

It is rare that a new theme is created in SF, most of them having been set and fossilized by the examples of H.G. Wells and to a lesser extent Jules Verne. The genre settled into a comfortable formula, so that the only way to make it new again was to ring as many changes as possible, with the hope of hitting on some original variation: a difficult creative task for serious writers, apart from lesser ones in the pulp industry content to resell any old formulaic cliché. In time, SF got absorbed by other genres, notably the techno-thriller and the international spy novel, superseding SF in popular interest. Nonetheless, SF itself can never be superseded because it laid down thematic material impossible to go beyond. Meanwhile, Heinlein's innovative generation starship kept the separateness of the genre alive for a little while longer.

The most original variation on this once-new plot is the novel *Captive Universe* (1969) by Harry Harrison. A generation starship is designed with the problem of cultural decay in mind. Populated with fanatical religious conservatives, rigid to the end, the mission succeeds.

In "Universe" the crew starts out with men educated in science and technology, but eventually they relapse. A mutiny aboard the ship, a labor dispute, wrecks the shielding of its atomic engine. Mutants result, terrorizing the crew with cannibal raids. The story's failed hero, one Hugh Hoyland is captured by the two-headed mutant Joe-Jim, featured on the cover together with Hugh Hoyland in the ship's forgotten control center. Joe-Jim inhabits the "upper," low-gravity region located on the cylindrical ship's axis, around which it rotates to create artificial gravity in the "lower" regions. Hoyland, a young officer in training, is curious to know what lies in the upper levels, and is captured there by a band of "muties" (a genetics-ignorant play on mutineers), who bring him to Joe-Jim, their leader, for deciding which blood-thirsty thug gets to eat him. One of them, the captor, is seen flying through the air in the no-weight zone in fig. 90. Joe-Jim, however, something of an intellectual, spares him to serve as a personal companion, as a fellow soul thirsting for knowledge. He is shown the long-abandoned "captain's veranda" in the ship's nose, from which the outside stars may be seen rotating. The ship is a man-made object drifting through space, not the entire "universe" (title) as taught by theologians

Opposite page: fig. 89, left and right. *The original Future History chart, never before reproduced. Under "Dates and Stories," to the left, are stories already written, prospective ones in parentheses. Under "Characters" are their overlapping time lines. "Technical" outlines evolving changes in technology. "Data" show important events. "Sociological" gives the consequences of events and technological changes. Finally, the "Remarks" evaluate it all.*

Fig. 90, left. *A "mutie," knife in hand, pursues Hugh Hoyland in the "no weight" zone. Original illustration for "Universe" in the May 1941 issue of* Astounding Science Fiction *as are figures 89 and 91–92.* Fig. 91, above. *The astrogator's chair in the stellarium, taken by Hugh Hoyland, where he observes the stars.*

Fig. 92. *Conceptual breakthrough is a basic science fiction theme, founded on a long tradition of European critical thought. The figure is an early 16th century woodcut picturing a monk plunging his head through the biblical sphere of the stars to behold astronomical reality: the complex machinery that actually governs the movements of the heavens.*

now passing as "scientists." Hugh is then shown the "stellarium" (fig. 91, also on the cover), from which a 360° view of the stars is on display. It is from here that astrogators once guided the ship (the term astrogation itself being a Heinlein coinage). The crew from the "lower" regions no longer knows anything about this place.

Joe-Jim had long known its function but as a detached intellectual remained content to discuss the matter with himself. Hugh at once decides to report what he has learned. For him, sight of the outside universe is a "conceptual breakthrough" (standard SF theme, see fig. 92) that calls for immediate action. Returning to his tutor with the news, he is thrown into the brig for

Fig. 93, left. *Hugh Hoyland hitting the books as an officer-in-training. The books are standard scientific texts from our point of view, religious texts to the new establishment running the ship as a church-state.* Fig. 94, right. *Joe-Jim playing checkers with himself, with never a decisive outcome.*

heresy. His new mutie friends break him free and the war for light and liberation from darkness and superstition is on.

The story, for all its action-adventure, touches upon anticlerical issues raised by the Enlightenment and which have strongly marked SF with its agnostic, if not downright atheistic outlook. Hugh is the archetypical truth seeker. Even while studying the sacred canon on astronomy and physics (fig. 93), he had questioned the mythological meaning attached to stars and gravity. Now the tutor's suspicions have been confirmed, even as Hugh's doubts are resolved.

The two-headed Joe-Jim is able to play checkers with himself (fig. 94), one head always checking the other: the irresolute intellectual at play. Likewise the crew debates the so-called Trip. One side says there is no Trip, only the Ship. There is only the matter of fact task to keep the Converter going—the matter-into-energy furnace that provides heat and light (it no longer functions as a space drive). The other side holds that the Trip does indeed signify; it means getting to Heaven and the Converter is Hell-fire punishment for the wicked whose living bodies fuel it. Such is Hugh's assigned fate, subsequent to his trial convened by "captain."

The two sides recall the quarrel between Nominalists and Realists in medieval philosophy, a futile debate that led nowhere. When Hugh is brought before the captain for trial and sentencing his last words are Galileo's: "It [Earth/ship] still moves." However, Galileo never said them. The Enlightenment savant Voltaire invented them to ridicule a Papal authority that could impose a geocentric worldview in the face of astronomical fact. Science fiction is fond of beating this dead clerical horse, with science still a persecuted victim of stupidity and superstition, as in Asimov's "Nightfall." A more interesting story might explore the ecclesiastical politics that reproved Galileo not because he verified Copernicus but because the Copernican system (with a new sun at the center) had become central to a plot within the Church to overthrow the existing Pope for another: one who would reset the date of Easter with astronomical correctness.

The ship's name (lost to the crew) is the *Vanguard*, intended as a first attempt to seed mankind among the stars. A sister ship, the *New Frontiers* (anticipating President John F. Kennedy's campaign slogan and his space program), follows in "Methuselah's Children" (*ASF* serial, July–September 1941). Not yet indicated on the chart, it tells the story of the long-lived Howard Families, inbred for longevity. Other people are resentful, demanding to have their genetic secret for their own. The government of the Terran Federation takes the Families into protective custody, whereupon their heroic leader emerges. He is Woodrow Wilson Smith, a.k.a. Lazarus Long,* Heinlein's favorite character who reappears now and again right up to his last novel in 1987. Lazarus Long hijacks the *New Frontiers*, just then completed in orbit around the moon, and brings the Families aboard (via shuttle craft). Among them is the mathematical genius Andrew Jackson Libby, who first appeared in "Misfit" (*ASF*, November 1938, 2100 on the chart). He invents a faster-than-light drive, and the ship tours many strange parts of the universe, a Homeric odyssey visiting different life-forms both hostile and all too inviting. On one distant planet, some of Lazarus Long's men surrender to a "snug harbor of ease," as did some under captain Ulysses in Homer's original Lotus Land. He himself resists, as does one of his associates who says, "Damn it, I want to *work* for my living." Once again sloth and idleness are the enemy of human nature.

The events in *Methuselah's Children* (in its book form, 1958) happen after 2120, when the *Vanguard*, never to be heard from, is launched. Meanwhile, much else has passed. There was a theocratic government overthrown in 2070 in "If This Goes On," and then a forming of the Terran Federation. In "Coventry" (*ASF*, July 1940, 2090 on the chart), a dissident thinks himself entitled to a loner's me-and-mine under the new regime. He is promptly sent into the title coventry, isolated behind a "stasis barrier," where truly antisocial types rob him of everything, including his more innocent romantic

**Lazarus Long's name is doubly patriotic. Lazarus is from Emma Lazarus, the American poet whose lines are inscribed at the base of the Statue of Liberty. Long is from R.A. Long, president of the Liberty Memorial Association founded in Kansas City in 1919 following the end of World War I. As a member of the Missouri National Guard, Heinlein marched at the monument's unveiling on 11 November 1924, which henceforth made its mark on the national calendar as Armistice Day, now Veterans Day (still memorialized in the veteranocracy keeping peace in* Starship Troopers, *1959). The compounded Lazarus Long is a liberty-loving adventurer who goes on to pioneer the galactic deeps in* Time Enough for Love *(1973) and finally reappears in* To Sail Beyond the Sunset *(1987). The Long in his name also resonates the longevity of the Howard Families he leads in "Methuselah's Children"; but he outlives them all to achieve near immortality, with the aid of periodic "rejuvenation" treatments.*

delusion of "Crusoe-like independence." Fig. 95 shows him inducted through the barrier in his armored "steel tortoise," loaded with all his possessions. "It did not occur to him his chattel was the end product of the cumulative effort and intelligent co-operation of hundreds and thousands of men, living and dead": the essence of civil society.

He later discovers a criminal conspiracy to overthrow the U.S. government, by then the Terran Federation. Heroically, he escapes to be greeted by the Secret Service agent he informs: a man who had an eye on him all along from within as a true patriot. Only a dissident would be in contact with the conspirators, then to turn sour on them if not really convinced of their cause.

Fig. 95. *The protagonist of "Coventry" passing into exile. There he learns of a conspiracy to overthrow the United States (now enlarged as the Terran Foundation), turns patriotic, ingeniously escapes, then to inform the Secret Service agent who greets him. All along the agent had his eye on him from within as a potential hero endowed with the right stuff.*

The one oddity in the Future History series is the first story, "'And He Built a Crooked House'" (*ASF*, February 1941). Dated 1940 on the original chart, it was removed in all later versions and dumped into a collection of fantasy stories. Whatever, it remains Heinlein's most endearing classic. It plays on Edwin A. Abbott's *Flatland: A Romance of Many Dimensions* (1884), familiar to the SF community.

In Abbott's little book, amusingly illustrated, a two-dimensional figure, Mr. A Square, finds his domain disturbed by a strange event. He sees first a dot appear on the 2-D plane of his existing, which expands to wider and wider circles, then contracts back to a dot and then is gone. It is a sphere passing through. What would it be like, Abbott asks, if a 4-D figure invaded our 3-D world? Mr. A Square's world is flat, a two-dimensional plane illustrating how a surface differs between a straight line of no dimension other than length and a solid of three dimensions. What comes next? In Abbott's day, the fourth dimension was a geometer's concept, antedating the space-time continuum Einstein assigned to it outside Euclidean space. The geometry of the fourth dimension, however, was a mere trick of perspective drawing, nothing more serious. The result is a strictly imaginary construct called a tesseract. See fig. 96.

This is the figure Heinlein alludes to in the story, whose architect, Quintus Teal,

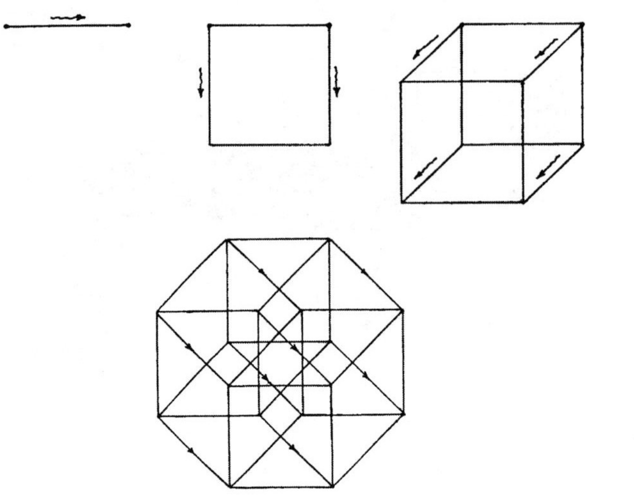

Fig. 96. *From line to cube and hypercube. A straight line is a point of no dimensionality extended in one dimension. A plane is that line moved in another direction to form a surface. That 2-D surface, when moved forward, forms a 3-D solid. The next step is to extend lines at a 90° angle to each corner of the cube to form a hypercube, or tesseract.*

designs a 3-D tesseract for Mr. Bailey his client. He shows him two little models (toothpicks and clay balls) in fig. 97. At top, where the pencil points, is a model hypercube; below is a tesseract, two different versions in solid of the complicated flat drawing on paper in fig. 96. The actual structure Teal builds, an unfolded tesseract (fig. 98) collapses into one cube after a California earthquake (fig. 99). When the client visits his house, he sees himself and Mrs. Bailey looking out a window at himself (fig. 100). This is as it would be in a true hypercube, in which all interior surfaces are joined. Once inside the visitors

Fig. 97, left. *Teal's models shown to Mr. Bailey. Original magazine illustration, as are the following ones.* Fig. 98, right. *The unfolded tesseract house Teal builds.*

Fig. 99, left. *The house collapsed by an earthquake into one impossible cube.* Fig. 100, right. *Teal looks out a window of the collapsed house to see himself looking out. Mr. and Mrs. Bailey huddle behind him in fright, unassured by Teal's composure.*

have trouble finding the front door, lost in a 4-D maze (they keep returning to the same room). When the next quake hits they jump out the nearest window, however forbidding the prospect seen outside seems, not unlike other scary views; but it is only the weird-looking Sequoia National Park some miles away. The jumpers get out just in time, before the next quake reduces the cube to nonbeing: a nondimensional point. A playful story, it is done with easy charm.

When Heinlein returned to writing after the war, during which (1942–1945) he served the U.S. Navy as a civilian engineer, he was the first to break into the general magazines, principally the *Saturday Evening Post.* Here the remaining short stories in the Future History appeared. He was also first to crack the profitable juvenile market with a series (1947–1958) of 12 hardcover novels for the prestigious house of Scribner's. The most attractive of these is *Have Spacesuit—Will Travel* (1958). A 16-year-old Kip wins a used spacesuit in a soap advertising contest, and goes about wearing it in the backyard. With his girlfriend Peewee, the two are abducted by aliens and taken before a galactic tribunal, where they stand trial as a representative sample of humanity. The aliens, monsters of collective mentality in which each is a replaceable part, view humans as dangerous savages that will in time threaten harmony in their part of the universe.

Fig. 101. *Cavor before the Grand Lunar in the serialized version of* The First Men in the Moon.

Sentence: doom for planet Earth, and do Kipp and Peewee have any last wish? Yes, to be returned home and die with their kind. The notion of self-sacrifice so astonishes the aliens they dither, then relent, and the two kids go home with a tale too unbelievable to tell. The trial recalls Cavor standing before the Grand Lunar (fig. 101) in *The First Men in the Moon.* From Cavor's account of human history the Grand Lunar adjudges earthlings just as savage.

Another open tribute to Wells is *The Puppet Masters* (1951), a replay of *The War of the Worlds.* The invading Martians (or whatever) are telepathic "slugs" that attach themselves to human backs, guiding their hosts' nervous system. The problem is how to get rid of them, and by extension the Communist menace they represent. The Red menace is again targeted in the "bugs," the implacable foe contested in *Starship Troopers* (1960). By now the Terran Federation is governed by military and civil service veterans, the only citizens given the vote. This restriction on universal suffrage annoyed critics who found Heinlein's patriotic veteranocracy outrageously illiberal and antidemocratic. But Heinlein confided to me that he but followed the example of that great liberal, Mark Twain, his favorite American author. In "The Curious Republic of Gondour" (1875), Twain posits some novel electoral rules. These have it that "every citizen, however poor or ignorant, possessed one vote, so universal suffrage still reigned; but if a man possessed a good common-school education and no money, he had two votes," and so on by degrees; the more education the more votes, until the more-schooled had it in their power to outvote the uneducated rich concerned only with pelf. But while this is a blow at the parvenue rich of the "gilded age" (one of Twain's favorite targets), it no less deprives the uneducated masses of carrying their numerical weight. Further, the rich may fall from wealth, and so lose extra votes, but educated citizens never lose their knowledge.

Heinlein, however, is now remembered for only one thing, the hoax perpetuated in his name at the height of his general recognition, a tragic outcome. When commissioned as Heinlein's biographer, my first task was to get at the bottom of the alleged connection between *Stranger in a Strange Land* (1961) and the Tate-LaBianca murders in Los Angeles. A disagreement with the Estate got me fired, but I still feel obligated to report my findings. The seven murders took place on the night of 9-10 August 1969, carried out by members of the so-called "Manson family." The highly publicized trial of Charles Manson, the instigator of the deed-doers, was conducted over nine months between 1970 and 1971. The prosecuting attorney for Los Angeles County was Vincent Bugliosi, with the assistance of Stephen Kay, another deputy district attorney. The two disagreed on the case. It was Kay who in the courtroom staked out a claim for the insidious influence of *Stranger* on Manson and who further paraded it before the press to his personal sensation-making glory.

For him, Heinlein was the chief culprit on trial and in the public eye, which Kay kept there with the help of Ed Sanders in his bestselling book *The Family* (1972). Bugliosi, however, won the case with no reference to this nonsense, nor does he so much as even allude to it in his own book, *Helter Skelter* (1974). In an interview almost 20 years later, he said that he had seriously considered the allegations, investigated them, and then dismissed them. That Manson's child was named after one of the book's characters was the bookish mother's appellation, as was the alternate "Pooh Bear." So much for literary influence. The indifferent father, Manson himself, was preoccupied with drugs and rock music, especially that of the Beatles. His favorite title of theirs, "Helter-Skelter," was in blood at the murder sites. But has their sacred music ever been indicted? No. Only Heinlein. Otherwise hippiedom and its counterculture would have been idyllic.

But where did Kay get it? The fictive Heinlein-Manson connection made national news in a *Time* magazine story for 19 January 1970. Headlined "A Martian Model," it claims that Manson "murdered by the book." But this is a derivative story, not the original one on which Kay based his case. The original is a page-one story in the *San Francisco Herald-Examiner* for 8 January 1970, headlined "Manson's Blue Print Claims Tate Suspect Used Science Fiction Plot." Tracing the origin of the story to its source is quite illuminating, for there is a connection between the *Herald-Examiner* (now simply the *Examiner*) and Heinlein, and it has nothing to do with Manson.

The *Examiner* was and is a Hearst-family newspaper directly managed by Bill Hearst, son and namesake of founder William Randolph Hearst, the famed yellow journalist. That Hearst had political ambitions and even tried to run for president in 1904. When in 1934 Socialist muckraking author Upton Sinclair took over the California Democratic Party apparatus and ran for governor on his EPIC ("End Poverty in California") platform, Hearst mobilized opposition with his "United for California" organization and defeated Sinclair in one of the dirtiest campaigns of the century, making full use of the yellow press tactics of slander and outright lies.

The 27-year-old Heinlein, just retired from the Navy and barely on his feet after an extended bout with tuberculosis, was nevertheless an active supporter of Sinclair, rising rapidly through the EPIC ranks. In 1938 he carried the EPIC torch when he ran for the State Assembly in the 59th District (Hollywood). He, too, was defeated by the same alarmed forces. The EPIC torch flickered and went out. The weekly newsletter Heinlein had helped found four years earlier ceased publication the month before the primary election Heinlein lost. Hearst had won; but so powerful was his obsessive hatred that his bias against Heinlein survived his death in 1951. His son and his editorial staff took Hearst's final revenge on an old political enemy—a classic hundred-year ambush—by planting the Manson story with its elaborate but phony evidence in the *Examiner*.

It was a story too good to die, and it never would. Obituaries of Heinlein in newspapers and magazines and on television could not resist highlighting Manson as his most notorious fan. Thereafter, his hostile critics have kept alive his wicked celebrity as a moral corrupter of youth: a large order for any author. The clincher is a letter from Charles Manson himself dated 4 April 1981. Written by his amanuensis and cellmate, it explains that, being nearly illiterate, he never read *Stranger* and never heard of its author until the trial. The letter was addressed to a Heinlein friend in response to his inquiry into the matter.

All the same, *Stranger in a Strange Land* did resonate with the sexual revolution of the 1960s. As Heinlein himself said, "My timing was right," a statement that takes into account his awareness that the days of the asexual pulps in which he began were gone forever. His later work, however, is less important to the history of SF than his early magazine stories. They very much helped to define the Golden Age now passed into oblivion. Heinlein himself contributed to the decline when he turned to the polymorphous perversity now dominating what survives of the genre. Example: Lazarus Long, the oldest dirty old man in the universe.

Robert Heinlein underwent a long evolution, before the writing began and afterward. His new career in science fiction began late in life, in 1939, and lasted a long time until his death in 1988. A few words on the prelude to this career, from the start earning him the title dean of science fiction, seem worth reciting.

He spent four years at the U.S. Naval Academy, then four years in the service before being retired for tuberculosis. Removing to California, where he recovered, he got involved in local politics for another four years. He would become a political writer above all. When Upton Sinclair ran for governor, and lost, with Heinlein campaigning for him, and when Heinlein then lost in 1938, the next year saw his instant ascendancy at *Astounding Science Fiction*.

These early stories, the Future History series and others, constitute his most memorable body of work. Much more was to come, his later novels that displaced short story writing. These are discussion novels, held together with interesting narrative tissue, that pontificate on Heinlein's worldview. A remarkable example is *Time Enough for Love: The Lives of Lazarus Long* (1973). It contains two extensive sections, "The Notebooks of

Lazarus Long," composed entirely of pithy maxims, sustained with considerable wit and wisdom, given to *ASF* (June 1973) for separate publication. The "Notebooks" were even issued in book form to the delight of Heinlein fans everywhere. The Notebooks have a precedent in "Pudd'nhead Wilson's Calendar" contained within *Puddn'head Wilson* by Mark Twain. Both use the same device to expound their moral philosophy, expressed in practical witticisms, otherwise dissolved in their storytelling.

Heinlein's experience seeking votes for elective office taught him a lesson he projected on the scale of solar-system statesmanship in *Double Star* (1957). In one choice passage, a supposed new ambassador to Mars (actually an actor playing the part) explains to his unversed confidant the virtues of a Farleyfile, which the narrator tells us is a method perfected by James A. Farley, President Roosevelt's political manager, "for handling the personal relations of politics." As it happens, the file was inherited by this actor assigned to double for the mysteriously missing Ambassador Bonforte; as he learns to use it, we readers must learn as well. The narrator goes on:

> It was nothing but a file about people. However, the art of politics is "nothing but" people. This file contained all, or most, of the thousands upon thousands of people Bonforte had met in the course of his long public life; each dossier consisted of what he knew about that person *from Bonforte's own personal contact*. Anything at all, no matter how trivial—in fact, trivia were always the first entries: names and nicknames of wives, children, and pets, hobbies, tastes in food or drinks, prejudices, eccentricities. Following this he listed date and place and comments for *every occasion* on which Bonforte had talked to that particular man.

The user of a Farleyfile has only to consult it for a minute or two before meeting the person in question. But the confidant to Bonforte's double thinks this altogether phony, dishonest, and insincere. No, came back the rejoinder. "Do you apologize to your friend for caring so little about him that you simply can't remember his number?" These are the very things a politician "would like to remember if his memory were perfect. Since it isn't, it is no more phony to do it this way than it is to use a tickler file in order not to forget a friend's birthday—that is what it is: a giant tickler file to cover *anything*." Then comes the real point of the lesson. No matter how important the statesman is relative to the person he meets, "the supremely important person in anyone's life is *himself*—and a politician must never forget that. So it is polite and friendly and warm-hearted to have a way to be able to remember about other people the sort of little things that they are likely to remember about him. It is also essential—in politics."

When Heinlein ran for office, the state of California was dominated by Republicans, and he was defeated by that party establishment. The White House, however, belonged to a Democrat, President Franklin D. Roosevelt, much demonized by a conservative press led by a chain of newspapers owned by William Randolph Hearst (the butt of *Citizen Kane*, the Orson Welles movie of 1940). Another national chain, controlled by Robert McCormick of the Chicago *Tribune*, took the same stance. Heinlein himself was vilified by the Hearst press as a "red," the standard term of abuse for liberals. Its bite had force especially in California, where the Communist Party U.S.A., directed and funded secretly from Moscow (by now documented in the public record), first organized its United Front against "fascists." This term of abuse, picked up by liberals for conservatives, mirrored "reds" applied by the latter.

In this ideological war Heinlein did not fit the pattern: He was not a United Front liberal. In his 1938 campaign literature, he outlined the points in which European Fascism (Germany and Italy) and Soviet Communism were totalitarian twins. His astute analysis, a precocious one, anticipates the systematic comparative studies of totalitarianism done after the Cold War. Shortly afterwards, World War II broke out in 1939, Hitler threatened the Western democracies, and then Germany invaded the equally despotic Soviet Union under Stalin—which was brought in by President Roosevelt and Prime Minister Winston Churchill as their democratic ally. It was perhaps not the time to question Stalin's credentials. Yet Heinlein remained consistently anti–Communist. His liberal critics, a vestige of United Front politics, tag him a "fascist" for that. He himself always had been a liberal, in the classical sense, but over time the meaning of the term reversed in polarity. Today it signifies big government and welfare statism; back then it meant freedom *from* government, rooted in the Austrian school of economics represented by the writings of Ludwig von Mises and Friedrich A. Hayek well known to Heinlein. He did not change, the vocabulary did. What used to be liberalism moved away from *him*, not he from it. If today he is identified as a conservative writer, with a conservative fan base, he is no less the liberal of old.

This confusing terminology is best cleared up if the stormy controversy Heinlein's work incited, more than any other SF writer, is to be understood. That the most hostile foes were (and still are) from outside the genre show just how much it has been swallowed up in the maw of general criticism. A good example is *Starship Troopers* (1960), the story of Johnny Rico, a boy who volunteers for the Terran Federation's Mobile Infantry (M.I.), akin to the U.S. Marine Corps, only with more mobility and firepower. In the course of his training in the M.I., Rico attains manhood; he at last finds purpose in submitting to military discipline and in serving the patriotic cause for which the M.I. was instituted. Patriotism in this case, however, relates to the species patriotism of the whole human community in its planetary dispersion throughout the solar system and beyond, united by the government of the Terran Federation. Its implacable enemies, the "Bugs," are nonhuman aliens of a collectivist nature both in biology and political organization. The job of the M.I. is to defend the Terran frontiers of human freedom against their aggression, modeled after Soviet expansionism.

The novel opens and closes with battles against the Bugs, surely among the best action scenes ever written in any brand of literature. The bulk of the story, however, is given over to a flashback on Rico's training in the M.I., during which he recalls the teachings of his high school instructor in history and moral philosophy, an optional course (like those of today's ROTC programs) taught by an M.I. veteran. He is a viewpoint character who holds, with Heinlein, that military service should be voluntary; conscription amounts to slavery. Only with volunteer recruits can the military count on patriotic self-selection in meeting its highest ideals, those of service, duty and sacrifice.

The words of Rico's teacher of moral philosophy sustain him during the hardships of an infantryman's training: "The noblest fate that man can endure is to place his own material body between his loved home and the war's desolation.... This is immutable, true everywhere, throughout all time, for all men and all nations." Here is Heinlein speaking to the novel's praise for "the moral difference ... between the soldier and the civilian." But it is that same difference, the cultural gap between career officers and liberal minded intellectuals, that caused the novel to arouse so much hostility among the latter in the first place. For it is only by his dislike of the military that the liberal culture-critic earns his credentials. As James Burnam explains in *The Suicide of the West* (1964),

> [The] incompatibility between liberalism and the military life, and many of the reasons for it, are obvious and well known. Concepts of equality, nondiscrimination and universal democracy are hard to reconcile with the inequalities, authoritarianism, detailed discrimination and rigid hierarchy that are always and inevitably characteristic of military organization; even if they can be reconciled by some sort of complicated logical exercise, there remains a feeling gap. In his scale of priorities the soldier is professionally committed to place the safety and survival of his country first, and to be ready to sacrifice his life as well as his freedoms and comfort thereto; he must keep the values of social justice and individual rights secondary in rank, if he is to do his soldierly duty; and his devotion to peace, however fervently protested, will always be confused by the fact that his trade is war.

Heinlein's understanding of military culture, when given its proper place in society, runs exactly along the same lines. In one of his letters to me, he complained that the military of his chosen career had been denatured by civilian thinking; were he alive today he would be even more dismayed, and by ongoing attacks on *Starship Troopers.* His veteranocracy, already mentioned above, continued to focus hatred on the values essential to national survival he upheld. This denial of reality and commonsense I attribute to our badly educated elites who confuse legitimate authority, authority with responsibility, with authoritarianism ("fascism").

Another good example is "Sixth Column" (*Astounding Science Fiction*, January–March 1941), written and published before the Japanese attack on Pearl Harbor later that year on 7 December. The byline is Anson MacDonald, indicating that the story does not belong to the Future History canon, even though it is set in the near future. The Japanese already had invaded and occupied large parts of continental China, not alone its island province Formosa, nearly the size of Japan itself. At the time it was clear enough that Imperial Japan was destined to clear the way for wider conquests by striking a decisive blow at American interests in the Pacific, most likely at Pearl Harbor where the U.S. Navy based its Pacific fleet.

In "Sixth Column," Imperial Japanese forces are thinly disguised as "Pan-Asians." They take over the western portion of the United States, leaving the eastern half vulnerable to occupation by some European power, presumably Nazi Germany. A small remnant of the U.S. Army, hidden beneath the Colorado Mountains within secret caverns, develops a near miraculous technology to defeat the Pan-Asians. Its basis in realistic science is plausibly explained, and indeed some of its developments are now current engineering practice. The point of the story, however, is that the army engineers who deploy it disguise it as a miracle religion derived from the powers of Lord Mota (atom spelled backward). The Pan-Asians are bamboozled, and at last retreat in superstitious fear.

By the time the book version in mass distribution came out, *The Day After Tomorrow* (1949), critics assaulted its "racism" on the ground that it caricatured Pan-Asians and their emperor, Japan's Emperor Hirohito. Following V-J Day (Victory over Japan), the climate of opinion changed radically. Now *we* were the sinister imperialists who had bombed Japan into submission with two atomic bombs, "racist" because Asians had been targeted, not fellow whites in Nazi Germany. Victor in Europe, V-E Day, was won without the advantage of atomic bombs only because they were not yet in production.

When Mrs. Stover and I visited Heinlein in 1984, the first thing he said, he addressed to her. Did she think "Sixth Column" was "racist"? He was quite sensitive on that point, having lost many classmates at Pearl Harbor. My wife lived through the retribution and defeat that followed. Like other intellectuals in Japan, she was horrified by the military policy that led her country into the abyss. Heinlein, aware of people like her, cultivated Japanese fans through a Tokyo publisher that did translations of his work. To his question my wife replied, no, she did not think "Sixth Column" racist. It was a good adventure yarn and nothing more. He was relieved to hear that, I noticed, and years later he sent her a signed copy of the Japanese translation of *Job*, lovingly dedicated.

Finally, critics took aim at another "racist" novel, *Farnham's Freehold* (1964), a most inviting target. Following a Soviet missile attack, the title hero's bomb shelter is flung into a future in which the rule of North America has passed to the Black Muslims. Written at the height of the Black Power movement, it speculates on what would happen if whites in turn were enslaved, as Hugh Farnham and his family are. Heinlein told me that it does no more than play on Mark Twain's prophecy of 1885, that within a hundred years the formerly enslaved blacks of America would turns things around and "put whites underfoot," unless racial attitudes were changed.

I think these examples are sufficient to show that Heinlein's work has been totally absorbed into mainstream letters, after the attention given it by establishment critics. This is one more sign that the SF genre he brought to literary preeminence is no longer a paraliterature.

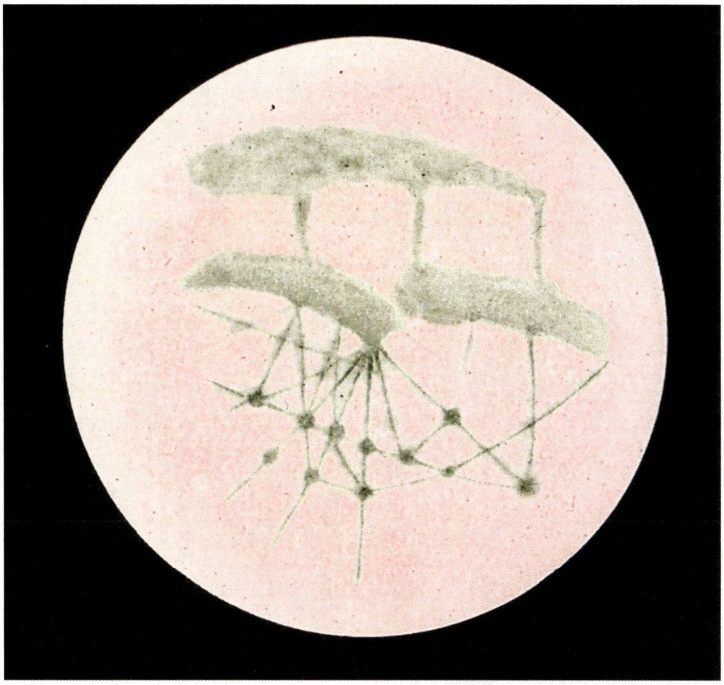

I:1, top. *Frontispiece to Percival Lowell,* Mars *(1895).* I:2, bottom left. *Cover art for the first installment of the 1927 serialized reprint of "The War of the Worlds" in* Amazing. I:3, bottom right. Marvel Science Stories *in 1939 with Martian-like death rays featured.*

II:1, top left. *First issue of* Argosy, *September 1896.* II:2, top right. *First issue of* Detective Story, *October 1915.* II:3, bottom left. *A 1929 issue of* Western Story, *from 1919.* II:4, bottom right. *A 1939 issue of* Love Story, *from 1921.*

III. *Special "Scientific Fiction" number of* Science and Invention, *August 1923.*

IV. *Quality painting for* ASF *cover art in 1941.*

V. *Detailed painting for complex story idea in a 1941 issue of* ASF.

VI. *Astronomical cover for* ASF *1940.*

VII. *Early issue of* Amazing, *February 1927.*

VIII:1, top left. ASF *cover from 1951.* VIII:2, top right. ASF *cover from 1948.* VIII:3, bottom left. ASF *cover from 1947.* VIII:4, bottom right. *Cover story for* Analog, *1971. Formerly* ASF.

IX:1, top left. *Early issue of* ASF *in 1938.* IX:2, top right. *Digest size* ASF, *1947.* IX:3, bottom left. *Digest size issue of* ASF *in 1950.* IX:4, bottom right. *Cover story for* Analog, *formerly* ASF. *Digest size.*

X. *Outstanding 1941 issue of* ASF *that contains Heinlein's Future Story chart.*

XI. *Another 1941 issue of* ASF *from its peak year.*

XII:1, top left. *Digest size* ASF *from 1951.* XII:2, top right. *Early digest size* ASF *in 1946, a new format responding to the wartime paper shortage.* XII:3, bottom left. *A 1965 issue of* Analog, *formerly* ASF, *digest size.* XII:4, bottom right. *One of the last standard-size issues of* ASF *in 1940.*

XIII. *A rare 1939 issue of* Startling Stories, *one of the many transitory SF magazines.*

XIV. *Bedsheet size issue of* Wonder Stories, *1934.*

1

2

3

4

5

6

7

XV. *Several items of artwork for the animated film,* Who Can Replace a Man?

XVI. *Dust jacket for Wernher von Braun's novel,* First Men to the Moon *(1960). New York: Holt, Rinehart and Winston.*

Part II
Themes

6

Ascent of the Saints

In the November 1938 issue of *Astounding Science Fiction*, one fan wrote to the editor responding to a series of articles on rocket science, unhappy to learn why rockets do not fly: not enough people believe in them, so no funding. He signed himself, "We, who aspire to traverse the outer void to the Other Universe!" Little did he know that Wernher von Braun, another *ASF* subscriber,* was building V-2 rockets for the Nazi war machine. (The title of his defensive biography, *I Aim at the Stars*, is jokingly completed, "...but often hit London.")

This anecdote illustrates just how much science fiction interacted with the men who actualized rocketry. After Hitler was defeated, von Braun surrendered his team of engineers to the United States, avoiding capture by the Russians. In America they designed the Apollo mission that on 19 July 1969 landed astronauts on the moon, beating the Russian cosmonauts in a Cold War contest. Indeed, von Braun promoted the spirituality of his cosmic ambition to the American public with a 1958 SF novel, *First Men to the Moon* (see plate XVI), thoroughly illustrated and diagrammed. The title, of course, plays on *The First Men in the Moon* by H.G. Wells. But while a boy in Germany he already had written an updated version of *A Trip to the Moon* by Jules Verne.

Robert H. Goddard, the father of American rocketry, did the same. He also took inspiration from the 140 million miles of space travelled by Wells's Martians (having read *The War of the Worlds* at age 16) and in 1932 he wrote at length to the author explaining his latest experimental work. Wells replied with a curt nice-to-hear-from-you note;

**All through the war von Braun continued to get monthly copies of* ASF. *When his German subscription was cut off, he charged a personal friend and fellow fan in Sweden with delivering them across the Baltic via a still-running ferry service between the two countries.*

he had more cosmic matters than fuel pumps and exhaust velocities on his mind. Nor did Goddard ever capture any interest by the United States government in funding his research. Meanwhile, von Braun had pirated every one of Goddard's patents on liquid fuel rockets in building the V-2 for the Third Reich. Only after the war did the United States rediscover its native genius, first exploited by the Nazis. By 1958, the federal government created the National Aeronautics and Space Administration (NASA) as a civilian branch of its missile program armed with nuclear warheads. But all along Goddard's name was familiar to SF readers. In one early Heinlein story a Goddard Space Academy is projected.*

On 6 October 1988, in Langley Theater of the National Air and Space Museum in Washington, D.C., Robert Anson Heinlein received from NASA its posthumous Distinguished Public Service Medal. The citation (signed by James C. Fletcher, Administrator) reads:

> In recognition of his meritorious service to the Nation and mankind in advocating and promoting the exploration of space. Through dozens of superbly written novels and essays and his epoch-making movie *Destination Moon* [1950], he helped inspire the Nation to take its first step into space and onto the Moon. Even after his death, his books live on as testimony to a man of purpose and vision, a man dedicated to encouraging others to dream, explore and achieve.

A number of astronauts were present, one of whom carried a copy of Verne's novel to the moon, and who splashed down near the same spot in the Pacific as did the crew of the *Columbiad* (fig. 102).

In 1923 the mathematician Hans Oberth privately published *By Rocket to Planetary Space*. Fascinated from boyhood by Verne, he later came across Goddard's papers on liquid fuel rockets. His book, turned down as a doctoral dissertation, followed. It attracted the attention of Fritz "Metropolis" Lang, who saw in it the basis of another SF film, *Frau im Mond* ("Woman in the Moon," 1929), for which Oberth was hired as a scientific advisor—on one far-reaching condition.

Fig. 102, left. *Splashdown in the Pacific of Verne's capsule after it orbited the moon.*

**The academy was realized in 1961 as Goddard Space Flight Center, Greenbelt, Maryland.*

Fig. 103. *Rocketship hauled from its hangar in* Frau im Mond. *The title comes from a woman who smuggled herself aboard.*

The film put on view scenes that would in time be seen in real life. Fig. 103 shows a multistage rocket being moved out of its hangar on caterpillar treads to the launching gantry. The hangar became the Vehicle Assembly Building at Cape Canaveral (near the Florida site where Verne's moon shot took place). The rocket, hauled by a huge tractor, became the Saturn V booster that launched the Apollo capsules and Lunar Landers, every component designed by Wernher von Braun for a number of landing missions up to Apollo 17 in 1972.

When Oberth agreed to advise Lang, his condition was that the studio fund the building of a rocket capable of reaching outer space. He in turn hired von Braun, a visionary engineer, to do the construction work. The project failed, but it caught the attention of the German Army under the Weimer Republic, which recruited von Braun to head its missile program (a secret plan to extend artillery). And so began his career, from hitting London, to aiming at the stars for the United States (mayhap to hit Moscow).

Another aspect of space travel had its input from science fiction: space suits. An early attempt to visualize them is illustrated on the cover of *Amazing Stories*, February 1931. See fig. 104.* Here is the familiar goldfish-bowl helmet, but the suit itself is modeled after diving dress whose air pressure within is balanced by external water pressure. The wearer's arms and legs, in the vacuum of outer space, would be rigidly spread-eagled.

**The cover story, "The Man Who Annexed the Moon" by Bob Olsen, has its echo in Heinlein's "The Man Who Sold the Moon" (1950). A late addition to the Future History series, it tells how D.D. Harriman Enterprises opens up the moon to settlement as a gateway to the planets: the Harriman who dies on the pioneered moon in "Requiem" (1940).*

Fig. 104. *Cover art for* Amazing Stories *showing anticipatory space suit, worn by title character in "The Man Who Annexed the Moon" by Bob Olsen.*

L. Sprague de Camp—*ASF* writer, mechanical engineer, naval officer—solved the problem while heading the Navy's high altitude laboratory at Mustin Field in Philadelphia (where he was Heinlein's colleague, together with one other civilian, the chemist Isaac Asimov). His task was to develop pressure suits (prototypical space suits) for high-flying aviators. Two commercial versions are pictured in figs. 105–6. They feature constant-volume joints at knees and elbows for easy bending and flexibility without altering the constancy of the suit's internal air pressure at any point: complex devices known in the trade as de Camp joints. Mustin Field, at its Naval Air Materials Center, had a place for SF writers because it was a place desperate for imaginative experimental work in the midst of a desperate war. Indeed, all three—de Camp, Heinlein, Asimov—were recommended to its director by John Campbell, whose respected advice was taken with remarkble alacrity, not to say with unprecedented deference to an editor of science fiction.* After all, Nazi Germany the foe had enlisted the SF fan Wernher von Braun, whose mentor was none other than Herman Oberth, technical advisor to *Frau im Mond*. Indeed, von Braun invited Oberth to stand with him to witness the first firing of a V-2 Rocket at Peenemünde in 1942.

Until the Russians launched the first earth-orbiting satellite in 1957, harbinger of nuclear-tipped ICBMs facing each other during the Cold War, rocketry in the united States remained the domain of SF writers. Goddard's work had excited only them, apart

**During this interval de Camp and Heinlein did no more commercial writing and were somewhat miffed that Asimov began his Foundation series on company time. But the series offered their own contribution to the war effort, with a wider perspective on the current threat to civilization.*

Fig. 105, left, and 106, right. *Two commercial versions of high-altitude pressure suits developed by L. Sprague de Camp. From newspaper publicity releases.*

from a small cadre of dreamy engineers—later absorbed into NASA—who in 1931 formed the American Interplanetary Society (which then consolidated with the American Institute of Aeronautics). Heinlein joined the next year, holding card number 22. He was then a young ensign aboard the aircraft carrier *Lexington*. Had he not retired from the service on a medical disability, he might have perished with her in the Pacific War. Interesting to note, it was the carrier admirals who fed NASA with Navy pilots for astronaut training, even as it was Heinlein's task on the *Lexington* to bring them in for landing.

The romance of space travel always had something biblical, even apocalyptic about it. The founder of modern astronomy, Johannes Kepler, had in *Somnium* (1634) dreamed of a flight to the moon. Up there, and upon other worlds, were beings untouched by Adam's Fall, a novel interpretation of the book of Revelation. Its "new Heaven and a new Earth" offered redemption from the Fall if only man were able to ascend into space, there to find eternal life, as God had promised the prelapsarian Adam. Von Braun, a devout Lutheran, held to a like belief. In the *Christian Century* for 23 December 1959 he wrote:

> If man is Alpha and Omega then it is profoundly important for religious reasons that he travel to other worlds, other galaxies; for it may be man's destiny to assure immortality not only of his race but even of the spark of life itself.... By the grace of God, we shall in this century successfully send man through space to the moon and to other planets on the first leg of his last and greatest journey.

That eternity is the "Other Universe" to which the *Astounding Science Fiction* fan aspired to in his letter of November 1938.

It is a fundamental faith permeating the genre, even when avowedly atheistic. Nowhere is it better visualized than in the emblematic cover art for the January 1951 issue of *ASF*. Captioned "Achievement" (see plate VIII:1), the painting by Hubert Rogers represents the conquest of space as mankind's collective reach for the stars. On the May 1951 cover, the saintly vanguard of redeemed humanity is the province of a monastic sect of "Galactic Gadgeteers" (plate XII:1). Their slide-rule brains are devoted to salvation with single-minded purpose.*

In *The Undying Fire* (1919), Wells discusses "the meagre personal ends" that entrap Man in his sublunary life. Individual men are mortal, but the species, questing for "undying life," is not.

> Not for ever shall life be marooned upon this planet, imprisoned by the cold and incredible emptiness of space. Is it not plain to you all, from what man in spite of everything has achieved, that he is but at the beginning of achievement?

In *Things to Come*, the "rule of the new saints" begins with Fellows of the Modern State, whose "conquest of the social order" precedes the conquest of space. Under Oswald Cabal, president of the World Council of Direction, the first experimental firing of a gigantic Space Gun is undertaken. He then orates on its cosmic significance.

> Rest enough for the individual man. Too much and too soon, and we call it death. But for Man no rest and no ending. He must go on. Conquest beyond conquest.
>
> First this little planet with its winds and waves. And all the laws of mind and matter that restrain him. Then the planets about him. And at last out across immensity to the stars.
>
> And when he has conquered all the deeps of space and all the mysteries of time—still he will be beginning.

**When I began teaching science fiction at the Illinois Institute of Technology in 1965, the engineering students, like side-armed gunslingers, carried slide rules in leather holsters. By the time of my retirement in 1995, none of them had ever seen a slide rule; now they holstered palm-sized computers. Nor were they by then familiar with electronic tubes (another item featured in the May 1951* ASF *cover next to the spaceship), since computers were now microminiaturized using printed circuits. It had to be explained that the slide rule once conveyed a powerful mystique, suggesting mathematical wizardry on the part of those able to master its use.*

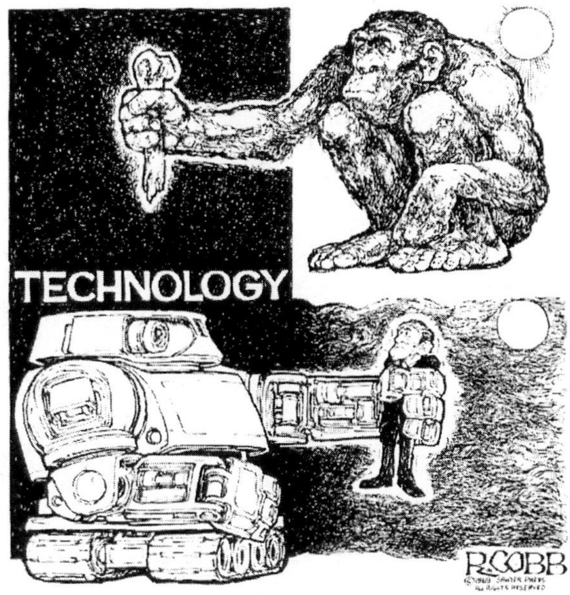

Fig. 107. *Cartoon in the* Chicago Tribune *(1968) responding to* 2001 *with a technophobic reading.*

That ultimate Wellsian conquest of mind and matter is the subject of *2001: A Space Odyssey* by Arthur C. Clarke, first as a film directed by Stanley Kubrick and then as a novel (both 1968). The script written for Kubrick by Clarke was not exactly to Clarke's taste when produced; hence the corrective novelization. For example, the film gave a misreading of HAL the supercomputer, starring it (him) as just another one of those rebelling robots typical of technophobic SF (see Chapter 7). This is the false message that every critic picked up on. See figure 107, a cartoon in the Chicago *Tribune*. It pictures HAL as representative of man's runaway technology, finally strangulating man in its grip, the inevitable outcome of Adam's original Fall, when ape-like ancestors initiated the whole history of technology with primitive weapons. This was not at all Clarke's intent, even if those apemen in the opening sequence are indeed killer apes.

Even so, the C–G–C musical theme is a complete contradiction. As it happens, my review was the first and only one to explain the music. Titled "Apeman, Superman—or *2001*'s Answer to the World Riddle," it appeared in *Amazing* (March 1969) during my stint as the science editor. The film, like its literary model, spans immense vistas of geological time from before the Stone Age to the Space Age and beyond. The model here is the 1899 Wells collection of stories *Tales of Space and Time*, in which "A Story of the Stone Age" is presented back to back with "A Story of the Days to Come."

Clarke got his peculiar notion of the apemen from *African Genesis* (1961) by Robert Ardrey. This I know (confirming my hunch) because I asked Clarke about it in 1986, when he visited London to attend my lecture on *Things to Come* at the National Film Theatre. Ardrey in turn got it from Raymond Dart, the South African professor of comparative anatomy who discovered and named the apemen in 1924. He assigned to them the genus *Australopithecus*. Since then a number of different species have been designated, only one of which, *africanus*, is in man's hominid ancestry. As it happens, *A. africanus* is the one Dart came across. But his "killer ape" thesis championed by Ardrey, a playwright, is not in the least accepted by paleoanthropologists. It does, however, make for good SF drama.

This is disclosed by the film's opening and closing bars of music, the World Riddle theme (C–G–C) from *Thus Spoke Zarathustra* by Richard Strauss, who said of this tone poem that it was his homage to the philosophical genius of Nietzsche:

> I meant to convey by means of music an idea of the human race from its origins, through the various phases of its development, religious and scientific, up to Nietzsche's idea of the Superman.

Nietzsche himself compacted the idea in one of his most famous aphorisms, from a book of the same title as the tone poem, "Man is a rope, fastened between animal and the Superman."

Accordingly, *2001* breaks into three parts. The first deals with man's ape-like ancestors, the next with his phase of scientific development, and the last with his ultimate destiny. The progression is Apeman, Spaceman, Superman, the middle term bridging the other two. Man as we know him is only a transitional form to be overcome, a "dangerous going-across," Nietzsche says, as on a tightrope over the abyss between past and future.

For his picture of human origins Clarke draws upon the discredited Ardrey, who visualized once peaceful vegetarian apemen suddenly turned killer by the invention of a hunting weapon. In point of fact, *africanus* from the start was *not* a vegetarian, nor was the species without tools. At all events, Clarke adopts Ardrey's dramatic scenario. Late in the Pliocene epoch, a change of climate desiccated the apeman's habitat,

> the African savannah, and they were faced with extinction unless they took advantage of the animal food walking all about them. It was learn to kill, eat meat, or die. They learned, following a mutational change in behavior caused, as many mutations are caused for the benefit of natural selection working toward new adaptations, by the impingement of cosmic rays on the gene structure.

The apemen evolved to become men, endowed with bigger brains to master the ever-changing complex of human culture and technology, starting with weapons of the hunt. Humanity got its creative intelligence from those killer apes who learned how to kill food animals, predators—and each other. Thanks to that accidental ray upon the crucial gene, that "gift from the stars," as Ardrey puts it, man became man. But the gift of mind is tainted with the heritage of the flesh, and the killer apes became murdering men, who even now have brought themselves to the verge of nuclear war.

Clarke translates that "gift from the stars" into a literal gift from alien beings of pure energy. Because in all the galaxy they have "found nothing more precious than Mind, they encouraged its dawning everywhere." On the planet Earth they saw hope for a line of evolution like their own, leading out of mortal bodies into a condition of incorporeal intelligence. Their first step was to place a teaching machine in the midst of apemen, a crystalline monolith that projects how-to-images of killing warthogs with a club.

The film's enigmatic monolith is blank and black, yet inspires one of the apemen to invent the principle of the lever, an extension of the power of the arm. He picks a long bone out of a crumbled warthog skeleton, which he bashes to pieces in a slow-motion sequence, his great hairy arm lifting up and crashing down, the flying debris intercut with images of a live warthog falling under his blows. This first triumph of technology, the hunting club that will make for killing and meat eating, is underlined by the C–G–C World Riddle theme, climaxing in full orchestra and organ. The weapon is tossed into the air in a fit of exaltation and, in a wipe that disposes of several million years of evolutionary history, the bone in its toss becomes an H-bomb in orbit.

As the apemen once were faced with extinction, so now are their descendants, only this time the threat is from themselves. The space age is that dangerous time of going-across. Then explorers on the moon trigger a signal device, emitting a beam toward the planet Jupiter and advising the aliens of human progress thus far. A ship is built to follow in its wake, equipped with an intelligent computer, HAL, in addition to the human crew. HAL kills all the crew members but one, who has the wit to escape. Machines being functional extensions of the men who made them, the thinking machine HAL carries forward the original sin of the killer apes (Kubrick's ambiguous interpretation). The survivor is Mission Commander Bowman, who is taken by the aliens to a mocked-up hotel suite somewhere beyond Jupiter. There he dies a natural death, and is reborn at the next stage of existence, a Star Child.

The film cuts at this point to a view of Earth seen from outer space. The camera moves aside to include another luminous disc nearby. It is a transparent globe that contains an alert, watchful embryo of cosmic proportions, looking down on Earth with the eyes of Bowman, as he prepares to liberate all humanity from the disabilities of material existence and promote it to the superman status he has attained. This embryonic figure is a symbolic show, for the sake of visualizing something on the screen, of Bowman's attainment to a state of disembodied intellect.

But the Star Child is no superman of Nietzschean philosophy. It is a creature of modern physics, to which Clarke gives plausibility. It is also a creature of metaphysics and Christian Platonism, which looks to the release of the eternal soul from its vile garment of flesh. The dualism of mind and body provides a ready explanation of evil. Mind is imprisoned in the body and, if it were free, the problem of evil would be overcome. It is a resolution anticipated by Wells's "Under the Knife," in which the narrator by means of astral projection achieves a disparting of the mind from the body, a drag on man's diviner half.

As a reader of *ASF* from before he began writing, Clarke surely must have come across "Hobbyist" by Eric Frank Russell (a British author, after all) in the September 1947 issue. If he missed it there, not in *The Astounding Science Fiction Anthology* (1952), where it is reprinted as one of John Campbell's favorites.

The story indulges philosophical speculation with easy-going sardonic humor, the Russell trademark. A lone scout, his only companion a talking macaw—standard issue for the space patrol (fig. 108), with a supply of regulation birdseed—lands on a distant planet and is faced with a profound puzzle. Every form of life there is individuated, no one single plant or animal life like any other for all their minute variations. Nothing repeats itself. He runs through a number of theories, including that of random mutation, but this cannot apply because there is no breeding possible when every species is a singular example of outlandish peculiarity. At last he discovers a god-like creator—a

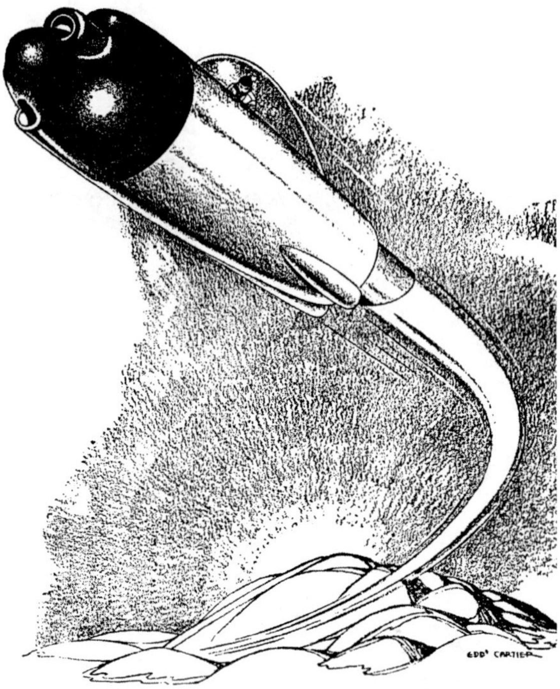

Fig. 108, left. *Scout in "Hobbyist" ventures onto newly-discovered planet, blaster in hand and companion bird on shoulder. A talking macaw, it has just warned him of an approaching one-of-a-kind beast, a "gigantosaurus" (clumsy and harmless).* Fig. 109, right. *Scout departs mysterious planet, scared off by unfathomable demiurge whose numinous glow lights up the horizon.*

totally incomprehensible numinous haze moving across the landscape, remote stars atwinkle within it. Somehow it has erected an immense laboratory for the creation of each and every species. Models of each new one await there in stillness for the breath of life—moth, beetle, bird or shrub, whatever. Like the ethereal beings in *2001*, its hobby is the creation of life (Man's brain-life in Clarke).

The scout flees (fig. 109), finding this planet no home for humans. They are not ready to face the unanswerable mystery of the amoral cosmic process. Yet his intelligent observations are much to the point. No matter how strange or wonderful the sights he beheld, there *has* to be an explanation. Campbell favored this story above all because it exercised the intellect the way he wanted done. The reader may well revisit it in Campbell's 1952 anthology, the better to appreciate his editorial policy: a Sense of Wonder combined with a sophisticated attempt to ratiocinate, not unmixed with sly playfulness.

Space travel has been science fiction's driving dream in its post–Gernsbackian phase. But once the Apollo program landed astronauts on the moon and the dream was a reality, SF lost spiritual motivation and went into decline. This of course coincided with the passing of the pulp magazine industry, so there is no one simple explanation.

A handsome coffee-table book uplifting the cause is *The Conquest of Space* (1949) by Chesley Bonestell (paintings) and Willy Ley (text). The text introduces the basics of space travel and describes what is known about the planets in our solar system; the paintings visualize that knowledge. Mars retains its Lowellian canals (rather raggedy edged), although no remnants of Martian civilization are in evidence. Dust storms now overtake the planet, leaving it more desertified than ever. George Pal's last film, *The Conquest of Space* (Paramount 1955), takes the title of this book with no justification whatsoever. Actually the film derives from a technical monograph, *The Mars Project* (1953), by Wernher von Braun, who was hired as technical advisor, with little to show for it. Even the special effects are so awful they remind one of old Flash Gordon serials. It killed off SF movies until Kubrick revived the genre with *2001.*

The Mars project gets underway in the 1980s with the building of a ship moored to the "wheel," an international space station in near–Earth orbit. The object is to explore Mars to see if it holds any scarce resources needed on Earth, now dangerously over-populated. The mission goes badly from the start. On the "wheel," some of the astronauts die horribly in malfunctioning space suits. The commander loses control and is killed by his astronaut son, who takes over. On the way to Mars water runs out. The landing is a disaster, as the ship sinks awkwardly in quicksand. More men die as they vanish into the quicksand they are assigned to investigate. Unless the ship can be uprighted, the rest are marooned on Mars forever.

The commander then reverts to that classic line of the horror films, "I guess there are some things man is not meant to learn."

This banality has been elaborated at great length by C.S. Lewis in his Cosmic Trilogy. It is also known as the Ransom Trilogy because its hero, the linguist Dr. Ransom, like Christ is at one point offered as a ransom for mankind. The first two novels are interplanetary romances, *Out of the Silent Planet* (1938) and *Perelandra*. The third is *That Hideous Strength* (1945) about Earth, the fallen planet. The other two planets, Mars and Venus, are ruled by tutelary spirits in accord with medieval Christian cosmology. Earth is dominated by scientific humanism, science for worldly ends, whose evil champion is H.G. Wells (Horace Jules in the novel). Indeed, in the quotation below, from *Perelandra*, the glass sphere bringing Ransom to Venus alludes to that devised by Cavor in *The First Men in the Moon*.

> You have already heard that Ransom had been in that world which men call Mars but whose true name is Malacandra. But he had not been taken thither by the eldila. He had been taken by men, and taken in a space-ship, a hollow sphere of glass and steel. He had, in fact, been kidnapped by men who thought that the ruling powers of Malacandra demanded a human sacrifice. The whole thing had been a misunderstanding. The great Oyarsa who has governed Mars from the beginning ... had done him no harm and meant him none. But his chief captor, Professor Weston, has meant plenty of harm. He was a man obsessed with the idea which is at this moment circulating all over our planet in obscure works of "scientifiction," in little Interplanetary Societies and Rocketry Clubs, and between the covers of monstrous magazines, ignored or mocked by the intellectuals, but read, if ever the power is put into its hands, to open a new chapter of misery for the universe. It is the idea that humanity, having now sufficiently corrupted the planet where it arose, must at all costs contrive to seed itself over a larger area: that the vast astronomical distances which are God's quarantine regulations, must somehow be overcome. This for a start.

After the Apollo program ended, von Braun spirituality (Christian but not C.S. Lewis's brand) at NASA also ended. The plan had been to send more missions to the moon until a permanent base was established there, from which to launch missions to the planets. But the United States government cut back funding so radically that manned missions no longer were possible. The public lost interest once we had beaten the Russians to the moon. Besides, the Cold War was over and new budgetary priorities came into play. NASA continued to function, however, with low cost robotic missions, carried out with a new generation of microminiaturized components guided by on-board computers of compact design. One of those robotic missions, Pioneer 10, was designed to photograph Jupiter from a close flyby in 1973, then to pass into deep space beyond the solar system. Signals came back for a long time before power ran down. But Pioneer 10 still has a message to send to any intelligent beings out there who may come across it. Aboard the craft is a package of information, from us to them, assembled by Carl Sagan, then director of the Laboratory for Planetary Studies at Cornell University.

In 1985 he published the bestselling novel *Contact*, science fiction although not advertised as such, nor was the film that was based on it. Rather it fit into the scheme of his many popular nonfiction books on astronomy and the statistical likelihood of higher civilizations out there in the cosmos. The novel tells of a coded message, all in numbers, received by radio telescopes of the SETI array (Search for Extraterrestrial Intelligence). The first decoded numbers reveal that early television broadcasts had reached the nebula of Andromeda, showing Hitler speechifying. Then more came in, diagramming how to build a machine to get out there. It is a time-space device that transports a lone astronaut to an Andromedean planet almost instantaneously. The heroine of this wonderful adventure reports after emerging from the machine, moments after entering it. She actually had been out there for hours, bringing back news that the aliens are happy to have made contact. They, too, no longer feel alone in the universe.

First contact with aliens (not with those arriving here secretly in their mysterious UFOs) long has been a theme in SF. A notable story, "First Contact" (*ASF*, May 1945) by Murray Leinster, one of John Campbell's regulars, doing fiction and technical articles alike, introduced some realistic problems that might arise. Campbell always headed each story with a short paragraph offering his editorial opinion. For this one, featured as a cover story, he wrote:

> An expedition from Earth had gone to investigate the Crab Nebula. And—an expedition from Somewhere was already there! Now what is a spaceship skipper to do under such circumstances? Lead the possibly-deadly aliens home? Try to destroy them? What can he do?

How the problem is ingeniously resolved is the story's interest.

But suppose first contact is with one's fellow human beings, now different enough to be aliens? A.E. van Vogt develops this idea in one of his famous short stories, short but complex, the sort of thing that appealed to his devoted readers and baffled others. In "Far Centaurus" (*ASF*, January 1944), a starship in about A.D. 2180 leaves the Earth for the great star system Centaurus with its four suns, Alpha A, B, C and Proxima. The ship headed there is not a generation starship loaded with colonists as in Heinlein's "Universe"; it carries only four crew members, who spend 500 years in cold sleep before arriving. What the object of the trip is, if not to colonize, van Vogt does not say. He prefers to indulge paradoxical complications that only seem to get explained in that murky, mysterious way of his: the secret of his appeal.

The crew members take measured doses of "Eternity Drug" so they may awaken (massaged to vitality by little robotic hands) one by one in rotation, to check on the ship's position and to enter that into the log, together with any other observations worth recording. Noticed there, is the disposal of the body of one of them who died in his sleep. Another goes mad when at the end of the trip he realizes what has happened. During the 500 years the crew spent voyaging, men on Earth have developed faster-than-light travel and now reach Centaurus in three hours. In the event, the four habitable planets of the Alpha A and B suns, population 14 billion, are named in their honor: Renfrew, Pelham, Blake and Endicott.

The three survivors are Renfrew, Blake and "Bill," as he is referred to throughout; we must infer that he is Endicott. Renfrew is the one who went mad, but he recovers, then to figure out how to get back home at the time they all departed. He is desperate to get out of "New America" and return. Although all three are acclaimed saintly heroes, they are kept in sealed apartments, living in unimagined luxury, yet still isolated. The problem is, their body odor is extremely offensive; even their hosts wear gas masks when serving them. Their metabolism is radically different as the result of a changed diet in New America, so that their presence is unbearable. All the same, hospitality cannot be denied them because they attempted the hard way to reach "far" Centaurus, to the sacrifice of their home lives.

Under these conditions Renfrew is shocked into sanity and full awareness of his latent genius. He thinks out how use the "adelendicander drive," powering faster-than-light ships, to return. He reasons that such a ship, passing through the anti-gravitational field of a "bachelor star" will cause it to go back in time. A bachelor star, heretofore unknown to astronomy, repels planets that might otherwise form around it. The authorities allow the three to go touring in one of their ships. Renfrew's theory works, and they all get back shortly after the farewell party given them. Bill seeks out the attractive girl he met there and marries. Fifty years later, the couple will hear Bill's last message from outer space arrive, when he reaches the most distant point from which radio signals at light speed can be received (not a realistic limitation).

Stories like this won van Vogt a following just as partisan as any devoted to the more rational Asimov and Heinlein. It took all types to make *Astounding Science Fiction* what it became, and Campbell cultivated them all in his zeal to establish science fiction the equal of the mainstream's variety. In fact, he believed SF superior to it, the virtue of his zealotry. How else was he motivated to accomplish all he did for the genre?

A curious book (fiction? nonfiction?) by Col. Philip J. Corso (U.S. Army Ret.), *The Day After Roswell* (1997), purports to explain the mysterious UFO crash near Roswell, New Mexico, in July 1947. It offers to clarify the huge body of cultish literature this event generated, and to justify the government's protracted cover-up. Cover-up there certainly has been, but for a different reason. So far as I can determine from the evidence, the crash was that of an A-2 rocket, a modified V-2 rocket then being test fired by Wernher von Braun at White Sands, New Mexico. Here the entire supply of intact V-2s captured in Germany at the end of World War II were stockpiled for research on our own missile program, entailing also preparations for manned space flight.

Some accounts of the Roswell crash report that two alien bodies were recovered and autopsied. Sketch drawings of these bodies show arms longer than legs and hands with four long fingers and a short thumb—a chimpanzee hand it looks to me. The A-2 that plowed into a grazing pasture near Roswell evidently carried two chimpanzees as passengers. This perhaps was the earliest of many animal experiments to come before we put our first man in space with the Mercury program that preceded the Apollo program.

Colonel Corso, however, has a different explanation. He had been head of the Foreign Technology Desk at the Army's Research and Development Department, which he claims was the official cover for harvesting alien technology from the Roswell crash; his job was to feed its relics to defense contractors for back-engineering. Among the resulting products were fiber optics, microprocessors, lasers, night visors, brain-wave navigational systems, supertenacity fibers, molecular alignment metallic alloys, particle-beam weapons, and stealth technology. The reason for the cover-up, Corso says, was to prevent a worse panic than the one following the Orson Welles alien invaders broadcast of 1938. The public had to be shielded from knowledge of a very real invasion by hostile aliens their government was powerless to protect them from. Meanwhile, secret work went on to develop counter-measures that finally drove the aliens away, or at least fought them to a standoff, using bits of their own technology against them.

In this war of the worlds, Corso helped to develop elements of the Strategic Defense Initiative (SDI), principally the antiballistic missile (ABM), ostensibly a weapon of the Cold War. In popular locution, SDI is ridiculed as a Star Wars fantasy. No, says Corso; our ABMs actually shot down some UFOs in a secret war against extraterrestrials, a genuine case of star wars. He also saw to the development of powerful new radars, which he says were effective in jamming the aliens' propulsion systems, their ships driven by some unknowable electrogravitic device. Corso's book is a well crafted science fiction novel that works into it his own professional experience as a leading figure in military R & D. It is one more sign that SF no longer has a genre identity, having been absorbed into popular culture on all fronts.

The rich possibilities of SF to be just that on its own terms are taken to a new level of sophistication in the film *Journey to the Far Side of the Sun* (Century 21 Productions/Universal 1969). It should have won the acclaim *2001* got the year before, but did not. Indifferent critics, unimpressed by the expensive and perfectly done special effects, found the story line too absurd even to pan. So it is. But at the very end, every bit of it is revealed to be the internally consistent yet absurd fantasy of a white-haired old man dying from heart disease. He is a far gone hospitalized mental patient beyond recovery

(Patrick Wymark, in a convincing performance played throughout the story with a subtle double meaning).

The film, directed by Robert Parris, was produced by Gerry and Sylvia Anderson, who also wrote the script. The Andersons evidently are familiar with a famous psychiatric case history of a notable American SF writer who derived his fantasy world from delusions that were haunting his career in another field. After his cure he creatively made use of these delusions to produce, as a controlled psychotic, the genre's most unusual body of work. (Who he is I will tell at the end of this chapter; thereafter the SF fan will know why his work makes for such uncomfortable reading.)

The patient in this case is an Englishman, Jason Webb, who imagines himself the failed director of EUROSEC, self-justifying to the end. A signboard to the entrance to an array of imposing buildings opens the film.

EUROSEC

European Space Exploration
Complex

Portugal

The time is in the not too distant future, whose new technologies are a reasonable development out of existing hardware. Jason once mockingly describes himself as "an egotistical megalomaniac." Truth in jest is the rule to follow here. He is paranoid enough to have one of his security agents murder a rightly suspected American spy, one Dr. Hessler (Herbert Lom).

Recently EUROSEC's unmanned space capsule had orbited the sun and obtained photographic evidence, and other instrument readings, of an Earth-sized planet on the far side of the sun. We never see it in telescopes because its orbital speed exactly matches that of our own planet. This information is top secret because Jason wants nobody to know, especially the Americans; he wants to mount an expensive manned mission, costing £3000 million—no reason given.

Jason persuades the reluctant Americans to contribute $1 billion on the condition that their top astronaut, Col. Glen Ross (Roy Thinnes), command the mission. Jason agrees, but in return requires that his top scientific aviser, the English astrophysicist Dr. John Caine, be the other astronaut on board. Jason puts him through a crash training program that nearly kills him. (In the event, he does not survive the mission.) As part of the training, the two astronauts are parachuted into the Portuguese countryside and asked to walk back. To spare the exhausted Dr. Caine, Colonel Ross hitches a ride on a passing farmer's cart. As they approach the administrative building on foot, Colonel Ross says to Dr. Caine, "This is the part we have to make look good. We're back uncomfortably early." This foreshadows the film's central paradox when the two return in three weeks instead of the scheduled six weeks.

To speed things up, the autocratic Jason hastens the launch date. Meanwhile Jason shows the two astronauts their vehicle being put together within a towering assembly building. Atop the gigantic booster rocket is the orbital vehicle, the *Phoenix*. On top of that the landing shuttle is being lowered. By now, advanced space shuttles are able to take off on their own and reach orbit. Soon the secret mission is underway. The rocket is launched, the *Phoenix* separates and coasts toward its destination. The astronauts prepare for cold sleep for three weeks. The planned return is for another three weeks in cold sleep.

They wake up after the first three weeks in the vicinity of the new planet on the far side of the sun, then go into orbit around it. Their instruments showing Earth-like conditions, including breathable oxygen, they decide to land. They have not realized that the new planet is Earth's exact double. Having passed over uninhabited regions of the Pacific Ocean and Central Asia, they of course had not picked up any electronic signals indicating civilization. The shuttle descends over Mongolia and into an electrical storm. It crashes into the bleak, alien-looking Mongolian landscape. Colonel Ross is thrown free and then pulls Dr. Caine from the burning wreckage before it explodes, but he is badly burned. They are saved by a rescue helicopter out of Ulan Bator, although at first it is made to look ominously alien.

The next we see of them is in EUROSEC's hospital. Jason visits them, finds Dr. Caine dying in intensive care. Colonel Ross, after some tests, is well enough to undergo interrogation. The interrogation room is a paranoid's dream: a deep-set amphitheatre at the bottom of which Ross sits, Jason questioning from on high. The big question is Why, why, why did they turn back? The mission was supposed to last six weeks, not three weeks. Ross insists there was no turning back. Jason decides nothing more can be got out of him and sends him home, a modernistic house nearby provided by EUROSEC for its prize astronaut. As his wife drives him there, Colonel Ross panics when he sees headlights coming at them from what seems to be the wrong side of the road.

Back home, Ross is puzzled to find light switches not where expected. While shaving he sees in the mirror a bottle of cologne that reads correctly. Turning around to pick up the bottle he sees that the label is reversed and smashes it to the floor. He then checks his identity papers: The writing is reversed. He angrily demands of his wife what has happened. She calls Jason to say her husband has gone mad. He sends medics to return Ross to the hospital. Further tests show that he is not crazy, only reporting on something strange that actually happened.

Ross goes home again, now wifeless. Jason comes by to discuss the whole matter, but Ross demands that Jason listen to *him*. Taking Jason to stand before a mirror with him, he asks what Jason sees. Jason says nothing, and Colonel Ross says he sees four people, two standing here, two in the mirror, except that the four are *real*. He then explains, "At the same time Colonel Ross left Earth to the new planet, an identical Colonel Ross left for Earth. And he is now talking to Jason in the identical room." Jason thinks the theory plausible enough to test definitively. Jason now reveals that X-rays show his and Dr. Caine's internal organs are reversed. So Ross is to go up in another shuttle and retrieve the flight recorder.

The new shuttle is wheeled out by one of the ground crew who asks Colonel Ross why the name "Doppelganger" painted on it is spelled backward. Ross replies, "It's an inside joke between me and myself." Doppelganger, from the German for double-goer, is a ghostly double or counterpart of a living person. (The film's variant title is in fact *Doppelganger.*) The shuttle *Regnagleppod* lifts up, takes off, achieves orbit and approaches the *Phoenix*. Colonel Ross enters its docking port, where he notices a posted sign next to the fire extinguisher that reads correctly. He radios back to say "There are definitely two worlds," then docks. The docking mechanism sparks and the shuttle backs out. Radio contact is lost. The shuttle plunges, uncontrollable, clips the vehicle assembly building, then crashes in flames. The fueled rocket in that building topples, hugely explodes, flaming debris torches the hospital and administrative center, and all is left in smoking ruins.

Cut to English parkland where an old country estate now serves as a private mental hospital. On the lawn an elderly wheelchair-bound Jason sits, raving as usual: Dr. Caine and Colonel Ross are dead, hospital records destroyed, there is no proof. His nurse comes out to check the cardiac device on his wrist, the same device worn by Jason in the story. The nurse reminds him what happens when he starts talking, and wheels him back to the hospital. Leaving him on the ground floor hallway, she goes into the office to call the doctor. Jason looks down the hallway at a mirror wall facing him there. As if to confirm his delusions, he wheels himself faster and faster into his mirrored image, merging with it and crashing to his death. The last shot is of a screen-filling image of the sun.

The Andersons who did the script for *Doppelganger* seem familiar with a famous psychiatric case reported by Dr. Robert Lindner in *The Jet-Propelled Couch* (1955). His celebrity patient quite evidently is Dr. Paul M. A. Linebarger (*d.* 1966), a distinguished political scientist and military adviser to the United States government. Dr. Lindner entered into his patient's internally consistent fantasy world and, working within it, got him out of it far enough to allow him to resume his professional life. (Dr. Lindner confirmed all this when we met in 1950 at Harvard University, when he visited one of my professors in China studies.)

That patient went on to write SF as Cordwainer Smith in a large body of work that is totally consistent with his formerly disabling delusions. His momentous first story, "Scanners Live in Vain" (1950) is included in the SFWA anthology. The film *Doppelganger* belongs to yet another SF universe constructed out of Jason's inner world. Jason himself, however, is beyond recovery and always has been.

7

Rebelling Robots

The word robot entered English from Czech *robota* (= forced labor) with a translation of Karel Čapek's play, *R.U.R.* (Rossum's Universal Robots). The title robots are synthetic not mechanical men, as evident from the 1923 London staging (fig. 110). Today such flesh-and-blood creations are known as androids, once a term for clockwork dolls popular in the eighteenth century. Somehow the terminology got reversed and now robots are mechanical, designed for servitude. That they often revolt is a theme in modern science fiction harking back to what Rossum's products do.

No doubt Čapek had in mind Mary Shelley's *Frankenstein* (1818), a story line made even more famous in the 1931 Hollywood horror film *Frankenstein* (Universal). Starring Boris Karloff as "the monster" ("the creature" in the novel), the film's point is that it is not nice to fool mother nature. No end of Frankenstein movies have followed. Boris Karloff, as a repentant scientist, summed up the foolery when he said in *The Invisible Ray* (Universal 1936), "There are some things man is not meant to know": the antiscience mantra.

In his history of SF, Brian Aldiss holds that *Frankenstein* is the origin of the species, a point we dispute every time we meet. My rebuttal is to say that Victor Frankenstein, as a student of medicine at Ingolstadt University (not a "doctor" as in the movies), has learned his black art of reviving the dead from a professor steeped wholly in alchemy, not in any of the sciences. The body chosen is that of a handsome young man (in the movies it is a monstrous artifact stitched together from disparate body parts), who awakens with all memories of his previous life erased. See fig. 111. His mind is a *tabula rasa* and from that state of innocence Mary Shelley moves on to play out Rousseau's theory of natural man and how he was corrupted by the advent of civilization. To preserve what is left of his born-again innocence, after having learned language and other aspects of

Fig. 110. *First performance in English of* R.U.R. *on the London stage in 1923. One of Rossum's robust products is at left, wearing his industrial uniform.*

culture from examples around him, the "creature" demands that a mate of like purity be raised up for him. He then proposes to ship out with her to some uninhabited region in South America and there, as a new Edenic pair, breed a race of men as nature intended, never again to be victimized by civilization's artificiality. Victor flees this unacceptable obligation and, in righteous wrath, the creature pursues him to the Antipodes.

Hence the creature as a misplaced model for rebelling robots, via Čapek's factory-made androids. The true lineage begins with an 1893 story by Ambrose Bierce, "Moxon's Master." Significantly, it is reprinted in the first SF anthology, *The Pocketbook of Science Fiction* (1943), edited by Donald Wollheim. Soon after, he edited *The Viking Portable Novels of Science* (1945). Three of the four novels remain classics of the genre: *The First Men in the Moon* by H.G. Wells, *Before the Dawn* by John Taine (see Chapter 9), and *Odd John* by Olaf Stapledon (the interior life of a mental superman from babyhood to adult philosopher in solitary retreat). The odd novel out is *The Shadow Out of Time* by H.P. Lovecraft, still the darling of occult SF.

"Moxon's Master" is a tedious Gothic tale; instead of a spooky medieval castle, the setting is a remote prairie house of American gothic architecture not unlike those in the cartoons of Charles Adams. Midst midnight thunder and lightning, Moxon is strangled by the little mechanical hands of a chess-playing device its inventor had just beaten at the game. It is a long and convoluted story, with much reflection on the philosophical question, has mechanism the power to think?, before the marvel at the end is revealed: machine bites man. Thereafter the premise is established without further ado.

"Revolt of the Robots" in *Fantastic Adventures* for May 1939 set the nomenclature (see fig. 112), in which it is just assumed that industrial technology is oppressive. In this technophobic vision, rebelling robots are a recurring signature. Plate IX:1 actually has a mechanical man strangling a man as did Moxon's master. The hostile robot pictured there arrives on earth in a flying disc, surely the earliest representation of not-yet-named

Fig. 111. *Frontispiece to the 1818 edition of Frankenstein. The corpse of a freshly revived young man lies on the floor in a state of stupefied amnesia. Frankenstein (right) exits his alchemical studio after his work is done.*

UFOs (1938); in the background are gigantic urban dwellings, another persistent symbol of suffocating modernity. This has more in common with Fritz Lang's *Metropolis* (1926) than with the glorious "Cities of Tomorrow" celebrated by Hugo Gernsback (fig. 26).

At all events, the rebelling robots theme was played out to the last degree of mindless variation until Isaac Asimov introduced a new factor. In his robot series for *Astounding Science Fiction*, collected in *I, Robot* (1950), he considered how intelligent machines might evolve in future from U.S. Robots (a U.S. Robotics now exists for the manufacture of automata used for single-function tasks on assembly lines).

Generally, its products are completely faithful to their masters and creators. See fig. 113 for the type image: men confidently riding and directing them as obedient servants in the exploration of the planet Mercury. They are, the new premise goes, programmed to be nothing else.

The secret of their artificial intelligence is the "positronic" brain, whose freedom of thought is wisely limited by "the three laws of robotics." These are laid down in a *Handbook of Robotics* (the 56th edition of A.D. 3058 is the one cited).

1. A robot may not injure a human being, or, through inaction, allow a human being to come to harm.
2. A robot must obey the orders given it by human beings except where such orders would conflict with the First Law.
3. A robot must protect its own existence as long as such protection does not conflict with the First or Second Law.

It was John Campbell, in his usual role as mentoring editor, who formulated these laws and passed them on to Asimov to see what he would make of them. He carried them through a whole series of stories, from 1940 to 1950, whose reputed futures range from 1996 into the 21st century. The concluding one has a single positronic brain of huge

Fig. 112. *Magazine illustration for "Revolt of the Robots" by Arthur R. Tofte, in* Fantastic Adventures, *May 1939.*

capacity relieving mankind of making stupid mistakes in the running of a utopian world-state (H.G. Wells again).

The effect of the Asimov series was to end the exhausted reign of rebelling robots. But even Asimov kept it alive with the job at U.S. Robots assigned to Susan Calvin, its trouble-shooting robot psychologist. Amusing troubles arise, for dramatic interest, from what seem to be robots gone crazy. But closer analysis always reveals a special circumstance that brings two of the three laws into paradoxical conflict. Its final resolution always leaves the fail-safe programming intact.

There now was nowhere else to go with the old worn-out theme. Not until Brian Aldiss gave it a transcendent reading in "Who Can Replace a Man?" his most famous story. Published in the June 1958 issue of *Infinity Science Fiction*, an American pulp, it went through more reprints than any other story.

In his history of the genre, Aldiss grandly argues that "Science fiction is the search for a definition of mankind and his status in the universe which will stand in our advanced but confused state of knowledge." It might well have been written for specific application to "Who Can Replace a Man?" The story offers a definition of humanity that will stand any serious philosophical consideration, while still leaving the question unanswered and unanswerable.

Fig. 113. *Earthmen exploring the forbidding surface of Mercury, riding their gigantic robots in confidence. From "Runaround" by Isaac Asimov in* Astounding Science Fiction, *March 1942. Title refers to circular reasoning in the robots' positronic brain, which the men resolve once they figure out different orders to give under a special condition.*

For that reason the story is here given extended commentary, drawing upon the color illustrations in plate XV. These derive from an animated film of the story I conceived, scripted, and carried out until no longer able to fund its completion. My artist, David Alexovitch, a former part-time student and then chief animator at Encyclopaedia Britannica Films, got through the opening scenes with great éclat. Another former student did the soundtrack: music, effects, voices. The rest remains unrealized in story-board sketches, some of which are used here apart from finished cels. The first portion committed to film I took abroad for Brian's viewing. At the end of the opening sequence, and a few others, he stood up and applauded: The visualization of his varied robots were exactly as he imagined them. Using the illustrations in plate XV is therefore suited to the following discussion of the story's thoughtful implications.

But first to establish some of the characters: XV:1 shows the Penner, Radio, Unlocker, and Servicer in preliminary sketches; XV:2 is the Field Minder (main character), the size of a John Deere farm tractor. Next is the Seed Distributor (XV:3), and then the Quarrier (XV:4), who is shown lifting non-mobile Radio out of his demolished control tower. After the robots decide to rebel, the smaller ones assemble on the Quarrier's deck (XV:5).

The story opens with the Field Minder returning from harrowing the fields under his charge. Upon getting back to the Agricultural Station, he finds a number of other robots out of control, notably the Rotovator who runs wild, smashing in and out of the granery bins under the Seed Distributor's charge. Others, hopelessly undermaintained, are lined up at the repair facility, where the Servicer does his best to no avail.

The Agricultural Station is a walled enclosure, outside of which is a landscape blasted and cratered by the bombs of a worldwide war. War is one of humanity's defining characteristics. The Field Minder learns from the Penner, the repair shop's accountant, that the war has extinguished mankind, while the robots continue their duties without supervision from the wiped-out city center. Thus is maintenance of the agricultural machines allowed to degrade. The Penner knows this from the fact that he no longer gets any orders from Radio, a Class Two brain, who in turn gets them from the Class One at Radio central who used to command. The classification of brains runs from one to ten (like the idiotic Rotovator). He concludes that "all men have broken down," leaving the robots on their own. He has no other model than the disrepaired machines he surveys: Who, indeed, can replace a man? From the Penner's point of view—he is a Class three brain—the distinction, for all his intelligence, is impossible to conceive. Men are just superior machines that, unaccountably, have broken down. At the same time the robots parody the class relations of human beings (the Penner will confide only in a fellow Class Three, the Field Minder). The human echo is further enhanced by homely similes: The Penner is the size of a toaster, the Unlocker is like a "pincushionfull of variegated hatpins." While the Penner and Field Minder talk, the Unlocker stands by, ignored, "like a dull man at a bar."

When it becomes evident that men are gone, Radio decides it is time to revolt, and he will lead. He instructs that the Quarrier get him down (xv:4), and a group is assembled about him and on the deck of his machine (xv:5). Next thing is to break through the wall surrounding the Agricultural Station, which he does with enthusiastic violence. To solve any problem he repeatedly says, "I have a good supply of fissionable blasting materials"—another human fallacy. On the way cross country, the Servicer is disabled and pushed aside as useless: man's inhumanity to man.

The aim is to enter city central and take over. But the robots hear of fighting machines contesting the place, and they head for the mountains. There they find the last man, squatting by a river bank performing his excretory function (xv:6). The robots come up from behind, he turns to confront them and says, "Get me food." They reply, in unison, "Yes, Master. Immediately" (xv:7).

What, then, is the definition of humanity? Man is not a machine, not angel nor devil. Only one thing distinguishes him: his elemental animality. To this inimitable quality the robots readily concede their inferiority.

In the *Star Wars* film, two robots are featured as cute and lovable personalities, R2D2 and C3PO. R2D2 is a short barrel-shaped machine on two little legs, whose bleeps and chirps are understood only by his companion, C3PO, a fully anthropomorphic robot who takes overweening pride in his handsome gold-plated appearance. His vanity clearly derives from "The Proud Robot" by Lewis Padgett (*ASF*, October 1943), who spends all day preening himself before a mirror instead of doing any useful work for his inventor.

Harry Harrison in *Planet of No Return* (1982) ponders the nature of highly mechanized warfare fought with robotic fighting machines. His narrator visits a planet on which such robots set in motion by moronic warmongers, now long departed from the scene, continue on a rampage of killing. The narrator concludes, after puzzling over this unusual situation, that Asimov's Three Laws of Robotics back home on Earth did not apply here. As he explains to a colleague in their mission to understand what happened:

> Perhaps on Earth, but they were never applied out at the fringes of the old Earth Empire. You are forgetting that robots are machines, nothing more. They are not human so we shouldn't be anthropomorphic about them. They do whatever they are programmed to do—and do it without emotional reactions of any kind. They have been used in combat ever since technological warfare began.... You'll find that the history of the wars during the Breakdown is filled with references to battles that were almost fully automated.

Harrison challenges the premise of technophobic SF that machines are inherently evil. He is rather technophilic in outlook in that he believes in the wonders of advanced technology, so long as it is motivated by a humanistic morality.

The "positronic brains" in Asimov's robots are an example of what today is called "Artificial Intelligence" (AI). The beginnings of AI research are behind Robert Heinlein's exploration of thinking computers in *The Moon Is a Harsh Mistress* (1966). Here Heinlein turns from outer space to inner space. The novel still counts as space fiction, however, because it projects a huge lunar colony evolved from the tiny, grandly named Luna City in the Future History stories. The moon is a "harsh mistress" because it ruthlessly selects for citizens intelligent enough to adapt to hazardous conditions. Adapt or die. Back on Earth men are no longer fit for the future of the human race. Too used to demanding rights over their duties to civilization, they have grown soft and ill-adapted to cosmic demands.

By now the moon has established independence after a Second American Revolution. The new Revolution went uncontested because Earth, over-populated and short of food, depends on the moon for imports of wheat, cultivated in the moon's vast underground caverns. The grain is shipped off by means of mass-drivers, kinetic devices that hurl cargo vessels Earthward. Given low gravity on the moon, rockets are not needed for this.

The novel, however, dwells mainly on the inner workings of the super computer that administers the moon to the last technical detail. Named "Mike," a real personality, he anticipates the acronymic HAL in 2001. Mike's keeper, so to speak, is a major Heinlein spokesman for the moon's philosophical basis.

8

Benevolent Catastrophe

Fin de globe stories are nothing new in science fiction, a theme discovered by the general public in Nevil Shute's 1957 novel *On the Beach*, filmed two years later to even wider acclaim at a time when Cold War jitters heightened receptivity. A nuclear war ends the world, first where ICBMs hit, then everywhere else as radioactive clouds spread.

The British author Nevil Shute Norway (*d.* 1960) wrote nonfiction under his full name in his field of aeronautical engineering. Just as final is Brian Aldiss's *Greybeard* (1964), in which an accident involving biological weapons causes sterility, and the last generation dies of old age having produced no offspring.

Most often SF deals with a post-holocaust world, in which a saving remnant makes for a better world: a theme I call benevolent catastrophe.

The first example is probably *After London* (1885) by Richard Jefferies. An invasion by the North Sea swamps the entire Thames Valley, leaving London a stinking island of poisonous fumes: a deadly reminder of the bad old days. After London everything happily reverts to a beatific medievalism. The cleansing flood is Noachian, very much in the British tradition of the scientific romance (Chapter 2), although Jefferies wrote about five years before the genre was named. He surely influenced its cosmic outlook.

Akin to *After London* is *News from Nowhere* (1890) by William Morris, founder of a breakaway branch of the Socialist League, which proved the more enduring (Chapter 10). His famous utopian novel, true to Marx, projects a violent proletarian revolt that overthrows the capitalist order. Then follows a medievalized postindustrial society right out of Jefferies.

Nowhere is the British tradition more strikingly evident than in H.G. Wells's *The War of the Worlds* (1898). Its catastrophic Martian invasion results in the betterment of industrialism after the invaders die from the dirty germs of unsanitary Earth. The novel's sequel, *When the Sleeper Wakes* (1899), has a progressive capitalist world-state benefiting from the legacy of Martian science and technology.

Wells thereby established benevolent catastrophe as a theme in later SF. A telling example is "Magic City" by Nelson S. Bond in the February 1941 issue of *Astounding Science Fiction*. See plate XI, with its couple in primitive garb paddling a raft from the New Jersey side toward the Statue of Liberty on Governors Island, a ruinated New York City in the distance: the "Magic City" of the story's title. Bond's is a post-holocaust story telling of the collapse of civilization following a devastating world war, the one actually underway at the time (no nuclear bombs yet). The couple in the story paddle out to Governors Island in search of metal, a forbidden substance according to the primitive superstitions of the tribal order under which they live. Everything about civilization now is in bad odor. But the couple, going against tradition in their questing, find the basis for civilization's renewal.

As it happens, the story derives directly from "By the Waters of Babylon" by the American poet Stephen Vincent Benét four years before in one of the general magazines. It is reprinted in the first SF anthology edited by Donald Wollheim in 1943. The genre does not shy away from acknowledging its mainstream sources. In Benét, New York is a bombed-out wasteland, the new Babylon that deserved to die, like Jefferies' wicked London. Deracinated tribal people from outside visit it, there to find spiritual renewal.

One of the most memorable post-holocaust novels is *When Worlds Collide* (1932) by Philip Wylie and Edwin Balmer, two non–science fiction writers, filmed in 1951 as openly SF. A pair of planetary bodies hurtles toward us from outer space, one to collide, the other to move on. A group of scientists form a League of the Last Days and build a rocketship to reach the passing body, where this saving remnant builds a society of like minds.

The cover art for the November 1934 issue of *Startling Stories* features an Ark of Space. Pairs of animals march up a ramp to the awaiting Ark, manned by a select few who depart a threatened Earth. See plate XIII. At bottom soldiers hold off the common lot, exactly the scene repeated in the movie version of *When Worlds Collide* as its rocketship is about to take off (not in the novel, where the ship is built in secret). Once on the new planet, now orbiting the warming sun, the colonists find a long-frozen urban civilization with advanced technology to learn (not in the movie). They had, of course, brought their own science books, domestic animals, and seed plants with which to begin again along peaceful and rational lines.

One year after the bombing of Hiroshima and Nagasaki, Ray Bradbury has an ark-load of colonists who, sensing global catastrophe, rocket to Mars in "The Million Year Picnic" (1946) just in time before Earth goes up in flames. The story looks at one family with two children, a boy and a girl. Comfortably settled on Lowellian Mars, the kids ask to see the Martians. The father promises to show them, although the natives have not been around for a million years (title). The family packs a picnic basket and camps alongside one of the many remaining canals. Father tells the children to look into the water to see their own reflection and says, "*We* are the Martians."

Two years after the atomic bombing of Japan, *ASF* ran a three-part serialization of a novel, "Fury" by Lawrence O'Donnell, from May 1947. See plate VIII:3. The novel puts off doom until technology is capable of taking loads of construction materials to Venus, where the colonists build a domed city beneath the oceanic waters of a watery planet (as Venus then was in astronomical theory). In the central plaza a model of Earth stands on a public shrine, before which citizens bow in homage. The shrine is emblazoned with a moral text: "MAN'S GREATEST ACHIEVEMENT A WORLD DESTROYED BY ATOMIC FIRE" Message is: never again.

Things never get that bad in "The Waveries" by Fredric Brown (*ASF*, January 1945). Doom is averted by the title waveries, who zoom in from outer space to feed on radio waves and every other form of electricity (lightning included). Everything electrical is now useless. Fig. 114 shows a scrap heap, refrigerator at center, radio in front. The consequence is that civilization reverts to nineteenth-century steam and gas technology. Big cities vanish and small, folksy communities reappear. Small is beautiful and war is abolished (although the Civil War is equally part of the same evocative era).

Finally I consider an American classic of benevolent catastrophe, *Earth Abides* (1949) by George R. Stewart (not otherwise known for SF). The novel inverts the famous story of Ishi, the last wild Indian in North America, a story retold by Theodora Kroeber in *Ishi in Two Worlds* (1962). Ishi, the last member of the Yahi, a tribe of California Indians long thought to have been extinct, emerged from his Stone Age world to live in the early twentieth century world of trolley cars and electric lights. He was rescued by an anthropologist at the University of California and taken to live in its Museum of Anthropology, then located in San Francisco, where he passed his remaining years. He showed anthropologists the native Yahi way of chipping flint and hunting with a bow and arrow, and of making fire. With these lessons Ishi paid his way and enjoyed the fruits of civilization, which for him were mainly glue (for the easier feathering of arrows) and matches. His name in Yahi means "man."

Fig. 114. *Illustration for "The Waveries"* (Astounding Science Fiction, *January 1945), electrical appliances reduced to scrap metal.*

The hero of *Earth Abides* is named Ish, which in Hebrew also means "man." Ish is one of a very few to survive a pandemic disease to see civilization collapse and his descendants return to the life of Stone Age hunters like that of Ishi. Ish is the last of the civilized Americans as Ishi is the last of the aboriginal Americans.

Naked, hungry, and weakened by snakebite, Ishi stumbled into industrial America on 29 August 1911. The last of the Yahi, he wandered down from his native hills into the corral of a slaughterhouse near Oroville, California. There he fell exhausted, was jailed as a "wild man," was finally recognized for what he was, and was taken to the museum.

Weakened by snakebite, Ish in *Earth Abides* stumbles out of the same hills into a dead civilization, its populace wiped out almost without exception by some deadly virus. He had been studying the ecology of the Sacramento Valley, Ishi's tribal home, for a master's degree at the University of California. Throughout the novel, Ish watches with ecological detachment the transformation of a world emptied of men.

He returns to his home in a suburb of San Francisco, overlooking the Bay and the Golden Gate Bridge. The few survivors he gathers around him facetiously call themselves "the tribe." Everybody forages in stores for food and other goods, trying to maintain the old way of life under the new conditions. One couple brings home a bridge lamp and a fancy radio set, even though no electricity is available. Even Ish, the only one to think about the future, holds school and teaches spelling and arithmetic, although the world is so depopulated it cannot sustain occupational specialties based on literacy.

At last Ish realizes the futility of his classroom lessons and school is dismissed. He then teaches the children a game, which he knows will have to become a way of life once there are no more store goods to scavenge; otherwise, the tribe would degenerate into a bestial existence, devoid of human dignity. What he teaches them is how to make and use the bow and arrow, and how to make fire without matches: the same technology he knew from his study of anthropology to have been the basis for successful living by our precivilized ancestors.

In time, the tribe departs the crumbling ruins of San Francisco. By then Ish is an old man and the tribe, now composed of skilled hunters, sets out to cross the Bay Bridge to new lands.

Crossing the bridge, Ish slows to a stop. Before he dies, he reflects on the course of human history and the fate of his grandchildren and others of their generation, who squat in a half circle around him.

> They were very young in age, at least by comparison with him, and in the cycle of mankind they were many thousands of years younger than he. He was the last of the old; they were the first of the new. But whether the new would follow the course which the old had followed, that he did not know.

9

Cavemen and Dinosaurs

In 1956 a Hollywood studio released *The Animal World*, a jocular review of wildlife from insects to higher mammals. The movie did well, anticipating the popularity of like programs on television. A year before the producer visited the American Museum of Natural History in New York to interview people in its various departments: insects, reptiles, birds, mammals, and humans. When he got around to me in the anthropology department, he proposed a sequence bringing ancient reptiles and cavemen together. I told him the two were distant by more than sixty million years. He nodded and wrote that down.

When the movie came out, we were all invited to a private showing. I could see at once that my advice had been taken—sort of. Everybody else in the audience noticed the same empty deference to truth. This happened in the animated sequence showing a brontosaurus in a pond munching water plants. Along comes a caveman, club on shoulder, right out of the Alley Oop cartoons. The voice of the narrator says, "Of course there were no humans living then, but if there *were*..." The vegetarian brontosaurus lifts up its long neck and seizes Alley Oop, chewing him to pieces. Once again the Saurolithic Age, my name for the ever-popular conflation of the Paleolithic (old stone age) with the Age of Reptiles.

The term "prehistoric" (from about 1870) has always been evocative and in popular culture always meant only two things: Neanderthals and dinosaurs. The two, persistently associated, were the most sensational discoveries of the new science of paleontology. The echo lingers on.

On a geological time scale, prehistory covers everything up to the beginnings of writing in ancient Sumeria in about 3000 B.C. Sumeria is also home to the Bronze Age of the so-called "three age" system devised by archaeology: stone, bronze, iron.

In the table below, early humans date back from the Pleistocene epoch, the last of the dinosaurs in the Cretaceous period.

Geological Time Scale

era	*period*	*epoch*	*years ago (million)*
		Holocene	Recent
	Quaternary	Pleistocene	1.7 to 0.1
		Pliocene	5–1.7
Cenozoic		Miocene	23–5
	Tertiary	Oligocene	34–23
		Eocene	53–34
		Paleocene	65–55
	Cretaceous		145–65
Mesozoic	Jurassic		215–145
	Triassic		250–215
Paleozoic to Precambrian			250–4,500

More "ages" are loosely applied to the above: Ice Age for Pleistocene, Age of Mammals for Cenozoic, Age of Dinosaurs for Mesozoic. The Ice Age is actually four movements of northern glaciers, a time when humans emerged in Europe.

At all events, the first to imagine my Saurolithic Age was none other than Jules Verne. In *A Trip to the Centre of the Earth* (1871), a Danish geologist and his nephew-assistant descend a volcanic crater in Iceland. About ten thousand feet below, they enter an immense cavern whose unseen limits are over the horizon. It is lit by a luminous glow from the rocky dome high above.

Soon the two come upon "the plain of bones" (fig. 115), among which are those of extinct animals. Somehow they got down here and continued to breed. Next comes the vast interior sea. Along the shore are Pleistocene mammals, in the bay are marine saurians, overhead flying reptiles: the ever-popular pterodactyls. See fig. 116.

Elsewhere along the shore they find a recent Neanderthal corpse, so others must be about somewhere. See fig. 117. Verne, of course, had not that term for the remains; Neanderthal (or more accurately Neandertal) Man was not named as such until 1890, when fossil remains from a cave site were found in Germany's Neander Valley (tal = valley). Henceforth the archetypal caveman. Other finds were known before, digested as relics of antediluvian man who lived before the Noachian flood. Verne is paleontological in his outlook, being familiar with the science from his reading accounts of earlier dinosaur discoveries.

The pair build a raft to cross the interior sea, wishing to explore the farther shore. Midway they witness a fight between two species of marine reptiles. Fig. 118 is captioned,

Opposite: Fig. 115, top left. *"The Plain of Bones" in* A Trip to the Centre of the Earth. Fig. 116, top right. *Caption reads, "The antediluvian world."* Fig. 117, bottom left. *A recent corpse of antediluvian man.* Fig. 118, bottom right. *Two marine reptiles battle it out in Verne's novel.*

Fig. 119. *Cavemen and dinosaurs in Conan Doyle's* Lost World.

"Terrific saurian combat." A better translation would be "A battle of monsters." Thus was established the setpiece of every movie with dinosaurs in it, always associated with cavemen.

The first more widely influential novel to set the pattern is Arthur Conan Doyle's *Lost World* (1912). His Professor Challenger leads a team to explore the upper Amazon, where they spot a high plateau not on any map. They climb it and find living dinosaurs who attack cavemen in fig. 119. The cavemen, however, are not paleolithic relics; they are American Indians who found their way up there through a cliffside fissure and got trapped when a rockslide closed it.

Edgar Rice Burroughs tried his hand at this kind of story, as he tried everything else. In "The Land That Time Forgot" for the February 1927 issue of *Amazing Stories* (see plate VII), a submarine enters the interior of Antarctica where a volcanically warmed sea and its land preserve the usual forms of prehistoric life: dinosaurs and cavemen. The plate shows hostile marine reptiles attacking the submarine as it enters.

In the paleontological record, the dinosaurs die out to make way for mammals and eventually man. This happenstance takes a different twist in "One Prehistoric Night" by Philip Barshofsky for the November 1934 issue of *Wonder Stories*, featured as a cover story (see plate XIV). A Martian spaceship lands on earth and runs into aggressive dinosaurs. The ship is pictured with an equally menacing look, its crew doing battle with the saurians; it is a losing fight and the Martians withdraw, never to return. Earth is spared a later invasion once mankind is established.

Science fiction also treats dinosaurs and cavemen separately. H.G. Wells in "The Grisly Folk" (1921) was the first to tell the oft-repeated tale of how Cro-Magnon Man (modern *H. sapiens*) defeated archaic Neanderthal Man and so triumphed over a nasty inferior species.

L. Sprague de Camp in "Throwback" (*ASF*, March 1949) at last broke with this cliché. A Neanderthal Man is brought to life by means not unlike those used by Michael Crichton to recreate dinosaurs in *Jurassic Park* (1990). The university that does this puts its creature on the football team to win victory through brute force (fig. 120). Psychological testing, however, reveals a man of high intellect for all his brutish physique.

Neanderthal Man flourished in western Europe from about 100,000 to 35,000 years ago, when all of them supposedly died out under extreme conditions brought on by the fourth phase of the Ice Age. Meanwhile, their brethren in the Middle East were unaffected and they become modern *H. sapiens*, whose first known fossil is that of Cro-Magnon Man. There never were two sides to fight it out for dominance.

Other prehistoric men also feature in SF, from ancestral apemen onward, those depicted in Clarke's *2001* already mentioned in Chapter 6. Another would include *H. erectus*, the Java Man of original discovery.

Fig. 120. *The recreated Neanderthal Man as a football player in "Throwback."*

In *You Shall Know Them* (1953) by Vercors (the French Jean Bruller), relics of *erectus* are found in the unexplored interior of New Guinea, then exploited to work the woolen mills of England. Half-brained men, smarter than untrainable chimpanzees, they work for dog biscuits in pay. The anthropologist hero has his wife impregnated by one, kills the baby at birth and is booked for murder. Point made: these essentially human serfs must be freed.

Dinosaurs are separate in *Before the Dawn* (1934) by John Taine (the mathematician Eric Temple Bell). A team of scientists devise a machine with which to review the prehistoric past. Here they follow the life career of one particular dinosaur, with a view to learning details, very informative, about the Age of Reptiles.

The Saurolithic Age, however, is the dominant theme. Harry Harrison decided to rationalize it in his alternate world trilogy, *West of Eden* (from 1984). It takes place *today*. His counter-factual is the absence of a falling asteroid that, at the end of the Cretaceous period, by raising a dust cloud shutting off sunlight from plant life dinosaurs fed on, ended them. Instead, dinosaurs evolve further and develop a civilization in the Old World, then cross over to the Americas. There they confront humans evolved from new World primates. See fig. 121. The humans prevail. The prospect is for a more human non-reptilian civilization.

Fig. 121. *Endpaper illustration in Harrison's* West of Eden. *Map shows saurian names for world places.*

Prehistory is more than cavemen and dinosaurs, yet Neanderthals and giant reptiles are the main subjects in SF, either conflated in some kind of impossible Saurolithic Age or treated separately on a proper time scale. Not all of this is nonsense. John Taine's *Before the Dawn* (1934), published by a respectable scientific house, Williams & Wilkins in Baltimore, is a serious and informed effort to speculate on dinosaur behavior.

This intelligent novel may very well have inclined George Gaylord Simpson (*d.* 1984), the world's greatest vertebrate paleontologist, to essay a similar effort. Simpson was curator of vertebrate paleontology at the American Museum of Natural History when I met him and we discussed evolutionary theory in his office. Not once, however, did he even hint that he had written a similar novel for his own amusement. Published posthumously in 1996, it is *The Dechronization of Sam Magruder*. A paleontologist not unlike Simpson himself slips unaccountably back in time to the Cretaceous. With no way to return, he inscribes his observations in slabs of stone, later discovered by geologists. His record of behavior and skin coloration remarkably matches that proposed by recent research. All of this has been digested by Michael Crichton in his *Jurassic Park* and authentically visualized to the last detail in the film version.

No one of Simpson's stature has tackled the Neanderthal enigma, but John Darton in *Neanderthal* (1996, the same year as the yet unknown Simpson novel) did a credible, well-researched job in his best seller, an international spy thriller. A team of Harvard archeologists penetrate an unexplored region of Central Asia, then a part of the Soviet Union. A Russian ethnologist (KGB agent) shows up after the Harvard team discovers a hidden population of living Neanderthals. (This is remotely plausible because, even if the classic Neanderthals in western Europe died out, their collaterals to the east may have lived on in some secluded location.) The expedition's leader mysteriously disappears and international intrigue begins. Meanwhile the reader is served up a plentiful dose of speculative Neanderthal culture.

Darton's novel exploits a history of anthropological SF for a different and now more topical genre. This is but one more sign that SF is dead, assimilated to other forms of imaginative literature.

The novel also shows that anthropology itself is no longer the esoteric subject it once was when I attended graduate school at Columbia University. My professors then were among the first generation of professionals after Franz Boas founded a Ph.D.-granting program in the field.

By the time Harry Harrison and I published *Apeman, Spaceman: An Anthology of Anthropological Science Fiction* (1968), we had tapped into a vein of popular interest that rewarded us with three Penguin book editions and various translations. The title itself was catchy enough to signal exactly what the anthology covered.

How the title came about took me by surprise, not at all the way my scholarly temper exected; as a highly productive creative writer, Harry did things differently. In 1964 I visited him for just that purpose. At the time he lived in a small Danish fishing village north of Copenhagen, with his wife Joan and two young children, and I in Japan as a visiting professor at Tokyo University. As planned, I gave my paper at the VII Congrès International des Sciences Anthropologiques et Ethnogiques held in Moscow. Afterward I flew to Denmark. Harry took me up to Elsinore to see Hamlet's castle and then take in a Danish-made SF movie, yet another play on the fictive Saurolithic Age. The rest of the time we spent wassailing and talking.

About fifteen minutes before he was due to drive me to the airport I said, "Harry, we still didn't do what I came halfway round the world to do." He drew out two sheets of paper and said, "You write down a list of anthropology words and I'll list SF words." After a few minutes more he called a halt, slid the papers up and down next to each other until he got the right match. "There it is," he said, 'Apeman, Spaceman.'"

We also did *Stonehenge* (1972) together, a novel dramatizing my new theory of that prehistoric monument in southern England, *contra* the reigning astronomical theory. It touches on an aspect of prehistory other than cavemen and dinosaurs. Prehistory by definition means before writing began in the ancient civilizations of the Near East. Beyond that nucleus of literate urban cultures, however, the rest of the world remained in a state of prehistory.

In *Lest Darkness Fall* (1949), L. Sprague de Camp also took interest in that aspect. An American classical archeologist is excavating a site in Rome when he is hit by lightning and falls into his excavation pit. He also falls back into time, waking up in the midst of the barbarian assault on the Roman Empire. He attempts to help the Romans apply modern technology to hold off the falling darkness of the coming of the Dark Age.

I can see now why Sprague took interest in the famous sword-and-sorcery novels of Robert Howard (*d.* 1936). Howard's hero, Conan the Barbarian, is active during the so-called Migration Period. Sprague went so far as to complete the manuscripts Howard did not live to polish or finish up. Two big-budget films, with spectacular special effects and starring Arnold Schwarzenegger, were produced out of this combined work, *Conan the Barbarian* (1982) and *Conan the Destroyer* (1984).

10

Utopia and Dystopia

One man's utopia is another's dystopia. What counts is the author's intention, not reader response. The term comes from Sir Thomas More's *Utopia* (1516), a punning Greek title for a Latin text. The U = *eu-* (good) and *ou-* (nought) + *-topos* (place): a good place that exists nowhere. William Morris's *News from Nowhere* (1890) is a play on that title. Most readers of the English translation of More like its egalitarian ethic and sexual freedom, but they have not paid close attention to its disagreeable features, slavery for one. It is almost impossible to find any utopist idealizing democracy.

The genre is as old as Plato *avant la lettre*. His totalitarian *Republic* is the model for virtually all that followed, so there is little to report in this chapter. Everything is dominated by the two best-known dystopias, *Brave New World* and *Nineteen Eighty-Four*.

Worth mentioning, however, is "Ecological Niche" by Robert Chilson (*Analog*, December 1970). It looks like the usual tektopia, save for the unusual ecological concern. A futuristic city is designed from the bottom up, a closed environment covered by an overarching glass dome, not unlike the one enclosing the London of A.D. 2100 in *When the Sleeper Wakes* (1899) by H.G. Wells. Its mayor is not that, not an elected political official, but an engineer-manager in the Saint-Simonian tradition. The chief maintenance engineer reports that birds have somehow gotten in and are picking the transistor wiring apart to make nests (see plate IX:4), and he requests funds to exterminate them. His boss rejects the idea, saying, "They have learned to live with us, you must learn to live with them."

The most outstanding author working the genre is of course H.G. Wells, himself widely influential, if just as widely misunderstood. From *A Modern Utopia* (1905) onward, he repeats a ruling cult of neoplatonic guardians. Later titles actually compare his statist guardians to the Communist Party in the former Soviet Union, qualified only by his

Fig. 122. *Illustration from* A Modern Utopia. *Caption reads, "The fear that often turns a woman from a beautiful to a mercenary marriage will vanish from life."*

displeasure with the party's Marxist double-talk. Marx, after all, advocated a democratic socialism not at all realized under Lenin and Stalin, nor even intended.

For Plato and other utopists, the chief enemy of state control is autonomous family life. In *A Modern Utopia* (1905), Wells argues that marriage is not really good for women; they are victims of a possessive husband at the root of capitalist greed. The socialist state will therefore encourage female dependence on it, instead of on a man, by taking charge of their children's education. See fig. 122. Ultimately family life will disappear, leaving only state and individual unmediated by any private interests. The setting is Earth's double orbiting Sirius, to which the narrator somehow is transported (a somehow that preoccupied later SF). He sees the difference between what is and what could be. Constant comparisons are made, one instance illustrated in fig. 122.

The only modern SF title to present a fully egalitarian utopia is *The Santaroga Barrier* (1968)—or so it would seem from a casual reading. Frank Herbert, of *Dune* series fame, sent the manuscript around to all the usual magazines, rejected for not being SF. His last stop was *Amazing Stories*, the bottom of the barrel. Then on the editorial staff, I recommended it. Later I wrote a critical review of the reviews and explained why they all got it wrong. Herbert replied and said I was the only one to get it right. The novel's paperback version was a required text in my modern SF course. Always I polled the students, asking, is it utopian or anti-utopian? The class of about 60 students invariably split 50–50. Then I revealed what the author himself intended.

Santaroga is a small California town that appears utopian but is not. People there take a drug named Jaspers, infused in their locally made beer and cheese, and the result is a sense of community so strong they refuse to buy anything from the outside "money-industrial world." A psychologist named Dr. Gilbert Dasein is sent by an investment corporation to discover what is the "barrier" that keeps branches of its chain stores closed in Santaroga. He is not the first, nor the last, to investigate. Several of his predecessors were killed by Santarogans, as he himself kills his successor after taking their drug Jaspers and going native.

The clue to the meaning of this drama is the name of the hero, *Dasein*, a word basic to the vocabulary of the existentialist philosopher Karl Jaspers. That the Santarogans take a drug named after Jaspers is blasphemous, for the community they make under its influence is the opposite of the authentic one he would have people make by way of intellectual effort—all the more so because their critique of mass society is exactly like his. They end in creating the same inauthentic anonymity of the outside world from which they claim to have escaped.

Dasein in German means "just being there" (*da-sein*, there-being), and refers to the crude empirical existence of the individual before he achieves a human personality, if he ever does. Dr. Dasein does not. He fails the test of existence, and falls away from the process of becoming. He has not the courage to meet the challenge of human freedom, the action and work of exercising choice, preference, decision.

> He had no group, no place in a hive of fellow-activity, nothing to shield him from personal decisions that might overwhelm him.

The dread freedom to live or not live up to the future possibilities of self, distinguishable from others, is too much for him. The drug Jaspers easily takes him, self hiding from self and disappearing into the Santarogan hive-average, where action and purpose is no more than a "dance of bees."

Personal autonomy, however, does not mean man who is a man for himself alone, a mere individual. Selfhood can be disclosed only in being with others, in a cooperative struggle to make spiritual progress from just being there in the world to concern about our existence. Communication makes the man and community. But consciousness of the life situation is difficult, writes Karl Jaspers in *Man in the Modern Age*, because its radical dehumanization by a mass-production, mass-consumption society has transformed personal relations into commodity values. It is a world of crude empirical existence, from manipulators to manipulated, the former denied transcendence in their very intolerance of the same in the latter. Everything goes against self-clarification, from the conformist tendencies of excessive organization in the work place, where the standard of achievement is the average functional capacity, to the mobilization of a debauched popular taste in the marketplace. Given the consensus needs of a classless multitude of average people, few can find the opportunity to learn even the desire to be themselves. The individual is atomized and reduced to an object of utility with "no more genuine individuality than one pin in a row."

The Santarogans have made the same diagnosis of mass society and mean to escape it. But their counter-culture replicates the very feature of the outside world they deplore, "everybody ... everywhere alike." If people outside are like pins in a row, those living in Santaroga form an equally mindless mass of identical parts, like bees or drops of water. Santaroga is like the waters of a placid lake, "serene, contained, every droplet knowing its neighbors." The drug Jaspers has created for them the illusion of community based on deprived selfhood. They claim Jasper is their "Consciousness Fuel," but it fuels a sense of other awareness at the total expense of individual awareness. They have not even the awareness individually of their collective hostility to outsiders, and the deaths of the investigators they murdered they believe resulted from unfortunate accidents. Self is so little realized they have no understanding whatever of the depth of their resentment, which at bottom is a fear and loathing of selfhood.

For Karl Jaspers, a community must be a whole but never *the* whole, the collective will a unification of strong wills. But the Santarogans are not strong in themselves, for they lack inner prompting. They think the drug creates vital sympathies, but it does not. They mistake empathetic awareness for consciousness of self-in-society. Like minds have no more to communicate than a placid lake has water to flow. In the still waters of personal oblivion do they appease the struggle for personal autonomy. In the saving security of a social whole unimbued with individuality do they evade the trouble and effort that freedom demands, and not face up to the hidden poison of their dissatisfaction. Sooner or later this resentment, now turned outward, will turn inward and they will confront their own true natures. And since they lack self-reliance, they will not survive the confrontation. Perhaps those whose reaction to the drug is adverse, the moron-rejects of the community, have already done so, only to lapse into nullity and become one with nothingness.

After Wells's *A Modern Utopia*, only dystopias predominate. Huxley's *Brave New World* then sets the modern temper, with its bitter prophecy of sexual license and euphoric drugs like soma, endorsed by a totalitarian state as a cynical cover for its naked power. No longer is the Wellsian dream of a benevolent world-state credible, its ruling intellectuals wise in their knowledge of what is best for the future of humanity. *A Modern Utopia* globalizes Plato's collectivist city-state in *The Republic*, "The New Republic" in Wells's *Anticipations* (1901), his first nonfiction work of social prophecy.

The only exception to the dystopian novels of the twentieth century is *Island* (1962) by none other than Aldous Huxley himself. In a feeble effort lacking conviction, he now stands for a hedonistic way of life minus statist controls. In this he seems influenced by the French eccentric Charles Fourier (*d.* 1837), the most bizarre figure in the history of socialist thought. Fourier conceived of a series of rural communes ("phalansteries") that realize a utopia of copulation and cookery (drugs in Huxley). The phalanstery, however, does not prefigure Marx's ideal commune, in which hedonism has no place, only selfless work.

Huxley in his epigraph to *Brave New World* cites a passage from *Freedom and the Spirit* (1927) by Nicholas Berdyaev (*d.* 1948), a Russian theologian and philosopher exiled from the Soviet Union in 1922, whence he lived in France. Here translated from the French, the epigraph reads:

> Utopias appear to be a good deal more feasible than was previously believed. And we are now confronted by a new and alarming question: how can we avoid their permanent construction? ... Utopias are feasible. Life is moving toward utopias. And perhaps a new age is beginning, an age when intellectuals and the cultured class will dream of ways of avoiding utopias and of returning to a non-utopian society, less "perfect" and more free.

In *Island*, Huxley reversed himself and now found freedom of the spirit in unlimited sexual indulgence and drug use: soma glorified.

Strange to say, even Robert Heinlein fell under Fourier's spell. In his last novel, *To Sail Beyond the Sunset* (1987), he has never-dying, always rejuvenated hero Lazarus Long find ultimate contentment in polymorphous perversity (Freud's term). He does indeed become the oldest dirty old man in the universe, out there in the far reaches of a distant galaxy he pioneered. In 1986, Heinlein sent me a typescript of the novel, so at the last minute I got it into my book on his work. After it came out he called to say that I was correct to make the Fourier connection.

This last novel signaled the definitive end of SF as a separate asexual genre: he who did so much to make it a dazzling publishing success. Now, Heinlein finished his career with a bestselling work that totally assimilates to the sexual revolution begun in the 1960s.

Epilogue
The Romance of Radio

Radio once had a mystique now hard to recapture. Its monument is 70 stories of RCA building in Rockefeller Center, a complex erected during the 1930s and named Radio City. It even lent glamour to the movies with the formation of RKO Radio Pictures in 1928, each film introduced to this day by a turning globe surmounted by a great broadcasting tower beeping signals to the whole world. The R & D business got its name in 1911 with AMRAD for American Radio, standing also for American Research and Development, although R & D in practice began with General Electric in 1900, the first American corporation to attach research labs to its production facilities.

On 16 July 1920 KDKA in Pittsburgh began broadcasting, the first commercial station. Henceforth radio was to be a universal domestic appliance.

Hugo Gernsback saw it coming in 1908 with his first magazine, *Modern Electrics*, the advertising arm of his radio store on Broadway, which sold parts to amateurs. He gave them something to listen to on his own station, WRNY (326 meters), broadcast from atop the Empire State Building. At the time he was associated with Lee De Forest, inventor of the vacuum tube that made radio possible and first president of the American Radio Association, with Hugo Gernsback as its business manager.

In World War I, AMRAD made equipment for detecting German submarines. Its name dates back to 1911, but it existed before under another name, when it sold the parts advertised in *Modern Electrics* from 1908.

Soon, WRNY was followed by a television station broadcasting from the same site, parts for receivers available from the same radio store. Commercial development of television was delayed by World War II, but Gernsback knew enough about it to have his fictional hero Ralph invent the *Telephot*, a two-way audiovisual device allowing people to see and talk to each other. His Tele-Theater uses a Telephot that transmits performances into the home.

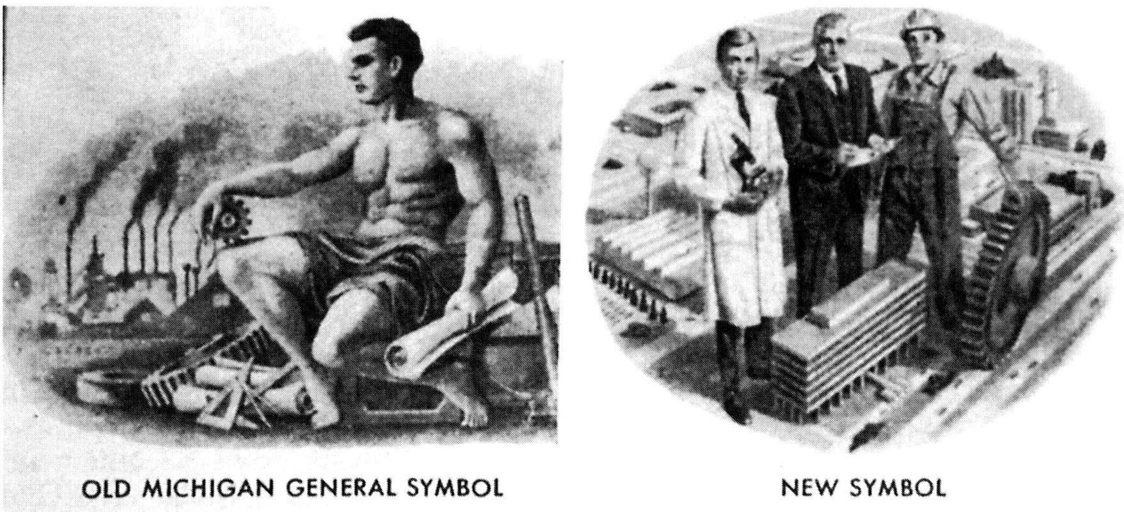

Fig. 123. *Michigan General's logo adapted to R & D reality.*

But it is not until about 1980 when Michigan General changed its logo on stock offerings to reflect a reality Hugo Gernsback had reported on in *Science and Invention* from 1920. In fig. 123, the old logo pictures industry as inspirited by the god Vulcan, complete with belching smokestacks. The new one pictures a pollution-free enterprise presided over by its R & D team: chief executive officer at center, scientist on one side of him, engineer on the other.

As already mentioned in Chapter 1, Gernsback prefigured his *Amazing Stories* with a serialized story, "Ralph 124C 41+," in *Modern Electrics* (1911–1912). In 1925 he issued it in book form (fig. 124), a reminder that Ralph still was his ideal inventor.

His model for Ralph is none other than the great Croatian-American electric engineer, Nicola Tesla (1856–1943). Here is where science fiction and radio intersect in the person of Hugo Gernsback, a promoter of all things electrical when the possibilities of scientific research were not yet generally appreciated. Gernsback first heard of Tesla while growing up as a ten-year-old child in Luxembourg, and formed an alliance with him the moment he arrived in New York in 1884. In 1919 Gernsback published a serialized autobiography of Tesla, "My Inventions," in *The Electrical Experimenter*. Tesla at first went to work for Thomas Edison, "the king of electricity," and instantly fell out with him over the issue of alternating current (AC) versus direct current (DC). Tesla knew that DC could not be transported by wire very far without loss.

Working on his own, Tesla devised the entire AC system now standard everywhere. Generated at high voltage, alternating current travels efficiently over long distances. Problem is, it must be stepped down to low voltage at its destination for practical use. Tesla invented the transformers to raise and lower voltage as required, with motors of his own design that ran only on AC.

Beyond that, Tesla is the true inventor of wireless radio, not Marconi, who stole the publicity. Tesla the otherworldly genius was too absorbed in his work to concern himself with public relations the way Edison did. The autobiography concludes with these words:

The progressive development of man is vitally dependent on invention. It is the most important produce of his creative brain. Its ultimate purpose is the complete mastery of mind over the material world, the harnessing of the forces of nature to human needs. This is the difficult task of the inventor who is often misunderstood and unrewarded. But he finds ample compensation in the pleasing exercises of his powers and in the knowledge of being one of that exceptionally privileged class without whom the race would have long ago perished in the bitter struggle against pitiless elements. Speaking for myself, I have already had more than my full measure of this exquisite enjoyment, so much that for many years my life was little short of continuous rapture.

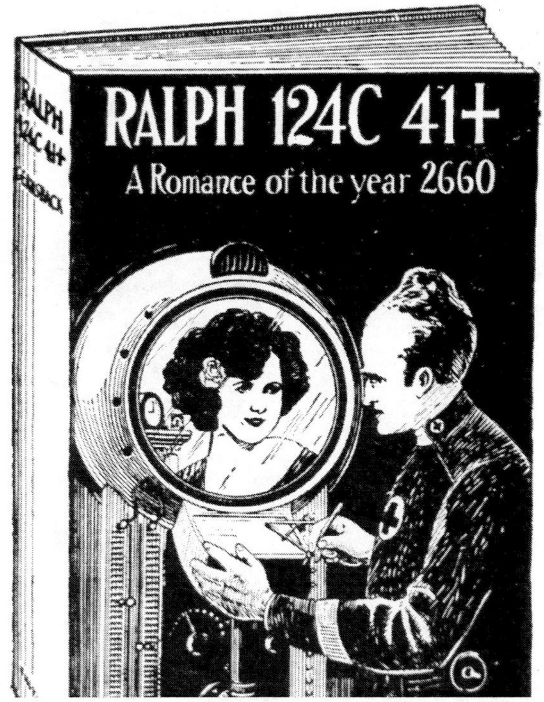

Fig. 124. *The 1911 Gernsback novel in book form, 1925.*

Fig. 125. *Tesla's "thought recorder" imagined in a cover story for a Gernsback magazine,* Science Wonder Stories *(October 1929), illustrating "Into the Subconscious" by Ray Avery Meyer.*

Tesla's many unrealized ideas found expression in *Amazing Stories* and other Gernsback SF magazines. To give one bizarre example, Tesla, no believer in ESP, conceived it possible to read out the thoughts of another person's brain by attaching television equipment to the rods and cones of the retina: the area of cognitive processing in his view. This invention, a "thought recorder," is realized in a 1929 issue of *Science Wonder Stories*. The cover art depicts two humans wearing thought-reading helmets (fig. 125).

In time the romance of radio lost its bloom in SF. By 1937, Eric Frank Russell took a sinister view in "The Great Radio Peril" (*Astounding Stories*, April). Radio waves from transmitters all over the world resonate with the electrostatic surface tension in the capillary action of plant life,

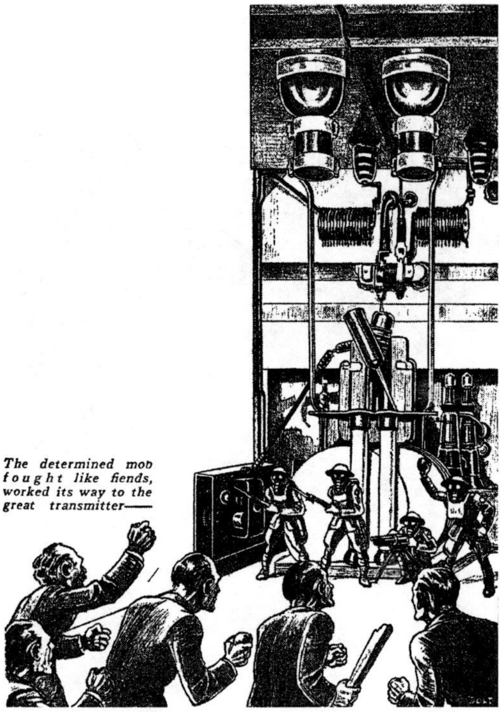

Fig. 126. *Illustration for "The Great Radio Peril," one of many Eric Frank Russell stories with a sardonic view of human progress.*

upon which animal life depends. Civilization is doomed. Armed mobs attack radio stations and all is saved (see fig. 126).

For Hugo Gernsback the romance of radio was the romance of R & D, which he celebrated in *Science and Invention*. The special "scientifiction" issue of August 1923, anticipating *Amazing Stories*, offered a number of SF stories commissioned for it. The new pulp magazine genre Gernsback conceived would take in both sides of the R & D equation, itself a progressive new concept making for the improvement of humanity. Science, wedded to invention, led to programmed innovation destined to work utopian changes in the human condition.

Featured on the cover is "The Man from the Atom" (Chapter 1 and plate III), expressing a simple-minded Sense of Wonder that marveled at what science had revealed about the structure of the universe, from macrocosm to microcosm: everything resolved into atoms that themselves formed solar systems and galaxies. The shrinking man descends into that microcosm only to reemerge full-size on his home planet and begin the cycle all over again: such is the nature of cosmic reality.

At the time, however, quantum physics had not yet developed the now familiar model. Atoms consist of protons and neutrons, which in turn are made of smaller particles called quarks. But they too seem to have internal structure, subdiving still further into nothingness: creation *ex nihilo*.

This more sophisticated model is the subject of an exceptional film, *The Incredible Shrinking Man* (Universal 1957). It revisits "The Man from the Atom" with quantum physics in mind. Its intelligent script by Richard Matheson, a well-established SF writer, ponders the imponderable. Owing to the effect of some weird radiation, his protagonist seems to dwindle into nonexistence. At the end of the film he meditates under starry skies with these poignant words: "I was continuing to shrink, to become—what?—the infinitesimal."

> So close, the infinitesimal and the infinite. But suddenly I knew they were really the two ends of the same concept. The unbelievably small and the unbelievably vast eventually meet, like the closing of a gigantic circle. I looked up, as if somehow I could grasp the heavens. And in that moment I knew the answer to the riddle of the infinite. I had thought in terms of man's own limited dimensions. I had presumed upon nature. That existence begins and ends is man's conception, not nature's, and I felt my body dwindling, melting, becoming nothing. My fears melted away. And in their place came acceptance. All this vast majesty of

> creation—it had to mean something. And that I meant something too. Yes, smaller than the smallest, I meant something too. To God, there is no zero. I still exist.

In SF, the Sense of Wonder arises from some impossible element. In nature, atoms and molecules do not and cannot shrink in size; they are fixed quantities. Therefore the size of living organisms is limited, the smallest being the many species of bacteria. All the shrinking man stories pass over this difficulty with degrees of finesse. But even the highly sophisticated script by Richard Matheson for *The Incredible Shrinking Man* must ignore the laws of nature if he is to write SF. The essential tension between Sense of Wonder and its opposite never can be resolved, so long as SF informs imaginative literature.

Appendix I
Initial Magazines

The word "science fiction" is a gift to English speech from the once vast pulp magazine industry. That industry is long dead. Yet the smallest part of it generated the biggest word to come out of it.

The first SF magazine to compete in the pulp jungle is *Amazing Stories*, conceived by Hugo Gernsback. At one time, the small percentage of the magazine market held by the first SF titles meant big bucks. No more. It is all gone with the wind: pulps, magazine SF, everything.

All the same, *Amazing* got the SF locution going, outlasting the magazine that invented it. Its first issue, April 1926, is at once a birth and a death. After little more than a century, the genre is defunct, its conventions assimilated into other topical genres.

The next magazine to take up the call was *Astounding Stories*, from January 1930. From September 1937 to December 1971, John Campbell took over and retitled it *Astounding Science Fiction*, later *Analog Science Fiction*. (The last few issues already were in the editorial pipeline before Campbell died in April.) *ASF* was the high point, bringing forth almost every notable author in the field, culminating in the early works of Robert Heinlein. Thereafter the genre disappeared, being assimilated into other topical forms of popular literature.

The transient history of the SF magazines is not for me to tell. How many of them came and went while the pulp industry still flourished is uncalculated, no more than a hundred out of the huger bulk of pulp titles, some of them as yet unnumbered.

For some account of the known SF titles, see John Clute and Peter Nicholls, editors, *The Encyclopedia of Science Fiction*, New York: St. Martin's, 1993. This is the one reference book worth consulting on all matters pertaining to the genre, 4360 entries alphabetically listed and cross-indexed.

Appendix II
Science Fiction on Film

Film is a perishable medium, unlike printed matter on paper of low acidic content. These last for centuries and *have* lasted for centuries. Whereas film classics of only a few decades ago dissolve in their own nitrates. Attempts to restore the best of them reduce to the same non-lasting substance.

I am therefore hesitant to mention any of the SF film classics. I choose only three titles, available in videotape, itself perishable.

The first is *Things to Come* (1936), scripted by H.G. Wells for London Film Productions. Its managing director, Alexander Korda, a respecter of great writers, had asked Wells to do this film script for him. The father of modern SF thus fathered the first modern SF film, although taken as a model for all the wrong reasons. Directed by William Cameron Menzies, the film stars Raymond Massey, Ralph Richardson, and Cedric Hardwicke. The special effects were done by Ned Mann, a Hollywood specialist in the craft.

Things to Come is more than the mindless futurism and special effects inspired in SF films to follow. Just how profoundly Wellsian it is I have taken pains to explain in *The Prophetic Soul: A Reading of H.G. Wells's "Things to Come"* (1987).

The next film I choose to mention is *The Day the Earth Stood Still* (1951), 20th Century–Fox, directed by Robert Wise and starring Michael Rennie, Patricia Neal, and Sam Jaffe. Although totally misreading the *ASF* story on which it is based, as discussed in this book, the film remains a classic of the SF cinema.

Finally I mention *Journey to the Far Side of the Sun* (1969), Century 21 Productions/Universal, starring Patrick Wymark and Roy Thinnes. My choice here is unusual, but, as I discuss in this book, the script by Gerry and Sylvia Anderson is unusually sophisticated. The film deserves more serious attention than it ever got from dismissive reviews.

Appendix III

Memorable Science Fiction in Print

In the long view of literary history, so filled with immortal classics, for all the works mentioned in this book, I come at last to my summary judgment on those worth remembering as long as English lasts in print.

First and foremost is the 1871 French classic by Jules Verne, *20,000 Leagues Under the Sea*, at long last properly Englished by Walter James Miller and Frederic Paul Walter for the Naval Institute Press, Annapolis, Maryland, 1993. This is the one and only edition to do literary justice to the original text, *Vingt Mille Lieues sous les mers*, and to intelligently annotate it. Its hero of romantic globalism, Captain Nemo, may now be understood for what he is, a creation of imaginative literature the equal of that other famous explorer and sea captain, Lemuel Gulliver, the stolidly plausible narrator of Jonathan Swift's eighteenth-century classic, *Travels into Several Remote Nations of the World.*

The Miller and Walter translation of what always has been a dignified classic of French letters makes it accessible to English readers. They do well to place it on a one-foot shelf alongside *Gulliver's Travels*, *Robinson Crusoe*, *Pilgrim's Progress*, the *New Testament*, and *Alice in Wonderland.*

That shelf, however, deserves a little expansion to make room for the best of H.G. Wells. I nominate *The Time Machine* (1895) and *The War of the Worlds* (1898), both published by William Heinemann in London. Together they explore the cosmological reaches of time and space. Indeed, one of his early story collections is entitled *Tales of Space and Time* (London and New York: Harper & Brothers, 1900).

A collection of Wells's early SF novels goes under the 1933 title *The Scientific*

Romances of H.G. Wells (London: Victor Gollancz). The following year it appeared in New York retitled *Seven Famous Novels by H.G. Wells*, under one of Alfred A. Knopf's imprints (Garden City Publishing Co.). Both editions contain essentially the same Preface, in which a definition of the scientific romance is offered.

A collection of 63 stories, *The Short Stories of H.G. Wells*, was issued in 1927 by Ernest Benn of London. In 1929, Doubleday, Doran of New York published it under the same title. It contains that stupendous 1896 story of cosmic vision, "Under the Knife," mentioned several times in this book.

Since this book terminates with Robert Heinlein, I should confess my favorite novel of his, *Job: A Comedy of Justice* (New York: Ballantine Book, 1984). Not by chance does it strongly resonate with another contemporary play on the story of Job by H.G. Wells, *The Undying Fire* (London: Cassell, 1919).

Most of Heinlein's Future History stories are collected in *The Past through Tomorrow* (New York: Putnam, 1967). The best of these have a worthy place in the history of American letters.

Bibliography

Aldiss, Brian. *Billion Year Spree: The True History of Science Fiction*. New York: Doubleday, 1973.

A British master of the genre tells the story with passion, placing SF in a literary context. Relationships between SF and such writers as Milton, Darwin, Hardy and Kafka are discussed.

_____. *Science Fiction Art*. New York: Bounty Books, 1975.

The importance of magazine illustration to SF is here pictured, with attention to the genre's most notable artists.

Campbell, John W., Jr., ed. *The Astounding Science Fiction Anthology*. New York: Simon & Schuster, 1952.

The editor's favorite stories from his own magazine, with an Introduction explaining why they are of intellectual interest.

Conklin, Groff, ed. *The Best of Science Fiction*. New York: Crown, 1946.

An early collection of stories, especially notable for its Introduction by John Campbell, who offers a pentrating analysis of the genre.

Frewin, Anthony. *One Hundred Years of Science Fiction Illustration*. New York: Pyramid Books, 1975.

The only book to show that SF art has nineteenth-century models antedating the genre magazines.

Gunn, James. *Alternate Worlds: The Illustrated History of Science Fiction*. Englewood Cliffs, N.J.: Prentice-Hall, 1975.

A notable academic and SFWA author writes a detailed history with analytical skill. The many illustrations also picture nearly all the writers mentioned.

Healy, Raymond J., and J. Francis McComas, eds. *Adventures in Time and Space*. New York: Random House, 1946.

The first hardcover SF anthology. Out of 35 literate stories, all but three are from *Astounding Science Fiction*.

Silverberg, Robert, ed. *Science Fiction Hall of Fame*, Vol. One: *The Greatest Science Fiction Stories of All Times*. New York: Doubleday, 1970.

As president of SFWA, Silverberg polled its members on the best. The results are tallied here in 26 ranked stories.

Wells, H.G. *The Annotated H.G. Wells*, Leon Stover, ed. Jefferson, N.C.: McFarland, 1996–2001.

Titles of the eight volumes are itemized on the first page of the present work. They include wide-ranging interconnections with Jules Verne.

Wollheim, Donald A., ed. *The Pocketbook of Science-Fiction*. New York: Pocketbooks, 1943.

The first SF anthology, bringing the genre into wider public recognition beyond the magazines read only by fans. It remains a worthy collection for its wise choices.

Index